YOUNG LIONS

YOUNG LIONS

CHRISTIAN RITES OF PASSAGE FOR AFRICAN-AMERICAN YOUNG MEN

BY REV. CHRIS MCNAIR

Abingdon Press

Nashville

YOUNG LIONS
CHRISTIAN RITES OF PASSAGE FOR AFRICAN-AMERICAN YOUNG MEN

ISBN: 0-687-09937-4

Copyright © 2001 by Abingdon Press

Scripture quotations in this publication, unless otherwise indicated, are from the *New Revised Standard Version of the Bible,* copyright © 1989 by the Division of Christian Education of the National Council of the Churches of Christ in the United States of America, and are used by permission. All rights reserved.

About the Author

The Reverend Dr. Chris McNair has worked with children, youth, and families in urban communities as a youth worker and pastor for more than fifteen years. He serves as the Executive Director of Christ's Children Ministries, an urban outreach ministry to unchurched youth and families in south Minneapolis. An ordained United Methodist minister, he has earned a masters of divinity in urban ministry and Christian education, from Asbury Seminary in Wilmore, Kentucky, and has earned a doctor of ministry degree, specializing in urban parish ministry, from Luther Seminary in St. Paul, Minnesota. Rev. McNair and his wife, Lisa, live and minister together and enjoy raising their three young children: Nathanael (7), Javan (4), and Ezra (2).

Young Lions is also known as Simba, a ministry of Christ's Children Ministries, a non-profit organization. Inquiries regarding the Simba Rites of Passage Program should be addressed to:

Christ's Children Ministries
3346 Columbus Avenue, South
Minneapolis, MN 55407

612-823-2977

Cover Design: Keely Moore

Copyright information for the photographs in the montage on pages 21 and 262 are as follows: 1, 2, 8, 11—*U.S. News and World Report* Collection, Library of Congress; 3, 10—Digital Schomburg Images of 19th Century African Americans, New York Public Library; 4—Rare Book and Special Collections Division, Library of Congress; 5, 7—Biographical File, Library of Congress; 6, 9—Lot 12735, Library of Congress.

MANUFACTURED IN THE UNITED STATES OF AMERICA

01 02 03 04 05 06 07 08 09 10   10 9 8 7 6 5 4 3 2 1

CONTENTS

From the Author 9

I. YOUNG LIONS PROGRAM

Overview

Young Lions in Action 12

Program Goals 14

The Symbol 17

Principles 18

Pledge 19

Code of Conduct .19

The Meetings

Weekly Format 20

Planning Chart 23

4th-Week Plan 24

Field Trip Permission Form 25

Yearly Calendar 26

Symbol and Ceremony 27

Keeping Track 28

T-Shirt Design 29

Young Lions Certificate 30

The Boys

Age Levels 31

Becoming a Member 33

Young Lions Application 36

Group Contract 37

Individual Expectations 38

Parent Involvement 39

Success Factors 40

II. MENTORS

A Mentor's Story 42

Getting Started 43

Mentor Contract 46

Mentor Training Sessions

    Session 1: Overview 47

    Session 2: Introduction 51

        Black Boys Handout 54

        Black Men Handout 58

    Session 3: The Need 59

    Session 4: The Program 62

        Philosophy & Goals Handout 63

    Session 5: The Meeting 65

    Session 6: Expectations 66

        Working With Boys Handout 68

Mentor Certificate .70

III. CURRICULUM

Curriculum Overview 72

    Unit 1: Career and Education 75

    Unit 2: Self-Awareness 96

    Unit 3: Heritage and Culture 116

    Unit 4: The Black Experience 143

    Unit 5: Family Awareness 167

    Unit 6: Growing Up 189

    Unit 7: Personal Responsibility 212

    Unit 8: Economic Responsibility 235

IV. HEROES & RESOURCES

African-American History Timeline 261

African-American Heroes 263

Reading Resources .285

FROM THE AUTHOR

FELLOW SERVANTS IN CHRIST,

The sight of children playing in my urban neighborhood is common; but when I see a group of young Black boys, I have mixed emotions. Part of me is full of hope at the thought of the potential and promise in those young minds. But part of me is saddened when I consider their environment, their family circumstances, and their school involvement.

Many of these children are defeated in life before it even begins because of chemical or physical abuse in the home and poverty and violence in the community. Many of our Black boys in these circumstances have their innocence stolen from them by witnessing violence regularly in the home and community or by having to grow hard in order to survive in the 'hood. Their lives are vulnerable and often forfeited to negative social dynamics, external circumstances, and inner emotional turmoil.

If only they had a chance at life, what would these boys become? Scientists, engineers, athletes, mechanics, carpenters? But many of them have little or no hope of a satisfying or fulfilling life.

We need a strategy to instill pride and hope in our Black boys to enable them to be the men that God created them to be.

Jesus Christ said that he came that we might have life, and that we might have it abundantly. I know that God's will for these children is to have joy, peace, and fulfillment in their lives. I also know that neither they, nor anyone, will have it apart from Christ. So I have hope; because in Christ, the potential and promise of these boys may be realized.

The concept of Young Lions came as an inspiration to me. In *Countering the Conspiracy to Destroy Black Boys* (Reading Resources, page 285) Jawanza Kunjufu's analysis of the condition of Black boys in our society is certainly apparent in my community. Kunjufu paints a picture of the effect of social structures and negative environments on young Black boys in inner-city communities. The situation he describes is sobering in its accuracy and familiarity. The phenomenon he articulates reflects exactly the kind of personality changes that I see among the boys with whom I work. His insights and suggestions regarding an African-American rites of passage resource were a catalyst for me to create a suitable vehicle to address the needs of Black boys in my neighborhood.

We need a strategy to instill pride and hope in our Black boys to enable them to be the men that God created them to be. One possibility is to develop a Christian rites of passage program for young boys. The Swahili word *simba*, meaning "lion," gives us a powerful image for such a program.

YOUNG LIONS offers a simple process, easily adaptable by any organization or group that works with youth. This manual is the result of creating a strategy for my urban community; it offers a curriculum and guide for a Christian, Afrocentric rites of passage program. Perhaps you will find it useful in your work with the boys in your neighborhood whether it is urban, suburban, small town, or more rural.

Young Lions has the potential for far-reaching impact in communities. As boys are influenced for Christ, they will, in turn, influence their families and peers. As families are influenced for Christ, the community will change. The noted author, lecturer, and former member of the President's Task Force on Hunger Dr. John M. Perkins said, "I am convinced that saving boys is one of the surest ways to heal the inner city. If we can reach the boys, we reach the entire community" ("Saving Our Children in a World Without Fathers," *Urban Family Magazine,* Winter, 1994). Intervention with Black boys is not exclusive of girls or other cultures. It is, rather, a strategy for creating a long-lasting impact for Christ on families and communities.

My prayer is that through Young Lions, the boys in your community will begin to realize their incredible value and worth in God's sight as God's children.

—*Chris McNair*
YOUNG LIONS author and
Director of Christ's Children
Ministries, Minneapolis,
Minnesota

> Intervention with Black boys can have a long-lasting impact for Christ on families and communities.

I. YOUNG LIONS PROGRAM

YOUNG LIONS
IN ACTION

If I were an African-American boy living in south Minneapolis, Minnesota, I know where I'd wind up on Saturday mornings and after school. I'd skip sleeping in, watching cartoons, or making a snowman in order to find out what it means to be a Black man—spiritually, socially, and culturally—at the Simba/Young Lions meetings in the basement of Park Avenue Church.

"Simba's fun and I learn a lot about my heritage," explains Anton Thomas, 13. "I know I can be proud of what color I am and not let nobody put me down about it."

By admitting only African-American males, Young Lions achieves a rare intimacy, a time for the men and boys to talk frankly. However, Young Lions isn't a separatist group but a specific strategy for reaching at-risk African-American boys.

"Some white people have offered to help with Young Lions, but these boys need more opportunities for positive interaction with Black males. That's why I've kept the group so focused," explains Pastor Chris McNair, Young Lions founder. Ultimately, that decision makes Young Lions a remarkable rites-of-passage experience that helps boys to come a little closer to what they may someday be: drug-free, well-adjusted Christian men with a solid sense of their African roots.

For the past three years, Thomas has participated in Simba/Young Lions nearly every week. There he meets "cool guys" who help him out with "stuff." For Thomas, "stuff" generally means his asthma problem. "When I get really bad asthma attacks, the guys say I need to deal with it. I need to take my medication and ask God to help me. God helps me," he continues, "whenever there's something going wrong."

In Thomas's peer group a lot can go wrong, and that's why Young Lions is so important. Without a positive place to belong and feel loved, many at-risk kids will fill that empty space with something else. "Even at age 11, many of these kids know they're vulnerable to getting on the wrong track in life," says McNair. That's why exposing youth to other options, to the hope and power of the Christian lifestyle in particular, remains the centerpiece of Young Lions's outreach. *Simba* means "lion" in Swahili, symbolizing strength and leadership—just what it takes to lift the heavy realities that burden too many African-American boys. High percentages of them are born into poverty; drop out of school; are murdered; land in prison.

McNair created the Simba/Young Lions program in 1991 with these grim statistics and neighborhood faces in mind. "It gets discouraging sometimes, seeing the gang banging, chemical abuse, and fatherless homes. But every time I walk out my front door," he says, "the little boys inspire me. It's worth beating the bushes for them."

Young Lions harkens back to ancient African traditions that kept communities close. That explains why Bill Fridge, Director of Safety and Security at Prudential Insurance, tells a story this morning with a colorful *kente* cloth around his neck. Around ten boys and their mentor counterparts sit in a circle listening to him.

"Your stealing days," Fridge exclaims, "are over!" As the story unfolds, we learn that Fridge, once a Gary, Indiana, cop, had to arrest a man he knew from childhood. "That guy was stealing back when we were kids. I had started going down that path too."

Fridge recalls that one day he was caught stealing a comic book and some candy. That he got caught on his first attempt may have been the handiest lifelong lesson he could learn. "I don't know which was worse," he says with mock seriousness, "getting caught or having to tell my mom and dad." As he trails off, the boys and men laugh uproariously at the predicament.

Underneath the humor, the boys sense the moral of the story. More than that, they see what kind of man Fridge has become. And they realize that his classmate wound up in jail after the arrest. His tale unlocks confession from some, stories of their struggles against harmful peer pressure. One cheerful kid who clowns around a lot and seems as innocent as his age, tells that a gang once asked him to help them steal a car. After explaining how he got out of the operation, the group discusses a variety of sticky situations other members have encountered and overcome. Painting graffiti, swearing, smoking—all the activities the boys mention lead to trouble. And trouble, mentors point out, can be avoided by making better choices about friendships and free time.

Making good decisions begins with getting information. That's why Young Lions men frequently tell about family, education, and career experiences. The need for information also explains why the Young Lions program deals with topics like self-concept, educational options, money management, personal hygiene, career and family issues, African-American history, and Christian faith.

"Our job," Fridge explains, "is to give the boys positive images of African-American men and expose them to the world outside of where they live." Engaging in regular service projects; dining at ethnic restaurants; and taking field trips to universities, airports, prisons, and museums encourage the boys to grow. The program continues attracting more youth every year.

"We don't want to just come in and out of lives," McNair explains. "So many of these kids miss a loving family. The authority that they've experienced may be so uneven, not having positive Black male images in their life." McNair says that 90 percent of the Young Lions ministry involves consistency, especially in waiting on the Lord. "When I can't see the fruit, when I only see boys slipping off the fence to the other side, I have to remember to be patient."

That patience produces results as simple and satisfying as watching a Young Lions boy walk away from a fight. And if a boy can walk away from the emotional heat of a fight, he's got the lion's share of what he needs to walk away from anything else that may undo him. That witness, McNair hopes, will touch families and the community for Christ—an invaluable mission accomplished boy by boy.

Excerpted from "Simba," by Pam Melskog (*Prism: America's Alternative Evangelical Voice*, May/June 1998 issue). Used by permission.

AN UPDATE ON ANTON

Anton Thomas is now eighteen. He has avoided negative community and family patterns and has graduated from high school, the first of his family to do so. Anton has a bright future ahead of him, being both drug and child free.

PROGRAM GOALS

YOUNG LIONS IS AN AFRICAN-AMERICAN MENTORING PROGRAM DESIGNED TO HELP YOUNG BOYS EXPERIENCE AND WORK THROUGH THE RITES OF PASSAGE TO BECOMING A MAN. THE GROUP ADDRESSES SPIRITUAL, EMOTIONAL, AND SOCIAL NEEDS.

GOAL

The goal of Young Lions is to teach Black boys what it means to be African-American men, spiritually, culturally, and physically. These three dimensions of self are explored thoroughly to infuse the boys with a strong self-image and positive self-esteem by knowing who they are in Christ.

The basic method by which this goal will be met is to invite Christian African-American men to engage the boys in personal relationships and thus model and teach Black, Christian manhood to them. The Young Lions curriculum provides a format and structure to facilitate this dynamic.

PHILOSOPHY

The Young Lions rites of passage program addresses the experience of Black boys from a holistic perspective of Christian ministry. Additionally, the Young Lions curriculum explores and affirms the innate spirituality and moral fiber of African-American culture. It provides positive experiences and dialogue about African-American culture, heritage, and traditions, placed in the context of Scripture.

The Young Lions group examines issues of male adolescence and puberty, addressing everything from personal hygiene to human sexuality. Young Lions provides an affirming atmosphere in which to examine the social and emotional aspects of daily life specific to the experience of Black boys. In Young Lions, the gospel is communicated in the context of Christian community and in a manner relevant to the experience of African-American boys.

The Young Lions methodology is to put nurturing Black men in a position to teach young Black boys for the purpose of instilling hope for who they can be. Young Lions works to cultivate and develop the inner person. Through actively engaging the curriculum, the boys will internalize positive Christian beliefs about who they are in the world and about their inherent value as creations of God.

Young Lions attempts to infuse Christian spiritual values so that the boys will gain and possess inner peace and strength to bring to bear on their external situation, whatever it might be. Young Lions is a program helping boys to grow like Jesus "in wisdom and stature, and in favor with God and man" (Luke 2:52, King James Version).

THEOLOGY

The Bible places great significance on teaching children. Proverbs 22:6 is a basic axiom for ministry to children and youth in urban neighborhoods: "Train children in the right way, and when old, they will not stray." To ensure lasting impact on a young person's life, Young Lions takes a holistic, long-term view of children's growth and discipleship. Children are to be highly valued and treasured in our communities.

We must recognize not only their worth as persons but also their significance for the survival of our families, communities, and society as a whole. As the psalmist says in Psalm 127, children are "a heritage from the LORD" (verse 3). They are certainly our hope for the future and provide a sense of security like "arrows in the hand of a warrior" (verse 4). Children bring blessing to our communities. And like the arrow on which the warrior depends, we must care for them; otherwise, we will lose face with our enemies.

The Bible illustrates many mentoring relationships from which we can draw wisdom: Moses and Joshua, Naomi and Ruth, Elijah and Elisha, Paul and Timothy. In each of these examples, we see the primacy of relationship and time invested as the ingredients for making a significant impact on youth. The impact is especially in their spiritual values and beliefs, which will enable them to grow in their own walk with the Lord.

In each relationship, the goal of the mentor was to see his or her charge grow to spiritual maturity and be used by God in a mighty way himself or herself. Jesus had this goal in mind in mentoring the twelve disciples. He looked beyond their present circumstances as fishermen, tax collector, and common people and saw them as leaders for the kingdom of God.

> Jesus looked beyond
> the present circumstances
> of his followers as fishermen,
> tax collector, and common people
> and saw them as leaders
> for the kingdom of God.

The essential nature of the mentoring relationship is that of discipleship. In mentoring the twelve disciples, Jesus ate, slept, prayed, and worked with them. He shared of himself so that they could carry on his work when he was gone. In the same way, the church is called to give of ourselves to one another.

The ministry of Young Lions is to make disciples of African-American boys and men.

The root words in Greek for *disciple* are *dis* and *capere*. *Dis* means "into" and *capere* means "to make" or "to shape." *To disciple* means "to embrace and assist in spreading the teachings of another" (*American Heritage Dictionary*, Fourth Edition). Christian discipleship involves molding people into followers of Christ.

The purpose of Young Lions is to shape African-American boys into followers of Christ and leaders of their families and communities. Discipling involves teaching and enabling through personal relationship. The mentoring relationship is the crucible in which new behavior is forged and tested by boys questioning what it means to be a man.

Finally, the linchpin of the theology behind Young Lions is to give the boys a sense of identity in Christ. Jesus is indeed relevant for the issues facing Black boys today, because he knew suffering:

* As a boy, Jesus himself faced extermination as King Herod ordered all Hebrew boys slaughtered in an attempt to kill the future king.
* Jesus experienced racism as a Jew in the Roman Empire, living in Roman-occupied Israel.
* Jesus spent most of his adult life with the poor, oppressed, and ostracized of his society.

In summary, Jesus knew what it was like to be discriminated against and to be feared and hated because of his ethnic background. He knew what it was like to live an endangered life; he knew what it was like to face prejudice; he knew what it was like to grow up male; and he knew what it was like to have limited economic resources. Jesus Christ can speak to the experiences and issues of Black males in America.

The aim of Young Lions is to enable African-American boys to achieve their God-given potential and to proclaim Jesus Christ to them, admonishing and teaching them with all wisdom, that they may grow into the likeness of Christ.

> The aim of Young Lions is to enable African-American boys to achieve their God-given potential... that they may grow into the likeness of Christ.

THE SYMBOL

Meaning of the Symbol

LION: strength and leadership
AFRICA: cultural heritage

Meaning of the Colors

BLACK – The culture of African-American people

RED – The struggle of African-American people and
the blood of Jesus

GREEN – The natural beauty of the land and
the growth of a Christian

GOLD – The richness of Africa's natural resources and
the promise of heaven

PRINCIPLES

A YOUNG LION IS

Strong
He is strong in mind, body, and spirit.

Intelligent
He thinks his way through life and applies himself in every situation.

Manly
He is becoming a man who is strong, responsible, and caring.

Brave
He is brave enough to be his own person and not follow the crowd.

A Leader
He leads the way for others by always doing what is right.

PLEDGE

I WILL STRIVE TO

◇ learn what it means to be an African-American man spiritually, physically, and culturally;

◇ respect God in my conduct and relationships;

◇ honor my family by using my God-given potential in every situation;

◇ show respect for myself by respecting others.

CODE OF CONDUCT

R-E-S-P-E-C-T

Respect God

by using clean and positive language and upholding moral standards for behavior.

Respect Others

by treating them the way I would like to be treated, encouraging them and treating them fairly.

Respect Self

by being positive in my behavior and participating in activities that will build me up and not bring me down.

WEEKLY FORMAT

The format of the weekly meetings has been purposefully planned and used successfully. Here is a description of the various parts and their meaning and purpose. The fourth week of each unit has a different format (see page 24).

OPENING ACTIVITY *(15 minutes)*

A good way to begin a Young Lions meeting is to prepare some sort of activity to involve the boys when they enter the room. This activity may be table games, board games, brain teasers, or group builders. Each session includes a suggested activity. The involvement heads off the awkwardness of boys who arrive early and quickly engages them before they get bored. Introductory activities also send a message to youth who arrive late. They find people busy having fun; they know that something is happening with this group and that it is a fun group. Providing snacks at the beginning of the meeting also gives the boys an incentive to be on time.

LIBATION/PRAYER

In African tribes, the libation was used to give thanks for the blessings of God, particularly for one's ancestors. In Young Lions, the libation follows the Old Testament tradition of giving thanks to God through a "drink offering" (Numbers 28:14-15). The libation is one way to teach the boys to pray and to allow everyone in the group, men and boys, to participate actively in worshiping God. Simply provide a plant of some sort and a cup of water. The person doing the libation can pour or sprinkle the water on the plant while giving thanks to God. He can give thanks for anything—family, food, shelter, special needs fulfilled, whatever. When that person has finished praying, the whole group responds: "In Jesus' name, amen." A different person will do the libation each week.

AFRICAN-AMERICAN HEROES *(15 minutes)*

Each week a different mentor will make a presentation about a figure in African-American history. Pages of basic information about each of the heroes are in Section IV of this book (pages 264–284). However, mentors may want to search the Internet or look up more information in the library. In doing so, they will make the story their own. Mentors need to avoid simply reading aloud but look for ways to engage the boys by making the presentations as interactive as possible. (See page 263 for helpful ideas to make a dynamic presentation.) Invite boys who can handle the responsibility to work with the mentor on a presentation. Each week add the figure's name to the **timeline** (see page 261).

TIMELINE

On page 262 is a photo montage of eleven of the African-American heroes referred to in YOUNG LIONS. You may use it in a variety of ways:

- Mount a copy of the page with the timeline and add the hero's name the week of the presentation.
- Challenge the group to identify the heroes. Have them work in teams or as individuals.
- Cut out the individual pictures and add them to the timeline.

1. Malcolm X
2. Jesse Jackson
3. Frederick Douglass
4. Ida B. Wells Barnett
5. W.E.B. DuBois
6. James Weldon Johnson
7. Marcus Garvey
8. Shirley Chisholm
9. Mary McLeod Bethune
10. Booker T. Washington
11. Thurgood Marshall

(See the imprint page for copyright information for the photographs in the montage, at right.)

ACHIEVEMENT ACTIVITY *(30 minutes)*

This is a focal point of the meeting. The object is to engage the boys in a project that is interactive and participatory and related to the unit for the month (for example: career and education). Activities take the form of one of these methods: hands-on, visual, dialogue/verbal, experiential, or written. The activities also become an opportunity for boys and men to work together.

The successful completion of the achievement activities for the month earns the boy an award. If a boy must miss a session, offer him a way to make up the work. You may want to include the fourth week's field trip as one of the activities that counts toward getting the award. In that case, completing three of the four activities can become the measure for getting the award. At the end of the year, give certificates (page 70) with a gold seal for each unit in which the boy has met the challenge. See page 28 for help in keeping track of achievements toward awards.

GAME OR CRAFT *(20 minutes)*

Many times the achievement activity will be time consuming, or it may itself be a craft project. However, if there is time, a brief game or simple craft project at this point of the meeting keeps the boys active and interested in what is happening.

STORYTELLING *(15 minutes)*

This significant part of the meeting is a chance for the boys to hear an African-American man's perspective on life issues. Each week, a different mentor will tell a personal story from his life, relating to the unit theme for the month. After the story, each boy is permitted one question.

GOD TIME *(15 minutes)*

This part of the meeting pulls everything together for a spiritual focus. Young Lions is a Christian rites-of-passage program, and Christian spirituality is a core emphasis. Spiritual values are a sorely missing ingredient in urban Black communities today. Helping boys internalize these values and instilling Christian belief are main objectives of the program. For our youth to have a chance in an often hostile world, they will need the spiritual strength of a personal relationship with God through Jesus Christ.

The devotional concludes the meeting with a look at God's perspective through Scripture related to the issue for that month. At the end of the devotional the boys are directed to record in their journals their thoughts about the issues covered that day and what they learned.

HARAMBEE CIRCLE

This ritual concludes every meeting. *Harambee* is a Swahili word meaning "Let's all work together." The men and boys gather together in a circle, joining hands. First, someone will close the meeting with prayer. Then the whole group will chant *Harambee!* four times, each time swinging clasped hands forward, and, on the fourth time, throwing hands up in the air.

✳

The meeting format may be adjusted to suit time constraints. The achievement activity and heroes should be scheduled every week while the other components may be rotated every other week. The meeting format should not be restrictive but, instead, should serve as a guide.

The group may spend time dealing with important issues that arise out of storytelling, for example. Be flexible and be willing to deal with such situations. These conversations in response to issues the boys raise are where Young Lions can really make a difference in their lives.

> ### Be flexible.
> ### Spend time dealing with
> ### important issues that arise.

PLANNING CHART

Fill in the name of the person leading the activity for each of the meetings.

UNIT_____

WEEKLY MEETINGS:	1ST	2ND	3RD
Opening Activity			
Libation/Prayer			
African-American Heroes			
Achievement Activity			
Craft or Game			
Storytelling			
God Time			
Notes:			

4TH-WEEK PLAN

The fourth week of the month is different each time. Often there is a field trip; sometimes there are other special activities. Suggestions for the trips and activities are in each unit.

These weeks also take planning to ensure success. Fill in the information needed. Add the name of the person who is taking on the responsibility for the arrangements and other planning. Whenever possible, have a boy work with a mentor in making arrangements. The practice will help the boys learn a vital skill.

Trip to:

Location:

Contact person:

Phone number:

Drivers:

Additional adults:

Any special instructions:

Cost:

Thank you sent:

Optional Activities and Sessions

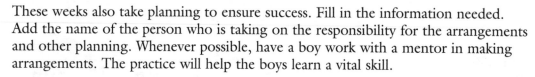

Activity name:

Page:

Supplies needed:

Leader(s):

YOUNG LIONS FIELD TRIP

The Young Lions are going on a trip to

_____

The purpose of the trip is to

_____

Time and place to meet to depart:

_____

Time and place to meet to return:

_____

What your Young Lion will need:

_____

For further information, contact

_____ Phone Number _____

I give permission for _____to go on the field
trip described above.   Young Lion's Name

_____   _____
Parent's Signature   Date

_____   _____
Contact Phone Number(s)

YEARLY CALENDAR

· · · · · · · · · · · · · · · · · · · ·

Getting Ready

June and July—Recruit Mentors

August and September—Train Mentors and Recruit the Youth

Sessions and Events

October—Unit 1: Career and Education

November—Unit 2: Self-Awareness

December—Unit 3: African-American Heritage and Culture

December—Special Event for Families: Kwanzaa Celebration

January—Unit 4: The Black Experience in America

February—Unit 5: Family Awareness

March—Unit 6: Growing Up (Personal hygiene and grooming)

April—Unit 7: Personal Responsibility (Conduct and work habits)

April or May—Overnight Retreat (Optional)

May—Unit 8: Economic Responsibility

Year-End Celebration

Give awards based on achievement activities.

Also give special awards at the end of the year
for attendance and participation.

SYMBOL AND CEREMONY

Symbol and ceremony are vital. Young persons are crying out for someplace to belong. They are desperate to fit in. It is crucial to create a sense of belonging to a specific group. Much of this may be achieved by a common symbol.

The symbol for Young Lions is a gold lion standing on its hind legs, roaring (see page 29). The lion is imposed upon an outline of the continent of Africa in the colors black, red, and green. Through good attendance, the boys earn T-shirts, sweatshirts, and hats with this insignia on them. (See page 29 for a black-and-white reproducible design. See the Young Lions webpage at www.ileadyouth.com/resources for a full-color version.) Throughout our community, the boys are constantly asked, "Hey, where did you get that; and how can I get one?" to which they reply with pride, "You have to belong to Young Lions."

Symbol and ceremony play a significant role in the Young Lions program. Here are several examples of ways to encourage and affirm the participants:

* **Give boys awards for meeting the requirements** of their Achievement Activities. At the end of the year, each Young Lion receives a certificate of achievement (see page 30). The boys receive one gold seal on their certificate for each month they have successfully completed their required Achievement Activity. Give awards also for attendance.

* **Develop some "Do the Right Thing" awards** to surprise youth caught in the act of doing something good. Do this either at your annual awards banquet or at your weekly meetings. For example, a young boy who refused to give in to negative peer pressure to engage in violence in a certain situation or who made the academic honor roll one semester might be rewarded and affirmed in front of the group. These unexpected awards provide incentive to the other boys to do what is right and self-affirming. A dollar bill can be a suitable award. What is important is not the expense of the award but the affirmation of being singled out for positive behavior.

* **Provide a positive alternative to gangs** and other forms of negative peer pressure facing young boys. Young Lions T-shirts, sweatshirts, hats, and so forth provide a positive group identity for the boys not only at Young Lions activities but also at school, home, and among their peers out in the neighborhood. Present T-shirts or sweatshirts as a reward for consistent involvement, for positive behavior, and for learning the Young Lions principles. The youth can wear these items with pride, being conscious of representing the Young Lions group and knowing that they have earned the right to wear them. Only Young Lions mentors and boys should be allowed to wear the symbol.

* **Hold a special event at the end of the year.** Bestow various awards in a public ceremony at a banquet. Make sure that each Young Lion (boys and mentors) is honored in some way. The tone of the ceremony should be special and affirming. Parents and family of the boys are given special invitations as well.

KEEPING TRACK

ACHIEVEMENT ACTIVITY AWARDS

The boys will consider it important that their work be recognized. Therefore, find ways to keep track of what they have completed as they work toward their achievement activity awards. Keep a file folder for each participant. At the end of each session, collect and file the completed projects. The boys then receive their folders at the awards ceremony at the end of the year.

ATTENDANCE

Keep an attendance chart so that you will know which youth attend which activities. This record will also give you a nudge to follow up personally if a young person is absent for some unknown reason. In addition, the chart can serve as a double-check for knowing which boys fulfilled which achievement requirements.

GOD TIME JOURNALS

Make copies of the appropriate pages for the God Time devotional and give a copy to each young man. Go through the material together, looking up and reading the Scripture, reading the devotional material, and answering the discussion questions. For the final personal reflection question, allow the young men to take a moment to write their thoughts on their handout.

Then collect the handouts and place them in plain manila folders labeled with the name of each individual youth. An option is to have the boys decorate a notebook or manila folder themselves.

At the end-of-the-year awards ceremony, give them the folder with all of their work from the year and invite them to take a few moments to reread what they have written. This review is one way for the young men to see how much they have grown.

LOGO AND CERTIFICATE

On the next two pages are two very helpful items:

* Page 29 has the Young Lions logo, which you may use to decorate T-shirts, caps, or other items for the group.
* Page 30 has a photocopiable awards certificate.

WEBSITE

Also, check out the Young Lions webpage on www.ileadyouth.com for full-color versions of the logo and certificate. Use a color printer to print the certificate. Use heat transfer paper (available at most office and computer supply stores and at some discount department stores) for a quick and easy iron-on transfer of the logo.

T-Shirt Design

YOUNG LIONS

© 2001 Abingdon Press

YOUNG LIONS

Congratulations to:

_____

for completing year _____ of the rites of passage program

at _____

on _____
   (date)

Harambee!

Signed _____

AGE LEVELS

Ideally, the Young Lions program can engage young Black males from elementary through high school age. The curriculum for Young Lions is designed primarily for elementary and middle school youth. An additional Young Lions group for high school youth is not required to do the Young Lions program; but as your group evolves and broadens its impact in your community, you will think of ways to expand to meet the needs of your youth.

Young Lions operates best in the context of a holistic program of Christian nurture, including Sunday school, sports outreach ministry, Bible clubs, and youth group. However, in the absence of such a comprehensive approach, Young Lions can still effectively reach young persons, especially if they are able to participate in the program for more than one year.

YOUNG LION CUBS

Elementary-age children of younger and younger ages are exposed to more and more mature issues through negative environments, media, and peer groups. Proactive measures among young children will yield significant fruit in the lives of urban youth. The key is developing a vehicle for preparing young men in your community to enter the Young Lions program. A group may be built around athletics, academics, or crafts—whatever holds the boys' interest. An elementary group for Black boys, Young Lion (or Simba) Cubs may be conducted as a school group, afterschool program, or neighborhood children's club. The program should focus on developing academic and life skills and on involving the boys with African-American men as role models. A suggested age range for Young Lion (or Simba) Cubs is nine- to eleven-year-old boys. Reaching this age youth is crucial (See "Fourth Grade Failure Syndrome," page 54).

YOUNG LIONS

Young people of middle school age (twelve to fourteen years old) experience inordinate stress and pressure in dealing with issues among their peer group, such as crime, violence, sexuality, and drugs. Dysfunctional family and hostile neighborhood environments contribute to the vulnerability of these young persons. The Young Lions group targets boys at a critical point in their development, when they are making choices and decisions that will have an impact upon the rest of their lives.

This age group can effectively evaluate choices and examine consequences for behavior; therefore, problem solving is a significant part of their development. They want to see principles demonstrated and lived out before them, which is why the mentor's role is so crucial. They are discerning the world around them, and they desire to test the evidence and facts about issues before committing their trust.

Young Black boys of this age need to participate in making decisions that affect them. Experiencing opportunities for leadership and being involved in group projects will address this need. Cultivate an open, relaxed atmosphere in which the boys may ask questions, express doubts, make decisions, and express themselves as individuals.

YOUNG LION WARRIORS

The development of high school age boys when they leave the Young Lions program is also a critical issue. A continuing high school Young Lion Warriors group can provide youth completing the Young Lions program an ongoing supportive network.

A Young Lion Warriors group may target teenage boys fifteen to eighteen years old. The group should focus on leadership development, spiritual discipleship, and college preparation or work readiness. The high school program should emphasize the mentoring relationship, matching youth with mentors who will have regular contact with them at least every two weeks. The boys and men may gather once a month formally as a group for discipleship and fun events.

Teenage youth should be given opportunities for leadership development. These include problem-solving situations and involvement in planning their activities. The program should be structured so that youth will have opportunities to lead and thus build their confidence through successful experiences. Their participation as leaders will also impart a sense of ownership and responsibility. At this age, youth also respond well to challenges for commitment and service, such as participating in service projects or being assistant counselors or junior mentors in the Cubs program.

Young African-American men in particular should be encouraged to make plans and set goals about their career choices at this age. Start them thinking early in their high school careers about creating options for the future. College trips and vocational experiences will stimulate their vision for what they can achieve in life. College preparation is critical, as many youth neglect to take advantage of resources available to them for information and scholastic readiness. Simple tasks such as making contact with colleges and filling out applications go undone for lack of direction or instruction. Provide exposure to various vocational trades that may interest the youth. Trade or technical school may be a better and more fulfilling option for some youth than college.

Ideally, the Young Lions program can engage young Black males from elementary school through high school.

Young Lion Cubs	9–11 years old	Adapt curriculum for more activities and less talk.
Young Lions	12–14 years old	Use curriculum as is, varying the content each year with choices from Optional Activities and Sessions.
Young Lion Warriors	15–18 years old	Focus on leader development, problem-solving, and planning skills.

BECOMING A MEMBER

RECRUITMENT AND APPLICATION

Distribute information flyers; speak to groups; and use any other appropriate means to inform youth and parents in your church, community, school, or neighborhood center of the Young Lions program. Provide youth and parents an opportunity to respond by returning interest indicators or permission slips or by attending an informational meeting about Young Lions. Follow up with a phone call and a visit, if possible, or a general meeting.

Youth enter the program through an application process in which they are interviewed with their parent(s) and learn the expectations of a Young Lions member. Both the boys and their parents are asked to sign the application to make a commitment for consistent involvement. The form also requires the boys to explain in their own words why they would like to be a Young Lion. (See page 36 for a copy.)

MEMBERSHIP REQUIREMENTS

In the information materials and meetings, make clear to the boys and their parents what the requirements and expectations of membership are:

Be the Appropriate Age or Grade Level

Determine the standards for age or grade level for your setting. (See page 31 for more information.) The Young Lions program is created primarily for boys grades four through eight. Every day, children are dealing with heavy stress and weighty issues. African-American boys can be emotionally and psychologically wounded at an early age through negative messages about their Blackness, through the media, by structural racism in social institutions, and by negative stereotypes and role models in urban communities. This program is meant to proactively deal with issues in a young man's life before he makes decisions that can have a negative impact upon his adolescence and adulthood.

Regularly Attend Young Lions Meetings

Consistent attendance is critical for a young man to get the most he can from the Young Lions program. Insistence upon good attendance helps in the development of a sense of responsibility. It also impresses once more upon the group the fact that belonging to Young Lions is a privilege. Rewarding responsible behavior is a positive way of reinforcing this. Determine small but meaningful ways to do so (see page 27).

CONTINUED MEMBERSHIP

Hold high standards for continued membership. Remind the boys of the importance of these commitments:

Know the Meaning of Being a Young Lion

All of the boys need to learn the principles, code of conduct, and pledge of the Young Lions as well as the meaning of the symbols and colors. Take a moment at the beginning of each meeting (after the Libation) for the boys to practice. New Young Lions should be able to recite these at the Kwanzaa celebration in December.

Attend School Regularly

Young Lions members should have good attendance not only at group meetings but at school as well. Education is a primary focus of Young Lions, and every opportunity should be taken to support schooling. Also, look for opportunities in the boys' schools, such as classroom visits, small groups, and special events, to use Young Lions curriculum to supplement public education with culturally specific learning. In addition to exposing all of the students to African-American learning, taking Young Lions teaching to school not only supports the boys who are a part of the group but also creates more interest by other boys, potential members themselves.

Exhibit Positive Behavior at School, Home, and With Friends

Young Lions represent Young Lions wherever they go. The standards for behavior in Young Lions apply not only at group meetings but also at school, home, or out in the neighborhood with their friends. Consistent participation in the program is rewarded with T-shirts and sweatshirts with the Young Lions emblem on them. Reinforce the fact that the boys represent Young Lions and must honor that association through positive conduct at all times. The shirts and sweaters can be a badge of honor, because only boys in the Young Lions program may wear them.

YOUNG LIONS CONTRACTS

At one of the initial meetings of the group, all of the boys who have successfully completed the application process will sign contracts outlining both the group (page 37) and individual (page 38) expectations of Young Lions. In the group contract, the boys resolve to grow and work together as a group. Individually, each boy makes a commitment to

1. be actively involved in the program;
2. be committed to his own personal growth and that of the group,
3. be respectful of himself, his peers, and God; and
4. be regular in his attendance, being present at a minimum of seventy-five percent of all meetings and activities.

RELATIONSHIPS WITH MENTORS

The main vehicle for teaching the boys the objectives of Young Lions is their relationships with the mentors. The dynamic between the boys and men at a meeting is wonderful and mysterious.

If given a choice, most boys would not readily choose to be part of a setting in which the number of men equals the number of boys in the group. Because of the significant presence of adults, the setting does not naturally seem to be a "fun" environment, but rather inhibitive and restrictive. Yet boys respond positively in this atmosphere to the attention of Black men. As genuine care and concern for the boys emanate from the men through their consistent involvement, the boys open up more and more. The boys will relax and be themselves and have fun, teasing and cutting up with the men. As they grow comfortable playing with the men, they will begin to feel comfortable opening up their lives to the men and talking about real issues in their daily lives.

The nature of the Young Lions program includes having fun and male camaraderie, but its main emphasis is on holistic education and Black male socialization. The purpose of the activities is to facilitate one-on-one relationships between the men and the boys. The main theme of Young Lions is to learn what it means to be an African-American man spiritually, physically, and culturally.

The dynamic
between the boys and men
at a meeting is wonderful
and mysterious.

YOUNG LIONS APPLICATION

Parent(s) or guardian name(s) _____

Student's name _____

Address
Phone # _____ Phone # _____

School _____ Grade _____

Birth date _____

In your own words, why do you want to join Young Lions? (Write your response on the back of this application.)

Will you attend the meetings regularly? _____

Will you conduct yourself with pride and with respect for yourself and others at school, at home, and with your friends as a member of Young Lions? _____

Having gone through the interview for membership in Young Lions, I understand the expectations and responsibilities that I will be called upon to fulfill. I pledge to apply myself to attend Young Lions meetings and to conduct myself in a manner appropriate for a member of Young Lions at all times.

Student signature _____

• • • • • • • • • • • • • •

As a parent of a Young Lions member, I pledge to encourage my son to be a consistent attendee of the weekly meetings and monthly field trips, and to show my support for him at home and through attending special family events.

*Parent signature*_____Date _____

_____Date _____

GROUP CONTRACT

THE MEMBERS OF YOUNG LIONS

for the term _____ to _____
       (MONTH/YEAR)   (MONTH/YEAR)

✓ As a group, we make a commitment to one another to learn together and encourage one another.

✓ We accept responsibility for regular attendance at meetings, representing Young Lions well through our proper conduct at all times, and for completing individual assignments.

✓ We will work together as a group, and we are committed to completing the Young Lions curriculum.

✓ We will work together, help one another, and succeed as a group.

Member Signatures

1. _____   2. _____

3. _____   4. _____

5. _____   6. _____

7. _____   8. _____

9. _____   10. _____

11. _____   12. _____

INDIVIDUAL EXPECTATIONS

AS A YOUNG LION, I AGREE TO

✓ Be actively involved physically, emotionally, and spiritually in every component of the Young Lions program.

✓ Be committed to my own personal growth and development through active participation in discussion, group projects, and activities.

✓ Be respectful of my peers, myself, and God in my conduct.

✓ Be consistent in attending at least 75 percent of all meetings and events.

. . . .

Signed_____

Date_____

PARENT INVOLVEMENT

Three criteria for the success of the program

are youth consistency, mentor consistency, *and parent involvement*. Provide opportunities for parents to be involved with the Young Lions program in significant ways. Ideally, the parents will be able to connect with the group on different levels, beginning with the beginning:

Start with the commitment. In order to participate in the program the boys *and their parents* go through an application process. This basically consists of a home visit during which the parent(s) and the child review a contract for membership in Young Lions (page 36), and then sign it. The contract describes the program and emphasizes the importance of consistent attendance. In signing the contract, the parent and child make a commitment to the Young Lions program.

Host a special event, such as Kwanzaa, that includes families, as a way to provide parents, youth, and mentors the opportunity to get to know one another.

Inform parents regularly about the group's activities. Be intentional about communicating to them when they drop off or pick up the boys as well as through more formal means, such as sending home written announcements. Using the field trip permission form (page 25) is one way to keep in touch. It also provides contact information in case of an emergency.

Schedule regular open house events to encourage parent involvement.

Invite moms as well as dads to visit meetings so that they know what the boys are doing. Have an open-door policy. Parents are welcome any time.

Facilitate regular contact between parents and their son's individual mentor and with the Young Lions coordinator as well.

Organize a boosters group. Perhaps one of the boy's parents would be willing to organize parents to assist with the program at special events and the like. Such a group may provide support for parents as well as help the program.

Invite parents to be drivers and additional adults on field trips.

Encourage fathers to apply to be Young Lions mentors.

Invite parents to the annual Young Lions Awards Banquet.

Young Lions provides opportunities for families to grow closer.

SUCCESS FACTORS

The success of a program such as Young Lions is dependent on consistent youth, mentor, and parent involvement. The Young Lions rites-of-passage program brings together these different aspects of a young man's world to build a strong sense of self within him so that he may be able to grow and be the individual that God has created him to be. The commitment of parent, mentor, and child to work together and the quality of their involvement will determine the success of the Young Lions program.

Consistency of adult mentors is of paramount importance. Work with a one-to-one ratio of men to boys, and have the men share the responsibilities for preparation so that they do not fall on one person. Have each man take responsibility for a different part of the schedule, or have two men take on the lesson theme for each month.

Consistent attendance by the boys is encouraged through various incentives and awards. The dynamic that draws the boys is not the games, field trips, and awards so much as it is the positive attention they get from caring, Christian, Black men.

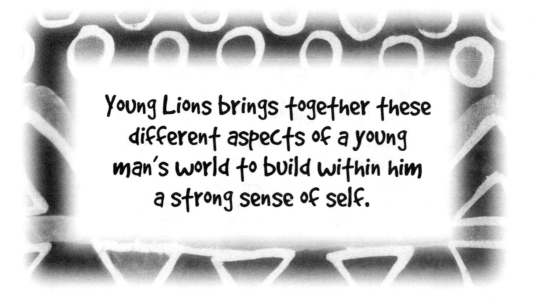

Young Lions brings together these different aspects of a young man's world to build within him a strong sense of self.

II. MENTORS

A MENTOR'S STORY

It's Saturday morning; and a group of eager, energetic inner-city teenagers pour through the door of Bill Cottman's house and catch the aroma of pancakes on the griddle. Wearing baggy pants, oversized T-shirts and sweatshirts, and athletic shoes of every size and shape, the teens are obviously glad to be part of this event.

Cottman waves his spatula and welcomes the boys to come and get it. Soon the group, which includes adult sponsors from Park Avenue United Methodist Church, a multiracial, inner-city congregation in south Minneapolis, is seated at a table and enjoying a spread of steaming pancakes, fresh sausage, and hot maple syrup.

Yet this morning's meeting of Simba (the Swahili word for "lion") is not just about breakfast. It is about teaching young, Black, inner-city boys what it means "to be a Christian African-American male," according to Cottman, a systems sales manager with Honeywell Corporation. With the mind of an engineer, he is always thinking of a creative, tangible way to teach the weekly lesson. Now close to 50 years old, Cottman conveys the calm and confidence of a high-level corporate executive. His personal warmth and sense of self-assurance helps put the boys at ease as they take off their jackets and pull up to the table.

Once breakfast is over and the dishes cleared, the energetic youth gather in the living room to listen to Cottman and other adults tell them about their own lives and faith.

"I graduated from Salisbury High School in Salisbury, Maryland, and then from Howard University, with an electrical engineering degree," he explains. "My father died when I was 12 years old. I have only a few recollections of my dad, and they are good. But it was my mother who raised me."

The highlight of Cottman's story on this day is about being in the delivery room to witness the birth of his only child. "I was proud to be there for my daughter's birth," he tells the young men. The boys ask questions about the experience, which sounds a bit overwhelming.

"Didn't you faint?" asks one teen.

"Why would you ever want to be there?" asks another.

"I wanted to reassure and comfort my wife," he responds. "I wanted to be able to say to my daughter that from the moment she entered the world, I was there for her."

For two young men in particular, Jamaal and Terrell, this morning's meeting is one more piece of the puzzle of what it means to be Black, male, and a believer—it means taking responsibility to love and raise the children you father.

UPDATE ON JAMAAL AND TERRELL

Jamaal, now 21, is enrolled in college and working a steady job. He volunteers as a mentor with the Simba program, working with neighborhood youth.

Terrell, after leaving Simba, became involved in a neighborhood gang and dropped out of school. He is now serving a term in jail related to a drive-by shooting.

Reprinted from "Teaching Manhood in the Urban Jungle," by Bob Moeller, *Christianity Today,* October 24, 1994, copyright © 1994 by Bob Moeller. Used by permission.

GETTING STARTED

The Young Lions program is designed to address the specific, holistic needs of African-American boys, especially but not exclusively in inner-city communities. After several years of doing ministry in an urban setting, I saw the need to expose young Black boys to more positive relationships and experiences than they were getting through school, family experiences, peer contacts, and even church. Many African-American male youth see the church and Christianity as irrelevant to their lives. The keys to meeting this need are providing examples of and relationships with strong African-American Christian males. The following are steps for recruiting and training men as mentors for Young Lions:

1. LOCATE MEN

Take every opportunity to discuss with other African-American men your vision for Black boys. The first step is to locate positive Black men. A good place to look for Black men who share a burden for addressing the issues facing Black boys is in the church. Other places are in other Christian institutions such as schools or colleges. Black men who work at schools or colleges, parks or community centers are there because they want to invest in youth; so it is worth your time to look for them at these places. Identify places where Black men gather in your community and make plans to visit to talk about what you are trying to do.

2. MAKE CONTACT

The next step is to make contact with these men. When recruiting men for your program, examine your existing friendships, networks, and social or work environments. Begin with those closest to you and work your way out in concentric circles of social relationships (family and friends, acquaintances and associates, strangers). Potential mentors may be friends, acquaintances, members of your church, neighbors in the community, young men that you know, college students, co-workers, and so on. Approach the men in your personal circle of relationships. Make contact with preexisting men's groups such as fraternities, support groups, men's groups at churches, and even clusters of friends. Make informal, personal contact with the men and follow up with a phone call.

3. BRING MEN TOGETHER

Invite several men to come together in an informal setting to discuss the issues facing Black boys and men. Come together to discuss common issues or current events having to do with African-American culture, racism, or discrimination. Various forms of communication include (growing in order of effectiveness):

a. writing a letter
b. making a phone call
c. personal contact and invitation

Don't start by asking the men to make a commitment or to begin a program. Bring them together just to talk. The challenge is to get persons to come to just one meeting to see what the group is like. Once a man comes to a training session or a typical Young Lions meeting with boys and sees the interaction between the men and boys, he will find it hard to refuse involvement. What invariably happens is that a meeting to discuss issues facing Black boys will turn into a dialogue about mutual issues, problems, and obstacles that all of you face in society as Black men.

4. SHARE THE VISION

At that point, the group will begin to invest personally in the vision of mentoring boys to help them become men. It is not the number of the men gathered that is critical to the success of the program but their commitment. A program of high quality will attract men of high quality.

Getting men to come to your meetings will take a great deal of work, patience, and thick-skinnedness on your part. Get the word out about the vision and the need through neighborhood newspapers, flyers, and posters, announcements at local churches, and so on. Persevere, and your efforts will bear fruit.

Although you may be successful in getting men to turn out to your training sessions, expect a certain amount of drop-out as you approach the point of actually doing something. But don't shrink from telling the men exactly what will be expected of them as mentors and asking them to make a commitment. For those who cannot commit to full-time mentoring, find short-term opportunities for them, such as assisting as a driver for a field trip. Often as men see the program in action, they will be more ready to commit to more later.

5. TRAIN MENTORS

When you begin meeting with the men, engage them in discussion on some of the issues. Focus on building up the group not on developing a program. Building rapport among the men is a critical step for the success of your Young Lions group. As the group engages in discussion and reflection, they will naturally begin to talk about their personal lives and experiences with family, faith, racial discrimination, and other issues.

Each man will bring different convictions and experiences that have shaped him. Each of them will have different reasons for wanting to be involved in Young Lions. This time together will allow you to affirm common ideals so that the group may be of one mind and purpose in working with the boys. It is not necessary that everyone agree with everyone else on every issue. What is necessary is that the men are able to work together and be in agreement with common group goals. The training sessions and content provide a structure for your men to meet several times before working with youth, building group cohesiveness and solidarity. The training meetings help develop a sense of unity among the men before they engage the boys. (See pages 47–69.)

6. ASK FOR COMMITMENT

The mentors are asked to sign a contract of commitment (page 46). The contract outlines the expectations of a mentor in terms of Christian commitment and lifestyle; involvement in the group, and being a role model by exhibiting positive relationships at home, work, and with peers. Men also commit to attending seventy-five percent of all activities, to trying to bring other men to Young Lions as mentors, to being an advocate for Young Lions by telling others about the program goals, and to participating in planning for regular meetings and special activities. The time commitment for men in Young Lions is to attend weekly meetings, to maintain consistent contact with one boy in the group, and to attend regular men's meetings.

7. CONTINUE DEVELOPMENT

It is important to encourage the men's continued development as mentors. The men should meet on a regular basis (once a month) without the boys being present. At this gathering, they may discuss issues or difficulties and receive insight and encouragement from one another. They may also brainstorm ideas and plan future activities. It is important for the coordinator to provide resources for development as well as training and spiritual nurture for the mentors. Remember, the success of the group is directly related to the well-being and comfort of the men.

8. BUILD SPECIAL RELATIONSHIPS

Mentors are encouraged to pursue a significant relationship with at least one boy in the group. In developing mentoring relationships what works best is for the Young Lions coordinator to observe which men and boys gravitate toward each other and work with them to develop those relationships.

Mentors are then asked to maintain regular contact with their "charge" outside the Young Lions meetings. This contact may be weekly, biweekly, or monthly—whatever the mentor, boy, and his parents work out. Mentor contact may take a variety of forms such as special trips, lunch together after a Young Lions meeting, or regular phone contact. In addition, mentors and their charges make personal contact weekly at the Young Lions meetings. Once the mentor and the boy have "chosen" each other, arrange for the mentor to meet the boy's parent(s) in order to lay out expectations for the relationship.

Each man's relationship with the youth may be different, but each relationship has tremendous value. Mentors must keep this fact in mind constantly. Emphasize the fact that their presence alone speaks volumes to the boys. A clear dialogue about mentor expectations and what is expected from mentors will make the men more comfortable with their roles.

Teach the men what to expect from the boys in terms of behavior and personal interaction. The structure of Young Lions is purposefully disciplined while remaining flexible. There are times to play games and times to get down to business. Adherence to this structure will assist in the development of genuine and positive relationships between the men and boys.

YOUNG LIONS
MENTOR CONTRACT

Expectations

✚ *Young Lions Mentors* are expected to be men who are actively seeking God and following Jesus Christ and demonstrating that relationship in their lifestyle.

✚ *Young Lions Mentors* are expected to exhibit a positive lifestyle free from any form of substance abuse or violent behavior.

✚ *Young Lions Mentors* are positive role models in their every everyday lives manifested in their relationships with their families, peers, and others.

Commitment

As a *Young Lions Mentor,* I commit to

— attending at least 75 percent of all meetings, events, and activities;

— recruiting at least one other man to join the Young Lions mentors;

— supporting Young Lions through telling others about our program goals;

— participating in planning and carrying out regular meetings and special events;

— pursuing a special mentoring relationship with one boy in the group.

Signature _____ Date _____

MENTOR TRAINING SESSIONS

The following material may be used for six consecutive meetings for mentor training and development. Another venue would be to hold a retreat to cover the material.

The basic format for each meeting or session with the men should be patterned after the Young Lions meetings with the youth. The suggested meeting format for the mentor training sessions has the following components (allow two hours for each meeting):

REFRESHMENTS *(15 minutes)*

Provide snacks for your meeting—doughnuts, muffins, coffee, and juice for a morning meeting, or something more substantial if you are meeting close to lunch time. Whenever you meet, food helps create a comfortable social dynamic of dialogue and interaction. While eating, the men can talk and get to know one another. Building relationships and camaraderie among the men is a primary focus of your training sessions. Whether you offer refreshments at the beginning or the end of each meeting is up to you.

ICEBREAKER AND INTRODUCTIONS *(15 minutes)*

In this part of the meeting, the men will introduce themselves to one another in a way that gives some insight as to who they are. This time is important for getting to know one another and preparing to work together. The more bonded the men are, the more effective the work among the boys will be.

LIBATION AND PRAYER *(5 minutes)*

As in the regular Young Lions meetings with the boys, open your gatherings with prayer and a libation ceremony. This is a time to give thanks and remember family and ancestors who have paved the way for the freedoms Black people enjoy today. Review the description of the libation ceremony (page 20).

PURPOSES OF GATHERING *(5 minutes)*

At each session, remind the men of the goals of coming together:

✚ **to discuss problematic issues facing Black boys in American society and in the local community;**

✚ **to examine ways Christian African-American men can respond to those issues.**

SESSION MATERIAL *(60 minutes)*

Work through the material for the six weekly training sessions (pages 49–69).

Session 1: Overview .49
Session 2: Introduction 51
    Black Boys Handout 54
    Black Men Handout 58
Session 3: The Need 59
Session 4: The Program 62
    Philosophy and Goals Handout 63
Session 5: . The Meeting 65
Session 6: Expectations 66
    Working With Boys Handout 68

DIALOGUE AND SHARING *(15 minutes)*

A primary focus of mentor training is to develop open discussion among the men. Maintain flexibility in your meetings to allow for exploring tangents and self-disclosing conversations.

CLOSING REMARKS *(5 minutes)*

These include summarizing the session's dialogue, emphasizing goals, praying together, and setting the agenda for the next meeting.

HARAMBEE CIRCLE *(5 minutes)*

Gathering in the Harambee circle is the way every Young Lions meeting ends. Have the group join hands in a circle and raise their arms together, chanting: "Harambee! Harambee! Harambee! Harambee!" *Harambee* is a Swahili word meaning "Let's all get together and push." In this setting, Harambee means working together to achieve a common goal.

✳

1. OVERVIEW............................

OBJECTIVES OF THIS SESSION

1. To begin to build a sense of group identity and common purpose among the men;
2. To introduce the issues facing Black boys in the community and to begin to define the problems that must be addressed;
3. To establish a dialogical format to frame ongoing discussions.

ICEBREAKER: WHICH ONE ARE YOU?

Have the men sit in a circle. Beginning with the group coordinator, go around the circle, and have each man introduce himself and answer this question:

If you were an animal, what would you be and why?

GROUP DIALOGUE

A. Get to know one another and the issues. The goal of Young Lions is to teach Black boys what it means to be African-American men spiritually, culturally, and physically. Before your group begins talking about the boys with whom you will be working, the participants need to talk about their own experiences as African-American men. Say something like:

> As Black men, you each know the importance of a strong self-image. This need is at the core of what we want to instill within the boys. However, before you begin meeting with them, let's explore where we as a group have been and from where each individual is coming. Each of us has had different experiences. In coming together, we join our individual strengths. Discussing our experiences with one another before we begin meeting with the boys will unify us. We won't focus on our differences; instead, we will focus on our strengths and the things upon which we agree.

Begin the discussion by asking these questions and inviting each man to answer:

✛ Why are you here today?
✛ Describe one way you have experienced racism or prejudice. How did (do) you deal with it?
✛ What do you feel are some critical issues facing Black boys today?

B. Introduce the problem-solving format you will be using in various discussions. Write out these questions for the group to see. Keep the list for future discussions.

✛ **What is the problem?**
✛ **What causes it?**
✛ **What is the solution?**
✛ **How do we implement the solution?**

Your group will spend the next five or six weeks working through these questions as a foundation for continuing dialogue about the needs of Black boys. This way of addressing problems is logical and clear, yet it is flexible and allows for group dynamics to develop. This process provides a structure for the men to have a dialogue and to struggle together with these issues.

In applying this format to the issues facing young Black males, the questions might be framed this way for your group discussion:

✛ **What are the problems facing Black boys in American society? in our community?**
✛ **What underlying causes lead to these problems?**
✛ **Think of some clear and effective solutions that may be applied to these problems.**
✛ **How can we as African-American men implement these solutions?**

Struggle as a group with the answers or non-answers. Don't settle for pat and easy solutions. Dig into the matter and examine the issues deeply. This discussion—hard work as it may be—is nevertheless a valuable time for your group of men to bond and talk about their convictions as well as their experiences.

For Next Session

Invite one or more volunteers to become familiar with Jawanza Kunjufu's series *Countering the Conspiracy to Destroy Black Boys*, Volumes 1–4, (African-American Images, ISBN: 0913543446); check Reading Resources, at the back of this book. Ask the volunteers to review the material as a foundation for the next session's discussion. Check your local library, bookstore, or Internet source for copies. If you are not able to obtain the book, the handouts for next week will be sufficient for informing the discussion.

Invite volunteers to track down statistics for your local area that pertain to the well-being of African Americans in your community or state. The library and the Internet are two possible sources.

2. INTRODUCTION ....

OBJECTIVES OF THIS SESSION
1. To introduce the men to the basic principles of and philosophy behind the Young Lions rites-of-passage program;
2. To reflect on the problems facing Black boys in American society through discussing statistical data and considering appropriate interventions;
3. To give the men a sense of the importance of their commitment to and presence in the lives of Black boys.

ICEBREAKER: I AM
Sit in a circle. Have each man take a turn introducing himself to the group and making an "I am" statement about himself (for example: "I am a father," "I am tall," "I am athletic," "I am a teacher"). Continue until each one has made ten statements. This exercise will give your group insights as to how each man perceives himself.

GROUP DIALOGUE
A. Use the handouts "Black Boys" and "Black Men" (pages 54–58) to expose the men to the issues and to promote discussion. Explore with the mentors the issues of the need for commitment and consistency by Black men working with Black boys. Encourage them to consider carefully their involvement in the Young Lions program, and challenge them to invite other men to become involved.

Men need to acknowledge and experience the urgency that faces urban Black boys and their communities. It is not a light task to take on the responsibility of mentoring and serving as a role model. Half-hearted involvement of a man who hasn't thought through his commitment may have a devastating impact on the life of a young boy. Don't ask for commitments yet, but start the men thinking.

B. Review these national statistical trends for urban Black males in America:

1. Homicide is the number one cause of death for Black males ages 15–24.
2. Nationwide 12% of Black teenagers drop out of school, but the rate is higher in the nation's 35 largest cities.
3. Thirty-three percent of Black children are born in poverty.
4. The pregnancy rate for African-American girls is 179 per 1,000 in contrast to 66 per 1,000 for white teens.
5. Only 14.6% of all African-Americans are college educated (compared to 25.9% of all US citizens).
6. One in four (25%) of all African-American men will have spent some time in prison during his lifetime.

1. Center for the Study and Prevention of Violence; 2. National Center for Policy Analysis and Johns Hopkins University; 3. Children's Defense Fund; 4. National Center to Prevent Teen Pregnancy; 5 US Census, March 2000; 6. prisoners.com/minority.html.

Examine these national statistics, but pay particular attention to your state and local statistics and trends. If your volunteer(s) from last week were unable to find comparable statistics for your community, discuss the men's perceptions of how accurate those national statistics are for their area. Don't get too caught up in the details. Together your group will have a feel for the vulnerability of the people in your community.

Try to discover underlying causes and trends that lead to such alarming figures. Discuss the effect of institutional racism on the Black community and on Black males in particular. Also look at how African-American people have responded to the problems. Jawanza Kunjufu's series *Countering the Conspiracy to Destroy Black Boys* is a good resource for this discussion.

The purpose of the sessions is not to rehash the obvious and repeatedly stated problems facing Black boys but for Black men to work together to seek and implement creative solutions. Emphasize positive and creative solutions already existing in the Black community through national or local initiatives. Some examples may include men's groups that are continuing to meet as a result of the Million Man March or other local examples of African-American men involved with the community and with Black boys, in particular.

C. The previous discussions in A and B will have set the stage for the presentation of the Young Lions program. "What is Young Lions?" is the question your group will answer. First, talk about the overall goals and objectives of the program:

> The stated goal of Young Lions is to teach Black boys what it means to be African-American men spiritually, culturally, and physically.

These three dimensions of self are explored in order to infuse the boys with a strong self-image and self-esteem by knowing who they are in Christ. Refer to pages 63–64 in detailing the goals and objectives of the program. At this point, you will also define the methods and procedures by which the Young Lions program addresses the needs of Black male youth.

The goals of the program will be met through a two-pronged approach:

✚ First, Christian African-American men will engage the boys in personal relationships and thus model and teach manhood that is both African American and Christian.

✚ Second, the YOUNG LIONS curriculum will provide a format and structure to encourage the interactive involvement of the men with the boys as well as content about being a Christian, African-American man.

For Next Session

Again, invite one or more volunteers to become familiar with Jawanza Kunjufu's series *Countering the Conspiracy to Destroy Black Boys,* Volumes 1–4 (African-American Images, ISBN: 0913543446). The material will be helpful in the next session's discussion.

Invite others to become familiar with *How Black Is the Gospel?* by Tom Skinner (out of print), or *A Black Theology of Liberation, 20th Anniversary Edition,* by James H. Cone (Orbis Books; ISBN: 0883446855). Both of these books will be good resources for the discussion in the next session.

Check your library, bookstore, or Internet source for copies.

BLACK BOYS

The Fourth-Grade-Failure Syndrome

The author Jawanza Kunjufu identifies the "fourth-grade-failure syndrome," in which bright, engaging, Black boys in the educational system reach a certain point in their development (fourth grade) and exhibit an abrupt change in personality and outlook on life. Kunjufu explores this dynamic further, making note of a boy's excitement about school and eagerness to learn demonstrated in early school years, and charts his attitude change to passivity and loss of enthusiasm and willingness to learn.

The fourth-grade-failure syndrome points to the unsuccessful transition of Black boys from elementary to intermediate grades in public schools. This dynamic plays out in the community as well. As boys grow older, it is obvious that at a certain age they begin to become harder. At around eleven or twelve years old, they enter a stage in life in which they have lost their childlike innocence and enthusiasm for life. This loss is reflected in their school performance and their interaction with others—adults and peers.

Kunjufu points to changes in the educational process, such as teaching strategies and classroom dynamics in the schools at that transitional point as a significant cause. But there exists as well the impact of negative influences in the neighborhood environment such as crime, violence, and drugs. At this age, boys may be more aware of family stress and dysfunction; and certainly, they are becoming sensitive to negative social messages about Black males through newspapers and other media and social policies. Black children suffer due to messages that tell them that they are inferior because they are Black; and this perception is reinforced by the media, police harassment, and social neglect.

BLACK CHILDREN SUFFER DUE TO MESSAGES THAT TELL THEM THAT THEY ARE INFERIOR.

Society's Messages

Black boys and Black children, in general, grow up in a society that communicates to them that they are unwanted. The vast majority of them grow up in communities in which they see their lives and the lives of people like them devalued through socio-economic trends and the prevalence of poverty, crime, and drugs around them.

Black children begin to develop a sense of inferiority even before they are old enough to enter the public school system. The pervasiveness of institutional racism, resulting in the warehousing of the Black poor in slums and ghettos, the lack of job opportunities for men, and an appalling lack of adequate housing is horribly insidious. It is not enough that society demonstrates that it views Black children as being substandard, but many of the children themselves begin to buy into the lie.

Black boys are viewed by mainstream society as threatening, so they experience more rejection and repression of their self-identity as children. Elementary school teachers are often white women who are trained from the perspective of a mainstream social perspective, which devalues "Blackness." Not only do they have no training or idea as to how to educate Black boys, but they also harbor an inherent fear of them. This dynamic is reflected in the church as well, where the Christian educators are also typically women.

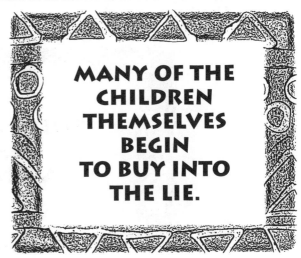

MANY OF THE CHILDREN THEMSELVES BEGIN TO BUY INTO THE LIE.

African-American boys have a strong need for firm guidance and supervision, personal attention, dependable relationships, and opportunities to channel their energies in positive ways. An educational system that measures intellect by a person's command of the written word excludes cultures that have an oral tradition perspective, so it will not bring out those students' best work. Mainstream society demands that a person conform to the majority culture in order to be accepted and allows no cultural self-expression. It repeatedly sends the message that an individual must either conform to the social norm or accept marginalization.

Target: Black Males

Black male youth feel this alienation explicitly. One young Black man who had dropped out of school and recently discovered that he was going to be a father was unsuccessfully looking for meaningful employment. He told me that the burden and stress he bears each day is so overwhelming that he can't allow himself to feel it. By forcing Black males to choose constantly between their own culture or the majority white one in order to survive, society devalues their Blackness and their self-identity.

The dynamics of growing up Black in America point to the need for Afrocentric and culturally specific educational programs for Black children, particularly Black boys. Statistics evaluating the progress of students in public schools consistently show Black males hugging the low end of the charts. The statistics on Black boys show disproportionately high rates in juvenile detention, of school dropouts, in labeling of learning disabilities, of the commission of crimes, and so on. Some alarming statistics point to the effective "erasing" of an entire generation of Black youth:

1. Life expectancy for Black males is 67.6 as opposed to 74.5 years for white males.
2. In major urban areas the probability that a 15-year-old African-American youth will be murdered by age 45 is as high as one in 12 (Washington, D.C.).
3. More Black men are in prison than in institutions of higher learning.
4. Black youth in urban areas are more likely to dropout of high school.

For whatever reason, the public school system in urban areas is not meeting the needs of at-risk Black youth; and these statistics demand a response. If Black boys were an animal species, Congress would declare them endangered.

All of these trends reveal a disturbing dynamic affecting Black males in urban America, which seems genocidal. Consider also the high rate of teen pregnancy, especially in urban areas, among Black females before age eighteen (5). This statistic points to the young Black males who are out there getting them pregnant but who are not ready to be fathers. Consider also that nearly one third of all Black children are born into poverty (6).

THESE STATISTICS DEMAND A RESPONSE.

Why Some Succeed

Common factors of resiliency among urban Black youth who succeed include independence, leadership ability, a high confidence level, and family togetherness (meaning that their families spend time together at least once a day).

This last factor points to the importance of stable families in the Black community. Debate continues about the significance of the prevalence of single-mother families in urban Black communities. The salient point for stableness for these families has to do with how the absence of the male adult affects child-rearing and the family's financial resources. Single-mother families in Black urban communities are usually poor families. However, whether it be single-mom, single-dad, or two-parent families, the stable family unit is critical.

Black boys who succeed in urban communities are those who exhibit self-motivation by occupying themselves in sports programs or getting jobs rather than hanging out with nothing to do. The scarcity of jobs for youth in urban communities severely curtails the opportunity for youth to choose an alternative to gang involvement. These youth and children show remarkable initiative in building supportive networks around themselves. Those networks, which function as an extended family, may include neighbors, positive peers, churches, parachurch organizations, and parks or community centers.

Black children have a crucial need for a sense of belonging to a community or larger society. Many of their families do not meet this need for them, so many turn to negative substitutes such as gangs. A primary need of all human beings is a need to belong, a need for community. Black males find it hard to fill this need in a society that repeatedly closes the door in their faces.

Statistical sources for pages 55–56 : 1. Centers for Disease Control and Prevention, 1998; 2. Heritage Center for Data Analysis, No. 00-05, 2000; 3. U.S. Census and Bureau of Justice Statistics; 4. Johns Hopkins University, 2001; 5. Black Women's Health; 6. Children's Defense Fund.

"IF WE CAN REACH THE BOYS, WE LIFT THE ENTIRE COMMUNITY."

The Goal and Beyond

If the goal of families and communities is to raise Black children to be well-adjusted individuals able to have and support families and contribute positively to society, then we must begin to look at specific measures designed to meet their particular needs. Such measures should teach and affirm cultural values such as "being Black" without characterizing the affirmation as being self-destructive or consumed by a hatred of whites. Intervention with Black males will turn back the inexorable tide of self-destruction evident in inner-city Black communities.

Reaching Black boys will affect everyone in the inner city, including girls and women. Whole families will see great impact as the boys grow into husbands and fathers; and whole communities will change as Black girls and boys see positive Black men as husbands, fathers, and leaders in their community.

John Perkins, author and founder of the Christian Community Development Association, a nationwide network of urban churches and ministries, states: "I am convinced that saving our boys is one of the surest ways to heal the inner city. If we can reach the boys, we lift the entire community."

The Young Lions program focuses on building positive self-image and self-esteem in Black boys. The program strives to affirm their value as unique persons in Christ and to affirm their culture as God-given. To do so is to give them inner resources so that they may cope with and succeed in a world that is often afraid of them and despises them because of the color of their skin.

(Excerpted from "Developing Simba: A Curriculum for Addressing the Needs of Urban African-American Boys," by Chris McNair.)

BLACK MEN

To say that African-American men are uniquely suited to address the needs facing Black boys is an understatement. Positive, self-assured African-American men are indeed the only hope for the children of the Black community as a whole.

Black boys simply will not see a better life for themselves unless they see an older man modeling it for them. Young Black men will not stay with their families or work to achieve their potential and become affirming and affirmed members of community unless they see other men staying and making it. Strong and firm, caring and self-assured men engender a positive response and motivation from the most hardened inner-city boys. They are naturally drawn to men who show an interest in them and genuinely care about them.

Boys respond to men from all walks of life: young men just starting out in life, mature men with families, retired older men—all men may have a significant impact on the life of a Black boy craving attention. Sports figure Charles Barkley was right—he is not a role model. A personal, enduring relationship with a man who cares will have much more value over time than the brief attention of the most popular celebrity. Urban Black boys are often crying out for structure and a firm hand giving loving direction.

However, they can sniff out a fake in a minute. They want and respond to "the real deal." In my experience of ministry in the inner city, I find that boys do not respond to me because I am a Christian or even because of the opportunities to do fun activities, but because they sense that I genuinely care about them. Positive male leadership is a critical component contributing to the development of male children.

Boys are often subject to female authority in schools and churches and even in their homes. The prevalent trend of absentee fathers and single mothers in urban areas leads boys to associate respect for authority and appropriate social behavior as being "feminine." It is incumbent upon public schools and community agencies to seek out positive male role models for urban Black boys. African-American men are the best possible resource for assisting emotional and often angry boys in redirecting their energies in positive pursuits.

(Excerpted from "Developing Simba: A Curriculum for Addressing the Needs of Urban African-American Boys," by Chris McNair)

POSITIVE, SELF-ASSURED AFRICAN-AMERICAN MEN ARE INDEED THE ONLY HOPE FOR THE CHILDREN OF THE BLACK COMMUNITY AS A WHOLE.

3. THE NEED ....

OBJECTIVES OF THIS SESSION

1. To identify some of the specific needs of Black boys;
2. To discuss viable solutions as to how those needs may be met and for the men to see themselves as a group implementing one or some of those solutions;
3. To recognize the power of the Christian gospel for meeting the needs of Black boys.

ICEBREAKER: GUESS WHO

Before the meeting, prepare index cards or small pieces of paper with the name of a famous or historical African-American figure on each. Prepare one card for each of the men in your group. Affix a card to each man's back as he enters the room, instructing the men not to tell one another what name is on their cards. When each man has a name on his back, the men must mingle and ask one another questions to guess what name they have. Limit the time or limit the number of questions to ten.

GROUP DIALOGUE

A. If you have access to Jawanza Kunjufu's series *Countering the Conspiracy to Destroy Black Boys,* use highlights from it to spark discussion. If you do not, ask the men to pull together a list of negative influences that have an impact on the boys of the community; and use the list to start the discussion.

Ask the men to speak openly and honestly about their impressions of Kunjufu's book. Some may agree with the author, and some may not. Most men will affirm many of his assertions but have reservations about a few. Talk about these differences of opinion.

Not all of the men will think alike or agree on all issues. However, through open dialogue, your group can come to common ground and be in agreement on how to work together to address the needs of Black boys in your community. Discuss the issues that point to the need for programs like Young Lions.

Use the reading to examine the issues facing Black boys in American society. Make a list or chart of different negative influences, and then discuss ways to have an impact on them. The participants should not assume that they can solve all of the problems, but this dialogue will suggest some specific areas your group can target. Discuss how Black men may make a difference in these areas as individuals in their relationships or workplaces and as a group.

Kunjufu outlines several dynamics that conspire to prevent Black boys from achieving their potential and maturing into strong and capable men. Review and discuss each of these dynamics: **low self-esteem, negative family situations, inadequate educational systems, peer pressure, social prejudice**.

✚ How can Black men respond to these issues?

✚ How can Black men respond to the crises facing Black boys? (Discuss the role of Black men in the family, community, and society as fathers, husbands, brothers, breadwinners, and leaders.)

✚ Do Black men have any obligation to respond to the crises mentioned?

These are all questions to which there are no immediate or automatic answers. These are questions for your group to struggle with in developing a group identity, common goals, and motivation. Struggling together in order to know what you are about and what you desire to accomplish is a key to the group's effectiveness.

B. Ask the men to examine their personal motives for wanting to be involved in a program like Young Lions. There is no wrong answer. Each man has different and personal reasons. Each man represents different experiences that have led him to this point. Recognize, however, and affirm the shared experiences of racism in your group. List the various motives for participating in Young Lions, which may include family, children, self, community, religion, among others.

You are not trying to build a group that sees itself as having all of the answers or being saviors of the Black community. Instead, you are bringing men to a realization of their own shortcomings as individuals and their strength as a group. As Black men, they are not coming to boys having resolved these issues but recognizing that they continue to struggle with their identity as Black men in a majority white society. What these men, in their maturity and wisdom, will have to share with boys is the experience having developed methods of coping that promote self-esteem and reconciliation among races as opposed to violence and hatred.

As you articulate among yourselves your struggles as Black men, attempt to identify common positive measures of coping and pursuing your goals in the face of opposition. Try to put words to the common factors that shape a code or standard by which you live. This will be your most valuable resource to share with young Black boys.

C. As a Christian rites-of-passage program, Young Lions affirms that Jesus Christ is key to developing such a code. Struggle with what this idea means. Christians often state that Jesus is the answer to any problem. How is Christ the answer to the crises facing Black boys and the Black community?

Read and discuss the material from the introduction to this Young Lions book (page 51–53). Invite the volunteers who have read *How Black Is the Gospel?* by Tom Skinner, or *A Black Theology of Liberation,* by James H. Cone, to give input from these sources.

As issues arise in the next few months, work at all of them from a Christian perspective; but be real and don't offer fake or insubstantial solutions. Struggle with each need. Pray together, read the Word, ask a pastor or spiritual leader to address the group on this issue. Each member of your group must be convinced of the relevance of Christ to the everyday experience of African Americans before offering a solution to the boys.

FROM THE PROGRAM GOALS

"The linchpin of the theology behind Young Lions is to give the boys a sense of identity in Christ. Jesus is indeed relevant for the issues facing Black boys today, because he knew suffering.

✠ As a boy, Jesus himself faced extermination as King Herod ordered all Hebrew boys slaughtered in an attempt to kill the future king.

✠ Jesus experienced racism as a Jew in the Roman Empire, living in Roman-occupied Israel.

✠ Jesus spent most of his adult life with the poor, oppressed, and ostracized of his society.

"In summary, Jesus knew what it was like to be discriminated against and to be feared and hated because of his ethnic background. He knew what it was like to live an endangered life; he knew what it was like to face prejudice; he knew what it was like to grow up male; and he knew what it was like to have limited economic resources. Jesus Christ can speak to the experiences and issues of Black males in America" (excerpted from page 16).

For Next Session

If you decide to give the men each a notebook for keeping Young Lions materials together, have them ready. Make photocopies for each of the men of the pages to be distributed in the next session (listed on page 62).

4. THE PROGRAM ....

OBJECTIVES OF THIS SESSION
1. To familiarize the men with the philosophy and goals of the Young Lions rites-of-passage program;
2. To review the Young Lions mentor helps.

ICEBREAKER: THE HUMAN KNOT
Have the men gather into a circle and stretch out one hand to reach across and grab the hand of a person across from them. Ask them to use the other hand to join with someone else in the circle. Be sure that no one is holding both hands with the same person. The task now is for the group to untangle itself without releasing each others' hands.

GROUP DIALOGUE
A. Distribute the Young Lions handouts of the "Philosophy and Goals" (pages 63–64). Review the material together, allowing for questions and dialogue.

B. Distribute copies of "Working With Boys" (page 68–69). Talk about the five keys listed there. Ask the men to provide examples from their own lives of how to live out those principles. Encourage the storytelling. Affirm the fact that no one does these things perfectly, but that with God's help the men will find their efforts bearing fruit.

C. Talk about the steps the boys take for becoming and remaining a member of Young Lions. Give the men copies of these pages:

Becoming a Member	33–35
Young Lions Application	36
Group Contract	37
Individual Expectations	38
Young Lions Symbol	17
Young Lions Principles	18
Pledge and Code of Conduct	19
Nguzo Saba (The Seven Principles of Kwanzaa)	138–139
Reading Resources	285–288

You might want to provide loose-leaf notebooks for the mentors so that they can assemble the papers into a handbook. Go through the notebook page by page, allowing the men to familiarize themselves with the material.

PHILOSOPHY AND GOALS

PURPOSE

Young Lions is an African-American mentoring program designed to help young boys experience and work through the rites of passage to becoming a man. The group addresses spiritual, emotional, and social needs and deals with issues such as personal hygiene, work habits, self-concept and self-esteem, knowledge of African-American heritage and culture, and education. The purpose of the curriculum is to involve boys in positive interaction with African-American men in preparation for adolescence and adulthood.

GOAL

The goal of Young Lions is to teach African-American boys what it means to be African-American men spiritually, culturally, and physically. These three dimensions of self are explored thoroughly in order to infuse the boys with a strong self-image and with self-esteem as a result of knowing who they are in Christ. The basic method by which this goal will be met is to provide Christian, African-American men to engage the boys in personal relationships and thus model and teach Black manhood and what it means to be an African-American Christian. The Young Lions curriculum provides a format and structure to develop this dynamic.

PHILOSOPHY

The Young Lions mentoring program addresses the experience of Black boys from the holistic perspective of Christian ministry. The Young Lions curriculum explores and affirms the innate spirituality and moral fiber of African-American culture. It provides positive experiences and dialogue about African-American culture, heritage, and traditions.

The Young Lions group examines issues of male adolescence and puberty, addressing everything from personal hygiene to a discussion of human sexuality. Young Lions provides an affirming atmosphere in which to examine the social and emotional aspects of daily life peculiar to the experience of Black males.

• •

In Young Lions, the gospel is communicated in a manner relevant to the experience of African-American males. The Young Lions program provides Christian rites of passage for Black boys. It addresses problematic issues facing Black boys from the perspective of Christian Black men.

The role of men in the Young Lions program is vitally important. Young Lions operates from three premises:

1. that Black boys growing up in the inner city will not see a better life for themselves unless they see Black men modeling it for them;

2. that Black boys will be naturally drawn to strong, firm, caring, and self-assured Black men who show a genuine interest in them;

3. that Black boys will be more than equipped not only to survive but thrive in life as they learn and embrace who they are in Christ.

Positive male leadership is a critical component contributing to the development of male children. Young Lions creates a medium for Black boys to receive instruction from positive Black men resulting in lives of realized potential and personal satisfaction.

Young Lions's methodology is to put nurturing Black men in a position to teach young Black boys for the purpose of instilling hope for who they can be. Young Lions's goal is to cultivate and develop the inner person. Through actively engaging the curriculum the young persons will internalize positive Christian beliefs about who they are in the world and their inherent value as creations of God. Young Lions attempts to infuse Christian spiritual values so that the boys will gain and possess inner peace and strength to bring to bear on their external situation, whatever it might be.

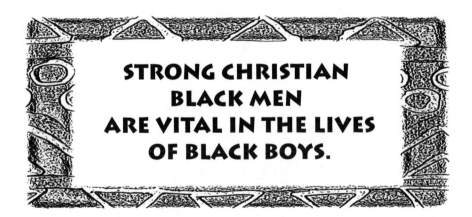

STRONG CHRISTIAN BLACK MEN ARE VITAL IN THE LIVES OF BLACK BOYS.

5. THE MEETING ....

OBJECTIVES OF THIS SESSION

1. To review and discuss the components of a typical Young Lions meeting and fourth week programming;
2. To familiarize the men with the YOUNG LIONS curriculum.

ICEBREAKER: TP AND ME

In the spirit of continuing to build strong connections within your group, today the men will play a toilet paper game. Bring rolls of toilet paper; pass a roll around the group, asking each person to take as much as he thinks he will need for the day. When everyone has taken some, tell the men that for each square of toilet paper they have, they must tell the group something about themselves.

GROUP DIALOGUE

A. Distribute handouts of the Young Lions weekly meeting format (pages 20–24). Review the material and discuss each component of the typical meeting structure. The men should be familiar with most of these by now, since the elements have been a part of their mentor training sessions. However, emphasize the specific purpose of each part of the meeting. Have the men look at the Planning Chart, and invite them to think about their willingness to lead in the various areas. It is not crucial at this point that they commit to leadership, but some may be ready by the end of this session to indicate a preference or a willingness to do a particular assignment in the first unit.

B. Talk about the fourth-week programming. Discuss the reasoning behind the field trips, optional activities and sessions, and practical things, such as insurance, drivers, ways to ensure that no one gets accidentally left behind. Show the men the Field Trip permission form and talk about the importance of communication with parents and having emergency contact information on hand at all times. Talk also about the importance of debriefing the experience with the boys. Encourage the participants to talk informally with the young men about what they found interesting or challenging about the trip or the activity.

C. Examine together the Curriculum Overview (pages 72–74). Carefully review and discuss the objectives and goals for each curriculum unit.

For Next Session

Give the men each a copy of the mentor contract (page 46) for them to think about for next session.

6. EXPECTATIONS ....

OBJECTIVES OF THIS SESSION
1. To discuss the expectations of mentors for involvement in the Young Lions program;
2. To covenant together for commitment of time and resources toward the success of the program.

ICEBREAKER: NAME ACROSTICS
Provide paper and a pencil for each of the men in the group. Ask each man to take a sheet of paper and spell his first name vertically in a column on the left side of the paper in large capital letters. Then ask everyone to write in a word that describes himself for each letter of his name. When the men are finished, ask each person to tell the group about his name acrostic.

GROUP DIALOGUE
A. At your final meeting you will want to get down to "brass tacks" and discuss the level of commitment required of the men and other mentor expectations. The temptation is to "water down" the expectations but remember it is quality, not quantity, that you want in the program.

Review the mentor contract (page 46) and discuss each expectation listed. Solicit the men's thoughts and input. Be prepared with some expectations you have personally in terms of their participation, sharing tasks, and other areas.

In your discussion on commitment encourage the men to bring forth real and personal issues. They may have concerns about conflicts between making time for Young Lions and making time for their own families. The men should be encouraged not to sacrifice family time, but to seek creative ways to free up time in their schedules to make a commitment to Young Lions.

Neglecting one's family in order to participate in Young Lions is contrary to the Young Lions program goals. Remind the men that the concern is not a commitment to a program, but a commitment to the boys with whom they will be developing relationships.

Many African-American men are searching for ways to contribute to addressing the issues facing the Black community. They are also searching for personal fulfillment and satisfaction through service and connectedness with other African-American men.

Black men may come with a view of "testing" Young Lions to see what it is like and if it will meet their needs. This "trying out" is entirely appropriate. The program coordinator must be sensitive to this dynamic and search for ways to minister to the mentors and enhance their experience in Young Lions. Men who have signed on as mentors often say that although the focus of the Young Lions program is on the boys, they themselves receive affirmation and support simply by gathering together and working together for a common purpose.

Conclude your time together by asking each man to respond personally to the question:

Why do you want to be involved in Young Lions?

Invite the men to sign the contracts, but give them the option to take home a copy and give signing more consideration. Also, for those who feel they cannot at this time make the full commitment, offer some ways for them to plug into the program from time to time or on a short-term basis. They may be more ready and able to make the greater commitment at a later time, especially if they have some positive experiences with the boys.

B. Talk about the first meeting of the Young Lions chapter with the men and boys together. Do you have the volunteers for the leadership for the first unit? Do they need to meet as a subteam to plan? Will an extra planning meeting at this point help the volunteers be more comfortable in their leadership? Encourage questions. Everyone needs to feel prepared. Close your meeting with a time of prayer and the Harambee circle.

Although the focus of the Young Lions program is on the boys, the men receive affirmation and support simply by working together for a common purpose.

WORKING WITH BOYS

Here are some basic principles for developing relationships with the boys. Every relationship will look different because each of the people involved is different. This list is not meant to be a formula but a guide.

1. BUILD RELATIONSHIPS

The relationships that develop between the mentors and the boys are at the core of the Young Lions program. Like all relationships, these will grow over time. The Young Lions program is a vehicle to develop these relationships. Through close, formal and informal, structured and unstructured interaction with positive African-American men, African-American boys will get a glimpse into what Black manhood is about.

The Young Lions program is based on tandem principles of role modeling and mentoring for influencing young men. Presenting positive images and accessible models of being a Black man is key to the mentor's role. As relationships develop, the one-on-one connection between men and boys comes into play and will influence boys on deeper levels of working out what it means to be a man.

The group will meet for a while before matching boys and men with each other. Those match-ups might develop naturally. After a time, some of the boys and men will be drawn to each other. The foundation of the mentor-mentee relationship is friendship. Being a friend and sharing your life is the basis of what being a mentor is all about.

2. BE YOURSELF

It is important to not enter into relationships with boys, trying to be something we are not. Children and youth respect honesty and realness. An older person trying to act "hip," or a middle-class person trying to act "street," will take that relationship nowhere fast. Genuine caring and concern are the qualities that will win over young people.

Young people will often test an adult's sincerity or commitment to relationship in a variety of ways. Acting out with bad behavior or shocking the person with their language or attitudes are two ways young people will test boundaries to see how and if an adult will correct or admonish them.

A good rule of thumb in dealing with negative behavior is to not sink to the level of the behavior exhibited. Don't respond in uncontrolled anger and never get physical in terms of discipline. Positive reinforcement through verbal affirmation and encouragement or special incentives are effective ways to influence behavior. Trips to a favorite fast-food place or pizza parlor or time with a mentor and his family are examples of special incentives to reward positive conduct. Incentives should always take the form of spending additional time with the adult. Time together rather than monetary rewards prevents getting into a pattern of bribing the boys for good behavior.

3. SPEND HIGH-QUALITY TIME TOGETHER

When spending time with youth outside a Young Lions meeting, consider a variety of effective and appealing activities. Again, put the emphasis on spending high-quality one-on-one time together. Spending time with a mentor and his family is also good; it is a great opportunity to model family values and lifestyles.

A quick word here is important. Young persons feel loyalty to their families no matter how abusive or detrimental they may appear to the outsider. Never compare families or give the impression that yours is better. Such statements will lead to resentment and contempt on the part of the youth.

Good activities to do together include sporting events, going out to eat, or going to the park to play basketball. Take the young man with you on one of your leisure activities (golfing; going to the gym, library, a concert or play; and so on). Sometimes, as a special treat, let your charge make the choice, subject to your approval.

Any positive activity in which mentor and mentee can spend time together is good. No matter what activity you do or where you go, this is a learning opportunity for that young boy as he observes you in different contexts. Watching a father care for his family at home, or working in the workplace, or spending energy in positive leisure pursuits is a dynamic that many African-American boys never witness; so these values are never instilled within them.

4. SET AN AGENDA

When you make time to do something with your charge, always be prepared with an agenda or something to talk about. Your agenda may be getting a boy to talk about his family or his school. It may be discussing a particular problem in his life. Consider beforehand what you want to accomplish or discuss in your time together. You may not get to that question or demonstrate the life skill you planned, but you will need to be prepared to provide focus for your time together. This kind of preparation ensures that your time together will be constructive.

Remember that the main purpose of being together is to get to know each other and strengthen your relationship. Sometimes, however, it is not talking but listening that is required and needed. Young people will open up to an adult who is genuinely interested in what they have to say, whether it is about a big problem they have or how their day at school went.

Observation is another skill needed by mentors. Even when kids are not talkative, you can learn something about them by how they dress, conduct themselves, act around their peers, and act around you. Don't be discouraged by quiet boys, but take the opportunity to employ these other skills to get to know them.

5. ENGAGE THE PARENTS

Parent involvement is also critical to a young man's success in Young Lions. Take every opportunity to meet the parents of the youth and pass the time of day with them. Although the quality of parental care will vary for each boy, every parent wants to be kept informed and to have an opportunity to meet the person with whom his or her son will be spending time. Your interest in his or her son will be an example to many parents. Once in a while, take time to sit down with the young person's parents and discuss his progress in Young Lions. Make visits to his home every now and then so that you have some insight as to the boy's home and neighborhood environment.

Each mentor should be given the responsibility of getting at least one boy to Young Lions meetings each week, either through a phone call reminder the night before or picking him up at his home. Picking the boys up and dropping them off at home afterward are natural times to meet and get to know parents, as well as the boys themselves.

YOUNG LIONS

Thank You to:

for serving this year as a Christian Friend and Mentor

Harambee!

Signed _____
Young Lion

Signed _____
Program Director

.... III. CURRICULUM

CURRICULUM OVERVIEW

Unit 1: CAREER AND EDUCATION

The goal of this unit is to explore career and educational opportunities through:

1. Examining the various future career options available to a person;

2. Seeing the connection between vocational dreams and goals and present tasks, responsibilities, and opportunities in education;

3. Envisioning and verbalizing plans and goals for one's life;

4. Witnessing and experiencing African-American men in rewarding and challenging careers.

Unit 2: SELF-AWARENESS

The goal of this unit is to develop an awareness and understanding of one's self through:

1. Discovering and being able to articulate one's strengths and weaknesses, gifts, and talents;

2. Being able to distinguish between self-esteem and self-image;

3. Showing self-expression through some form of art;

4. Learning that each person is important because God created him and loves him.

Unit 3: AFRICAN-AMERICAN HERITAGE AND CULTURE

The goal of this unit is to learn about the culture and heritage of African Americans through:

1. Developing an understanding of the roots of American Black culture in African heritage;

2. Cultivating a knowledge of the history, geography, and peoples of Africa;

3. Gaining a stronger sense of self-identity through African heritage;

4. Enjoying hands-on exposure to African tribal customs and traditions.

Unit 4: THE BLACK EXPERIENCE IN AMERICA

The goal of this unit is to learn about the Black experience in America through:

1. Developing a working knowledge of the Black historical experiences of slavery and the civil rights movement;

2. Exploring and understanding issues of racism and how they have had an effect upon society;

3. Developing a personal appreciation for the impact of African-American men and women in American history on society today and on personal lives;

4. Coming to an understanding of the potential of one's own contribution to African-American life and history.

Unit 5: FAMILY AWARENESS

This goal of this unit is to assist youth in developing an awareness and understanding of family through:

1. Gaining a knowledge of and appreciation for family history and family traditions;

2. Learning the value and importance of the family system and their places in it as fathers and husbands;

3. Developing a sense of appreciation for their own families as they examine various positive family structures, particularly the extended family network;

4. Participating in positive family activities to experience family togetherness.

Unit 6: GROWING UP

The goal of this unit is to learn about issues of adolescence through:

1. Engaging in open discussion about human sexuality in order to erase misconceptions and myths and to promote responsibility;

2. Examining the physical and emotional changes that come with puberty;

3. Developing a regimen of personal hygiene that is culturally affirming;

4. Participating in and experiencing appropriate cultural and social rites of passage leading to adulthood.

Unit 7: PERSONAL RESPONSIBILITY

The goal of this unit is to build a strong sense of personal responsibility in the boys through:

1. Building self-respect through examining personal responsibility in relationships, behavior, and self-image;

2. Realizing the impact of one's behavior and conduct on self, family, and society;

3. Exploring how to make positive choices and decisions for daily living;

4. Personally observing the effect of positive and negative choices in the lives of African-American men.

Unit 8: ECONOMIC RESPONSIBILITY

The goal of this unit is for the boys to learn principles of economic responsibility through:

1. Learning to apply the principle of delayed gratification in order to gain desired goals;

2. Examining the dynamics of employment and job readiness through roleplaying;

3. Developing an appreciation of the values of hard work and consistent effort for achieving financial goals;

4. Exploring the principle of cooperative economics *(ujamaa)* by working together to develop a business.

Plus . . . .

Field Trips: Each month, the group will participate in a field trip that pertains to the topic for that month.

Open Houses for Parents: Parents have the opportunity to be involved through open houses for parents at Young Lions meetings.

Special Events: These are held during the year and may include the Young Lions family opener, a family field trip, the Kwanzaa celebration, an overnight trip in the spring, and the Young Lions awards banquet at the end of the year.

CAREER AND EDUCATION

If you ask young men, particularly elementary age Black boys, what they want to do or be when they grow up, you will usually get the following response: "I want to be a professional football (or basketball) player." The idolization of public sports figures coupled with the worship of riches and material gain in our society indoctrinate youth to give such an answer. African American young men who see their culture represented by the media in a positive light only when associated with sports or entertainment are especially susceptible to this indoctrination.

The aspirations are not bad in themselves; but they are, in the vast majority of cases, unrealistic—not to mention unworthy of the potential of our Black young men. The fact is that only one percent of all athletes who compete in sports at the college level go on to a lucrative career playing in a professional league. A young person with this dream has only one chance in a million of seeing it fulfilled.

Our young men must be taught that other aspirations such as becoming a teacher, scientist, businessman, or construction worker have just as much value as those related to the field of professional sports. They need to know that their talents, skills, and interests other than sports can lead to lifelong careers that are just as fulfilling.

In this unit, the boys will explore their gifts and abilities and begin to realize their potential for leading personally satisfying lives.

UNIT OVERVIEW

This section focuses on developing a sense of future. The activities help the boys consider what their lives will be like at different points in the future: as teenagers, as they reach adulthood, at middle age, and so on. The young men are also encouraged to see themselves in the future as college students and career professionals, fathers and husbands. The young men have successfully completed the section when they are able to articulate specific steps to take to achieve their particular goals for the future.

UNIT LEARNING GOALS

The young men will

✚ Discover through field trips and other activities various career and vocational fields and educational opportunity options;

✚ Examine the relevance and value of education for daily living;

✚ Learn principles of delayed gratification for setting and achieving life goals;

✚ Identify their gifts, skills, and preferences, which may lead to future career choices.

UNIT SESSIONS
1. Career ABCs
2. Interviewing the Men
3. This Is Your Life!

ADDITIONAL SESSIONS AND ACTIVITIES
Bridge to Your future
Choosing a Career
Career Day
Career Photos
More Career Interviews
A Letter to Yourself

SCRIPTURAL THEMES

Ecclesiastes 2:24-26; 3:12-14—A person can do nothing better than to find satisfaction in his or her work. To that person, God gives wisdom, knowledge, and happiness.

1 Corinthians 12:4-7—There are different kinds of gifts, different kinds of service, and different kinds of working, but the same Spirit.

Colossians 3:15-17, 23-24—Whatever you do, work at it with all your heart, as you are working for the Lord and not for people.

UNIT 1 CAREER AND EDUCATION
Session 1
CAREER ABCs

FOCUS: To challenge the young men to consider the various potential career and vocational choices open to them.

Meeting Outline

		Notes
OPENING ACTIVITY & LIBATION	*15 minutes*	
AFRICAN-AMERICAN HEROES	*15 minutes*	
ACHIEVEMENT ACTIVITY	*30 minutes*	
GAME/CRAFT	*20 minutes*	
STORYTELLING	*15 minutes*	
GOD TIME & HARAMBEE CIRCLE	*15 minutes*	

Preparation

 Assign a mentor to review the life of W.E.B. DuBois (page 264) and make a presentation to the young men.

 Photocopy session activity sheets and collect pencils.

 Gather materials for the craft: magazines and scissors. Ask the mentors to bring magazines representing African-American culture.

 Assign a mentor to do storytelling.

 Gather Bibles and create God Time journals (see page 28) for the devotional.

Session 1

OPENING ACTIVITY *(15 minutes)*

Going to Africa: This game is a brainteaser. Have the boys and mentors sit in a circle. The leader of the game begins the game by saying, "My name is Sam Jones, and I am going to Africa. I am taking soup and a jumpsuit." Tell the group that each person in the circle must introduce himself and tell what two items he will be taking on his imaginary trip to Africa. The clue is that the first letters of the items must match the first letters of his own first and last names. However, none of the other participants knows the clue. The participants know only that the object of the game is to make a correct introduction. If a person's introduction is correct, the leader tells him that he may go. But if it is incorrect, he tells him that he may not go to Africa at this time. The game continues around the circle until everyone has made a correct introduction or until time is up.

LIBATION/PRAYER

See page 20.

AFRICAN-AMERICAN HEROES *(15 minutes)*

W.E.B. DuBois: Listen to the presentation about this African-American champion (see page 264). Discuss these questions, and invite the Young Lions to ask their own questions as well:

- ✚ Who was W.E.B. DuBois?
- ✚ Why is his life noteworthy?
- ✚ What did he accomplish?
- ✚ What were his views on education, career opportunities, and the self-improvement of Black people?

Note the life of W.E.B. DuBois on the African-American history timeline. (See page 261.)

ACHIEVEMENT ACTIVITY *(30 minutes)*

Career ABCs: This exercise is designed to help the boys think of various career and occupational opportunities. Hand out the "Career ABCs" activity sheet and have the group work together to write in as many career options as they can think of for each letter of the alphabet. Take time to describe each vocation as it is mentioned to be sure that everyone understands what it is. Then have the young men and mentors gather into small groups. Ask each of the boys to pick his favorite five careers from his sheet. Have the boys discuss with their small-group members their choices, giving reasons why they chose those careers.

CRAFT *(20 minutes)*

Careers Collage: Give each young man scissors and a stack of magazines. Instruct the participants to thumb through the magazines, looking for pictures that represent various careers and vocations in which they might be interested. Instruct the young men to cut out these pictures and save them for next week.

STORYTELLING *(15 minutes)*

Choosing a Career: Ask one of the mentors you selected before the meeting to tell a personal story having to do with work or choosing a career. Tell the group the following guidelines for storytelling:

1. Everyone must be silent while the mentor is telling the story.
2. After the mentor is finished, the listeners may ask questions.
3. Each young man should be prepared to ask at least one question about the story.

GOD TIME *(15 minutes)*

Ecclesiastes 2:24-26; 3:12-14: Ask one of the young men to read aloud the Scripture passage, and ask another to read aloud the devotional message from the God Time activity sheet. Talk about these questions:

✚ How can work be a thing of satisfaction?
✚ How can people please the Lord through their work?
✚ Do you think that God cares whether people feel good about the work they do?
✚ How can we get help from God about our career choices?

After the discussion, have each young man record in his journal his personal response to the lesson. Have the young men answer this question:

✚ What is one thing I learned today about work?

HARAMBEE CIRCLE
See page 22.

CAREER ABCs

LIST THREE CAREERS OR OCCUPATIONS
FOR EACH LETTER OF THE ALPHABET.

A

B

C

D

E

F

G

H

I

J

K

L

M

N

O

P

Q

R

S

T

U

V

W

X

Y

Z

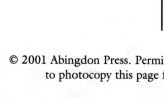

GOD TIME

READ ECCLESIASTES 2:24-26; 3:12-14.

What is the meaning of life? That is what the writer of Ecclesiastes is trying to figure out. He has tried everything—riches; earthly pleasures (drugs, sex, possessions); and even human wisdom—and none of them has given him a sense of satisfaction and purpose (Chapters 1–2). The key to satisfaction and fulfillment in life is having a sense of purpose.

Augustine was an African theologian (a person who studies the nature of God and religious truth), who went through the same struggle to find meaning for his life. He was a rich young man who wanted for nothing. Whatever felt good to him, he did it. But he was still unhappy. Both Augustine and the writer of Ecclesiastes realized that the only sense of satisfaction a person can have is in knowing God.

Life is a gift from God. Living for God pleases God and gives us satisfaction and a sense of fulfillment. The writer of Ecclesiastes concludes: "Fear God, and keep God's commandments; for that is the whole duty of everyone" (12:13b). Personal satisfaction and fulfillment are important factors in considering career or vocational choices.

✛ What is one thing you learned today about work?

UNIT 1 CAREER AND EDUCATION
Session 2
INTERVIEWING THE MEN

FOCUS: To assist the young men in seeing various career and educational options for themselves through examining the experiences of the mentors.

Meeting Outline

		Notes
OPENING ACTIVITY & LIBATION	*15 minutes*	
AFRICAN-AMERICAN HEROES	*15 minutes*	
ACHIEVEMENT ACTIVITY	*30 minutes*	
GAME/CRAFT	*20 minutes*	
STORYTELLING	*15 minutes*	
GOD TIME & HARAMBEE CIRCLE	*15 minutes*	

Preparation

◇ Assign a mentor to review the life of Frederick Douglass (page 265) and make a presentation to the young men.

◇ Photocopy session activity sheets and collect pencils.

◇ Gather materials for the craft: posterboard, glue, and pictures that the young men cut out last week.

◇ Assign a mentor to do storytelling.

◇ Gather Bibles and God Time journals (see page 28) for the devotional time.

Session 2

OPENING ACTIVITY *(15 minutes)*

Twenty Questions: As the young men and mentors arrive, start a game of twenty questions. The young men take turns choosing a person, place, or thing; and the rest of the group is allowed twenty questions to discover what it is. Ideas should focus on the subject of career and education.

LIBATION/PRAYER

See page 20.

AFRICAN-AMERICAN HEROES *(15 minutes)*

Frederick Douglass: Listen to the story of his life—how he educated himself; escaped from slavery; and became an accomplished speaker, author, and statesman (see page 265). Discuss these questions, and invite each of the Young Lions to ask his own questions as well:

+ Who was Frederick Douglass?
+ Why is his life noteworthy?
+ What were his personal accomplishments?
+ What did he achieve on behalf of Black people?

Note the life of Frederick Douglass on the African-American history timeline.

ACHIEVEMENT ACTIVITY *(30 minutes)*

Career Interview: This activity is designed to give mentors and young men significant one-on-one interaction and to allow the mentors to talk with the young men about their career experiences. Give the Young Lions the assignment of interviewing two or three of the mentors present.

Hand out the "Career Interview" activity sheets (page 85). Give each interviewer two or three copies—one for each person he will interview. Allow about six minutes for each interview and at the end of that time rotate the young men so that they are with different mentors. No more than two Young Lions should be with each mentor at any time.

At the end of the time, ask the young persons to introduce to the group one of the mentors they interviewed.

CRAFT *(20 minutes)*

Careers Collage: Continue the activity from last week. Give each young man a sheet of posterboard and some glue. Instruct the Young Lions to glue onto the posterboard the magazine pictures they cut out last week. The participants may position the pictures in any way they choose. When everyone is ready, have each young man present his collage to the group and explain his interests.

STORYTELLING (OPTIONAL) *(15 minutes)*

Choosing a Career: Since the mentors have told their stories in their interviews, this part of the meeting may be optional this week unless you have additional time. If additional time is available, have the mentor you have chosen before the meeting offer a personal story having to do with work or choosing a career.

GOD TIME *(15 minutes)*

1 Corinthians 12:4-7: Ask one of the young men to read aloud the Scripture passage, and ask another to read aloud the devotional message from the God Time activity sheet. Talk about these questions:

✚ **Do you think that God cares about what occupation you choose?**

✚ **What are the most important factors to you in choosing a career? Making money? gaining prestige and fame? having personal satisfaction?**

✚ **Does helping others play a part in your choice?**

After the discussion, have each young man record in his journal his personal response to the lesson. Have the young men answer these questions:

✚ **What gifts has God given me?**

✚ **How can I use my gifts to please God and help others?**

HARAMBEE CIRCLE

See page 22.

CAREER INTERVIEW

USE THESE QUESTIONS TO INTERVIEW A MENTOR:

Mentor's Name _____

1. What goals or dreams for your life did you have when you were a child?

2. Have you accomplished any of those goals or dreams so far? Which ones?

3. What goals do you currently have for your life?

4. What kind of work do you do? Describe a typical day at your job.

5. How did you choose your occupation?

6. How did you prepare yourself to do the job you have?

7. Do you have any hobbies? What are they?

8. Are you married? Do you have any children? If so, what are their ages?

9. What do you enjoy most out of life?

10. Name three things you value most in life.

GOD TIME

READ 1 CORINTHIANS 12:4-7.

What do you want to do with your life? You are unique and special, and God has given you unique and special gifts. First Corinthians 12 talks about the different gifts God has given the family of God. God gives us gifts for two reasons: to honor and serve God and to help one another.

In considering what you want to do with your life, think about the abilities and skills that God has given you. If you do not know what abilities you have, ask God to show you. Ask others who know you what they see in you. Think about what you do that you enjoy. Pay attention to what you are learning about yourself in these ways.

In the not too distant past, it was illegal for Black people to learn to read and write. However, through the struggles of your ancestors and God's grace, today you can get an education. You have many opportunities for developing your God-given potential through education, work experience, and other special learning opportunities. Recognizing your gifts and increasing your skills will give you many opportunities as you grow older.

✚ What gifts has God given you?

✚ How can you use these gifts to please God and help others?

UNIT 1 CAREER AND EDUCATION
Session 3
THIS IS YOUR LIFE!

FOCUS: To encourage the young men to look ahead at landmarks and specific events in their future that they may work toward.

Meeting Outline

		Notes
OPENING ACTIVITY & LIBATION	*15 minutes*	
AFRICAN-AMERICAN HEROES	*15 minutes*	
ACHIEVEMENT ACTIVITY	*30 minutes*	
GAME/CRAFT	*20 minutes*	
STORYTELLING	*15 minutes*	
GOD TIME & HARAMBEE CIRCLE	*15 minutes*	

Preparation

◇ Assign a mentor to review the life of Mary McLeod Bethune (page 266) and and make a presentation to the young men.

◇ Photocopy session activity sheets and collect pencils.

◇ Assemble materials for the game: a coin and a rag.

◇ Assign a mentor to do storytelling.

◇ Gather Bibles and God Time journals (page 28) for the devotional time.

Session 3

OPENING ACTIVITY *(15 minutes)*

Mingle: The players must mingle around the room until the leader calls out a number. Players then gather into groups of that number and sit down together. When everyone is seated, give the groups a question that everyone in the group must answer. The questions should be ones that help the mentors and young men get to know one another better. Example: What is your middle name? favorite hobby? After all of the groups have finished with the question, everyone gets up and mingles again until the leader calls out another number.

LIBATION/PRAYER

See page 20.

AFRICAN-AMERICAN HEROES *(15 minutes)*

Mary McLeod Bethune: Listen to the presentation about this famous African-American woman (see page 266). Discuss these questions, and invite the Young Lions to ask their own questions as well:

✚ Who was Mary McLeod Bethune?
✚ She was nicknamed "the Great Educator." Why do you think she got that name?
✚ What is the history behind Bethune-Cookman University?

Note the life of Mary McLeod Bethune on the African-American history timeline.

ACHIEVEMENT ACTIVITY *(15 minutes)*

"This Is Your Life!": Have the young men gather with mentors in small groups to work on the "This Is Your Life!" activity sheet (page 90). Instruct the boys to write or draw pictures or symbols of important events they foresee in their future. (Example: "When I am sixteen, I want to get my drivers license.") They should also be prepared to explain the steps they must take to achieve those goals. The purpose of this activity is to help the young men envision their future and set goals for having the kind of life they want.

GAME (20 minutes)

Reflex: Have the group of mentors and young men divide into two teams and line up in two single-file lines, one person behind the other, everyone facing the front. Teams must then sit on the ground close together. The designated leader must sit at the front of the two lines, and an assistant must sit at the end. Each person in the two lines must hold the hands of the person in front of him and behind (still facing the front). Everyone has his eyes closed, except for the first person in each line, the designated leader, and the assistant.

In front of the assistant is a rag, which is within reach of the two people at the end of the two lines. The leader flips a coin and reminds everyone (except the two persons at the front of the line) to keep eyes closed. If the coin lands with heads, the race is on! The ones at the head of the two lines squeeze the hand of the person behind them. Each person passes the squeeze back as quickly as possible until the last person's hand is squeezed and he can pick up the rag. If it is tails, they do nothing.

The assistant at the back of the two lines is the scorekeeper. The team that picks up the rag first wins a point. If a team picks up the rag but the coin flip was tails, then that team loses a point. Rotate the positions in the line until everyone has a chance to be up front and in back. The team with the most points at the end wins.

STORYTELLING (15 minutes)

Becoming Educated: Have the mentor you asked before the meeting tell about a personal experience from his life, regarding education.

GOD TIME (15 minutes)

Colossians 3:15-17, 23-24. Ask one of the young men to read aloud the Scripture passage, and ask another to read aloud the devotional message from the God Time activity sheet. Talk about these questions:

✛ What does it mean to work at something with all your heart?
✛ When you work hard at school or in a job, who are you trying to please? Yourself, family, boss, teacher, others?
✛ How can a person honor or please God through school?
✛ Why should we give thanks to God when we work hard, or do a good job at something?

After the discussion, have each young man record in his journal his personal response to the lesson.

HARAMBEE CIRCLE

See page 22.

THIS IS YOUR LIFE!

This is an exercise in looking forward and setting goals for your future.

Use the chart below to mark events and goals that you are looking forward to at different ages in your life. You can list anything from getting your drivers license to getting married. Plot the way you would like your life to be. Include educational goals, career and vocational choices, and marriage and family. Remember that God says that God has hopeful plans for your future, and that God can bless you better than you can imagine (based on Ephesians 3:20).

How old are you today?

_____

What are your goals for age sixteen?

_____

at age eighteen?

_____

at age twenty-five?

_____

at age thirty?

_____

at age fifty?

_____

at age sixty-five?

_____

My name is   **The date is**

_____   _____

GOD TIME

READ COLOSSIANS 3:15-17, 23-24.

The key to pleasing God and finding personal fulfillment in your work is your attitude. Having a good and positive attitude toward doing the best you can is the most important part of work. This is true regarding chores at home, schoolwork, or a job for which you get paid.

According to the apostle Paul, you should please God by doing the best job you can do at whatever you are doing. This attitude will, in turn, make you happy and give you peace.

Have you ever been asked to do a chore, and your mom or dad had you do it over again since you hadn't done it well? It just makes sense to do a good job the first time so that you can have more time to do what you want to do. Doing it right the first time also gives you a sense of accomplishment.

So do the best you can at whatever your job is. Have the attitude of doing it for God, not for your teacher, for yourself, or even for your parents; and God will reward you.

✚ How can you honor and please God through your schoolwork?

UNIT 1 CAREER AND EDUCATION
Session 4
FIELD TRIP SUGGESTIONS

Visit a Local College or University

Schedule a visit to a local campus. Your visit may include lunch at the cafeteria, activities at the gym or recreation center, a tour of the campus, and maybe even a free T-shirt. Campuses will usually conduct these visits for youth groups free of charge. Make arrangements with the college or university in advance.

Visit a Mentor's Place of Business

Ask one of the mentors to schedule a visit for your group at his workplace. The visit may include a tour of the business and maybe a lunch in the cafeteria (or a trip to your favorite fast-food restaurant afterward).

Schedule a Career Day for the Young Men

Ask each of the young men to choose one career that he is interested in. Then arrange for him to spend time on the job with someone in that field. The young men could be asked to give an oral or written report about their experiences at a later meeting.

Check Out Special Events

Go to a play, show, or museum exhibit with a career or education theme. Check the newspapers and entertainment listings for current and special events in your area.

Keep On Learning

Field trips are wonderful learning experiences in themselves. However, to help the youth get the most from them, do two simple things:

1. **Prepare the youth:** Give them some introductory information; talk about expected behavior; identify a question for them to be thinking about.
2. **Debrief the trip:** Ask the group what surprised them, what was interesting to them, what made them think. Have a group conversation or give the youth paper and pencils and have them write a journal page about the trip—or do both. Gather the journal pages and add them to the individuals' folders.

UNIT 1 CAREER AND EDUCATION
Optional
ACTIVITIES AND SESSIONS

Bridge to Your Future

Use the activity sheet (page 94) as it is or as a model to lead your group's discussion. Encourage the boys to visualize what they want their lives to be like in the future: what jobs they will have, where they will live, and the kind of family they will have. Once they articulate this, assist them in defining the steps they need to take to achieve their goals in life in the areas of education, relationships, finances, and so forth. This activity may also be done on large sheets of paper folded into sections.

Choosing a Career

The goal of this activity sheet (page 95) is for the boys to choose an occupation in agreement with their personal likes and abilities. In answering and discussing these questions, the boys will learn more about themselves and will be able to articulate their preferences. The exercise then challenges them (with a mentor's help) to translate those likes and preferences into various career and vocational options.

Career Day

Ask the boys to each choose one career that he is interested in. Then help each boy arrange to spend time on the job with someone in that field. Have the boys give an oral or written report at a Young Lions meeting about their Career Day experiences.

Career Photos

Have the boys choose a career field of interest to them. Arrange to have the uniform or clothing of someone in that field at your next meeting and take pictures of the boys dressed like the professional they are interested in becoming; for example, a judge, lawyer, policeman, businessman, teacher.

More Career Interviews

Find out what careers interest the boys, and invite some men in those fields to come to your meetings. Have the boys form small groups and interview the men. Or, look for Internet sites or computer programs on careers or skills and interest surveys.

A Letter to Yourself

Ask the boys to write a letter to themselves fifteen years into the future. The letter should address what kind of job or occupation they are in and how much education and experience they had to acquire to get where they are.

BRIDGE TO YOUR FUTURE

In this activity, you will think about the kind of life you want in the future. Identify the steps you need to take in the meantime in order to achieve those goals. Write in the **first** column a brief description of your life today in each area (family, home, and so on). Then write in the **third** column your dream about what you want your life to look like in the future. Last, write in the **second** column what you need to do to achieve those dreams.

	WHERE YOU ARE NOW	STEPS TO REACH YOUR GOALS	WHERE YOU WANT TO BE AS AN ADULT
Family			
Home			
Education			
Career/ Employment			
Relationships			

CHOOSING A CAREER

Some activities I most enjoy doing are

_____

The best way to motivate me is

_____

I am happiest when I am

_____

The most important things to me in life are

_____

I work best when I am

_____

Some people I know who have cool jobs are

_____

One thing people should know about me is

_____

One goal I have in my life is

_____

The way I feel about money is

_____

My greatest strength is

_____

My biggest weakness is

_____

One thing that I have done that I feel proud of is

_____

One thing that I have never done but that I would like to try is

_____

After I consider the statements above, possible career choices I would like are

_____

AWARENESS OF SELF

The psyches of urban Black boys are under attack from their earliest years by institutional structures, media messages, and social environment. Racism steadily deals terrific blows to the self-esteem of young African-American people, and discrimination reinforces an inferiority complex created by a social history of enslavement and segregation. These negative dynamics show up in the inordinate number of young Black men in the penal system and the unemployment line and in their number among school dropouts. For urban Black males to emerge from such constant stress with a positive and accurate self-image intact is rare.

The primary objective of the Young Lions program is to teach young Black boys who they are spiritually, culturally, and socially. This self-knowledge is key to overcoming the negative images surrounding Black children and the stress they endure trying to succeed in a society driven by mainstream values that exclude them. This knowledge of self will produce strong self-esteem, inner resources to draw upon, and a sense of community with ancestors gone before in times of struggle and with those struggling alongside them in the present.

To know who they are in Christ is paramount. They must know that they are precious to God—that God cherishes them. They must know by their own experience the truth of the Scriptures: that if they have Christ, then truly they have everything.

UNIT OVERVIEW

This unit is to help the young men develop a positive self-image and self-esteem and to know who they are in Christ. Seeing themselves positively, they will be better equipped to operate in the broader society and have meaningful personal relationships. The activities in this section are geared to help the young persons think through how they see themselves and who they would like to be. The theme for the month is that it is not how a person looks on the outside, or even how others perceive him, that determines his identity. The key is who a person is on the inside.

UNIT LEARNING GOALS

The young men will

+ Increase their self-esteem through seeing themselves as unique creations of God and through their identification with Christ;

+ Know themselves better intellectually, emotionally, and spiritually;

+ Develop an accurate self-image as African-American males in society;

+ Engage in reflection and self-examination.

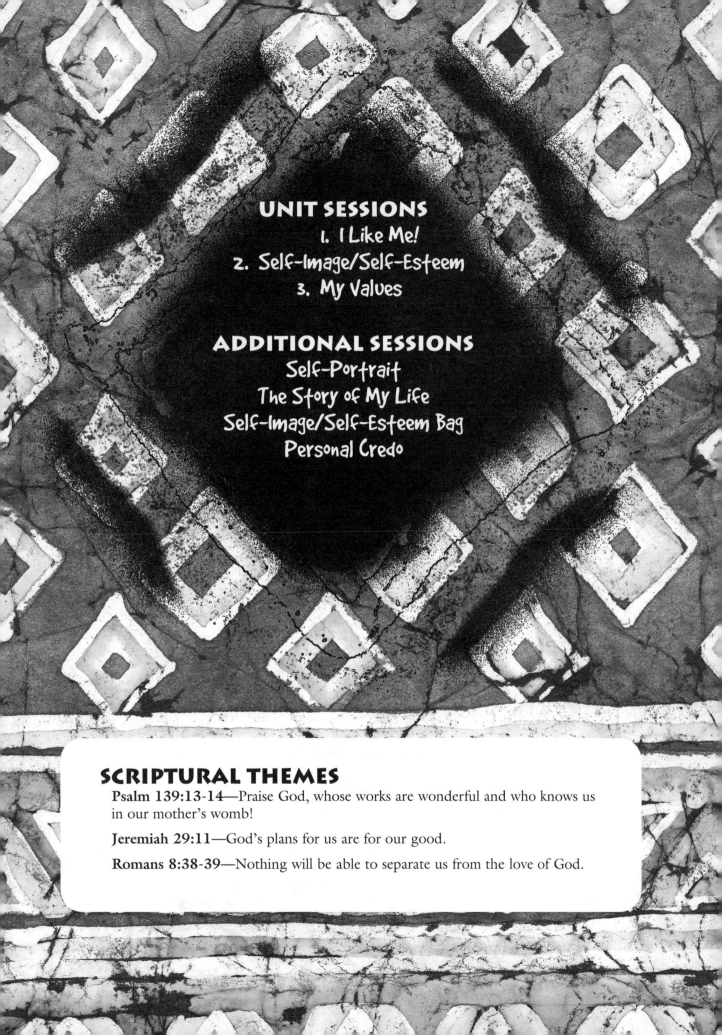

UNIT SESSIONS
1. I Like Me!
2. Self-Image/Self-Esteem
3. My Values

ADDITIONAL SESSIONS
Self-Portrait
The Story of My Life
Self-Image/Self-Esteem Bag
Personal Credo

SCRIPTURAL THEMES

Psalm 139:13-14—Praise God, whose works are wonderful and who knows us in our mother's womb!

Jeremiah 29:11—God's plans for us are for our good.

Romans 8:38-39—Nothing will be able to separate us from the love of God.

UNIT 2 SELF-AWARENESS
Session 1
I LIKE ME!

FOCUS: To challenge the young men to identify traits and characteristics they like about themselves.

Meeting Outline

		Notes
OPENING ACTIVITY & LIBATION	*15 minutes*	
AFRICAN-AMERICAN HEROES	*15 minutes*	
ACHIEVEMENT ACTIVITY	*30 minutes*	
GAME/CRAFT	*20 minutes*	
STORYTELLING	*15 minutes*	
GOD TIME & HARAMBEE CIRCLE	*15 minutes*	

Preparation

 Assign a mentor to review the life of Malcolm X (page 267) and make a presentation to the young men.

 Photocopy session activity sheets and collect pencils.

 Have on hand rolls of toilet paper for the opening activity.

 Gather materials for the craft: large sheets of newsprint or butcher paper, and washable markers.

 Assign a mentor to do storytelling.

 Gather Bibles and journals for the God Time devotional.

Session 1

OPENING ACTIVITY *(15 minutes)*

Introduce Yourself: Have the group gather into a circle. Pass a roll of toilet paper around the group, asking each person to take as much as he thinks he will need for the day. When everyone has taken some, ask each person to tell the group one thing about himself for each square of toilet paper that he took.

LIBATION/PRAYER

AFRICAN-AMERICAN HEROES *(15 minutes)*

Malcolm X: Listen to a presentation about Malcolm X (see page 267). Discuss these questions, and invite the Young Lions to ask their own questions as well:

- ✚ What is Malcolm X famous for?
- ✚ Why did he take *X* for his last name?
- ✚ What was his message to Black people?
- ✚ What did his message have to do with positive self-image for African Americans?

Note the life of Malcolm X on the African-American history timeline.

ACHIEVEMENT ACTIVITY *(30 minutes)*

I Am: Give each young man the "All About Me" activity sheet. Ask the young men to turn the paper over to the back side, label the sheet "I Am," and number along the left edge from 1–10. Repeat the phrase "I am" ten times in a forceful tone and pause so that the young men can write the rest of the sentence. For example: "I am *Black*"; "I am *beautiful*"; "I am *tall.*" After the first four or five times, the youth will have more difficulty thinking of personal characteristics to list. When the group is finished, divide the Young Lions and mentors into small groups and have them talk about their lists.

All About Me: While the young men and mentors are still in their small groups, have the youth fill out these activity sheets. They can individualize their lists by adding information of their own choosing for numbers 9 and 10. Then invite them to talk with one another about their personal preferences for food, hobbies, and so on.

CRAFT *(20 minutes)*

Body Silhouettes: Have each Young Lion pair up with a mentor (if there are enough of them) or with another young man. Give each person a large sheet of newsprint or butcher paper. The partners are to take turns lying on his sheet of paper and allowing his partner to use a marker to trace a life-size outline of his body on the paper. Have each participant put his name at the top of his silhouette (and otherwise decorate it with a border, and so on). Save the silhouettes for next week.

STORYTELLING *(15 minutes)*

Personal Storytelling: Have the chosen mentor tell a personal story having to do with self-esteem or self-image. Review with the group the guidelines for storytelling:

1. Everyone must be silent while the mentor is telling the story.
2. After the mentor is finished, the listeners may ask questions.
3. Each young man should be prepared to ask at least one question about the story.

GOD TIME *(15 minutes)*

Psalm 139:13-14: Ask one of the young men to read aloud the Scripture passage, and ask another to read aloud the devotional message from the God Time activity sheet. Talk about these questions:

+ How do you think the person who wrote this psalm felt about himself?
+ How did he feel about his relationship with God?
+ Did he feel important to God? Why, or why not?
+ How do you feel, knowing that God created you in your innermost being?
+ How do you feel knowing that God knew you before you were born?

After the discussion, have each young man record in his journal his personal response to the lesson.

HARAMBEE CIRCLE

ALL ABOUT ME

1. My Ethnic Heritage

_____

2. My Favorite Food

_____

3. My Best Time of Day

_____

4. My Age

_____

5. My Favorite Game

_____

6. My Hero

_____

7. My Hobby

_____

8. Title of a Book About Me

_____

9.

_____

10.

GOD TIME

READ PSALM 139:13-14.

You are unique in all of God's creation. When God made you, God broke the mold. Hold up your hand and look at your fingers. Notice the squiggly lines on your fingertips. Those are your fingerprints. You are the only one in the world with those special fingerprints. You are the only you who ever will be in this world. You are special to God.

Because you are special to God, you should be special to yourself. If you are special and important to God and to yourself, what everyone else thinks of you just isn't all that important. Your life means something, because it means something to God. So don't live your life trying to please your friends. Be your own person. Find out what pleases God, and do it.

✚ What did you learn about yourself today?

UNIT 2 SELF-AWARENESS
Session 2
SELF-IMAGE/SELF-ESTEEM

FOCUS: To help the young men learn to distinguish between self-esteem (how they feel about themselves) and self-image (how others perceive them).

Meeting Outline

OPENING ACTIVITY & LIBATION	*15 minutes*	*Notes*
AFRICAN-AMERICAN HEROES	*15 minutes*	
ACHIEVEMENT ACTIVITY	*30 minutes*	
GAME/CRAFT	*20 minutes*	
STORYTELLING	*15 minutes*	
GOD TIME & HARAMBEE!	*15 minutes*	

Preparation

◇ Gather various card and table games for the opening activity.

◇ Assign a mentor to make an African-American hero presentation about the Black Panthers (page 268).

◇ Gather materials for T-shirt skit: T-shirts, scissors, markers.

◇ Gather materials for craft: newsprint, markers.

◇ Assign a mentor to do the storytelling for the day.

◇ Gather Bibles and God Time journals for devotional time.

Session 2

OPENING ACTIVITY *(15 minutes)*

Table Games: Gather the young men and mentors into small groups of four or five and give them each a game to play (card games, board games, and so forth).

LIBATION/PRAYER

AFRICAN-AMERICAN HEROES *(15 minutes)*

Black Panthers: Listen to the presentation about the Black Panthers (see page 268). Discuss these questions and invite the Young Lions to ask their own questions as well:

✚ Have you ever heard of the mottos "Black Power" or "Black is beautiful"? Where did those phrases come from?

✚ What were the Black Panthers about?

✚ Do you think they were popular or unpopular? Explain.

✚ Do some Black people have special ways of greeting one another? What are some of them? Explain their significance.

✚ How well did the Black Panthers promote a positive self-image for African Americans?

Bring out the African-American history timeline and note the significant events discussed.

ACHIEVEMENT ACTIVITY *(30 minutes)*

T-Shirt Skit: Have one volunteer stand in front of the group, wearing one of the T-shirts you brought for this demonstration. Ask the group to think of negative things they have heard people say to other people and then repeat them to the volunteer. For every negative comment snip a cut in the volunteer's T-shirt. Then ask the group to repeat negative comments they have heard in their own household. Again make the cuts with the scissors.

When finished, slowly spin the volunteer around in front of the group and explain how every negative comment affects a person's sense of self-worth. It is said that every negative stroke a person receives from others requires seven positive strokes to patch up the damage to the self. A person's self-worth can be constructed by how he believes others on the outside perceive him (self-image) or how he feels about himself on the inside (self-esteem).

Send the volunteer out of the room to put on another T-shirt underneath the cut-up one. Ask the young men what the difference is. Ask them for ideas on how to develop and keep a strong self-esteem. Discuss building a strong self image based on your inner perception of yourself so that you cannot be negatively affected by other people's outside perception.

Self-knowledge in Christ is the way to a strong and accurate self-image. We can gain self-esteem by realizing that God made us and that we are precious to God.

CRAFT *(20 minutes)*

Body Silhouettes: Take out the body silhouettes from last week. Distribute the markers and ask the young men to complete their life-size self-portraits. Have them draw symbols or write words or phrases on the silhouettes that describe who they are, what their strengths and gifts are, what their hopes are. Have them talk in small groups or in pairs about what they have described about themselves in this activity.

STORYTELLING *(15 minutes)*

Personal Storytelling: Have the chosen mentor tell a personal story having to do with his sense of self-worth.

GOD TIME *(15 minutes)*

Jeremiah 29:11: Have one of the young men read Jeremiah 29:11, and have another young man read the devotional section of the God Time activity sheet. Ask:

✚ Do you ever dream about what you want your life to be like? Talk about it.

✚ What do you think God means about having plans for you?

✚ What kind of plans does God have?

✚ Ephesians 3:20 says that God is able to do infinitely more for us than we can possibly imagine. How does that make you feel?

After the discussion have each young man write his personal response to the lesson in his journal.

HARAMBEE CIRCLE

GOD TIME

READ JEREMIAH 29:11.

God created you for a purpose. God created people (Adam and Eve) because God wanted fellowship; God wanted friends. God created you specifically to be in a relationship with God—to be friends!

God wants you to have a good life. A good life means following Jesus and loving God first, and loving your neighbor as you love yourself. You have to love yourself before you can love anyone else.

Nobody grows up and decides he wants a bad life, but some people don't know to or choose not to put God first and love their neighbors (and themselves). But if you do, God will make your life better than you can imagine.

Jesus said to put God first in your life and everything else will be taken care of. God's plan for you is for you to have joy, peace, and love all the days of your life.

Complete the following sentence:

✚ I feel good about my life because

UNIT 2 SELF-AWARENESS
Session 3
MY VALUES

focus: To lead the young men tn an examination of what is important to them and how their value systems affect their choices.

Meeting Outline

		Notes
OPENING ACTIVITY & LIBATION	*15 minutes*	
AFRICAN-AMERICAN HEROES	*15 minutes*	
ACHIEVEMENT ACTIVITY	*30 minutes*	
GAME/CRAFT	*20 minutes*	
STORYTELLING	*15 minutes*	
GOD TIME & HARAMBEE CIRCLE	*15 minutes*	

Preparation

 Assign a mentor to review the life of Marcus Garvey (page 269) and make a presentation to the young men.

 Photocopy session activity sheets and collect pencils.

 Assign a mentor to do storytelling.

 Gather Bibles and journals for the God Time devotional.

Session 3

OPENING ACTIVITY *(15 minutes)*

Picture Charades: Divide the young men and mentors into small groups and give each group a marker and posterboard or large sheets of paper. Have a member of the group take turns coming to the front of the room to receive the charades clue. He must then run back to his group and draw a picture of the clue, but he cannot say or write any words. The first group that guesses the clue raises their hands and wins a point.

LIBATION/PRAYER

AFRICAN-AMERICAN HEROES *(15 minutes)*

Marcus Garvey: Listen to the presentation about Marcus Garvey (see page 269). Discuss these questions and invite the Young Lions to ask their own questions as well:

✚ Who was Marcus Garvey?
✚ What was his dream?
✚ What were some of his accomplishments?
✚ How did he help Black people in his time develop self-respect?

Note the life of Marcus Garvey on the African-American history timeline.

ACHIEVEMENT ACTIVITY *(30 minutes)*

What Do I Value? Hand out the "What Do I Value?" activity sheets for the young men to complete. In small groups with their mentors have them complete the activity sheets and discuss the results.

GAME *(20 minutes)*

Wink 'Em: Have the young men and mentors form two concentric circles, one inside the other. Have the players in the inside circle sit in chairs, facing inward, with the players in the outside circle standing directly behind the chairs. The outside circle will have one more player than the inside circle. The chairs should be spaced so that players can easily pass between the chairs. One of the chairs should be empty.

The object of the game is for the person standing behind empty chair to fill it with one of the seated players. The way he does this is to wink at a seated player, who then must try to move to the empty chair. Meanwhile, the standing players must focus on the seated players' heads while keeping their hands behind their backs. Whenever a seated player is winked at, the standing player behind him tries to stop him from moving by moving his hands from behind his back and tagging him. If the player who is winked at is tagged, he must sit back down; and the winker must wink at someone else. If the player who is winked at is not tagged and is able to change seats, the player behind the new empty chair must fill it by winking.

After a while, swap the players in the inner and outer circles.

STORYTELLING *(15 minutes)*

Personal Storytelling: Ask one of the mentors whom you have chosen before the meeting to share a personal story having to do with how his values affected a choice he had to make.

GOD TIME *(15 minutes)*

Romans 8:38-39: Ask one of the young men to read aloud the Scripture passage, and ask another to read aloud the devotional message from the God Time activity sheet. Talk about these questions:

- ✠ Have you ever felt separated from God's love? Tell about it.
- ✠ Why do you think God loves us so much?
- ✠ The Bible teaches that if God loves us, we ought to love others (1 John 4:11). Whom should we love? What about persons who are hard to love?
- ✠ The Bible teaches that love is the greatest personal attribute a person could have. Do you agree or disagree? Why?

After the discussion, have each young man record in his journal his personal response to the lesson.

HARAMBEE CIRCLE

WHAT DO I VALUE?

Rank in order the following values, from the most important (1) to the least important (12) to you.

_____ honesty

_____ financial security

_____ an exciting life

_____ concern for others

_____ health

_____ religion

_____ self-respect

_____ loyal friendship

_____ education

_____ family

_____ other:

_____ other:

My top three values on this list are _____

_____

My lowest value on this list is _____

Something I learned about myself is _____

_____

_____

GOD TIME

READ ROMANS 8:38-39.

God loves you. The Bible teaches that God loves you enough to send the Son for you (John 3:16). God loves you just as you are, right now. God doesn't tell you to go get cleaned up before loving you, God loves you right now. God's love is unconditional. God doesn't ask you to earn the love. It is impossible to be good enough to earn God's love, but God gives it to us freely.

So, since you know how much God loves you, what are you going to do now? How does this knowledge change the way you live or act toward other people?

The Bible says in 1 John 4 that if we say we love God but hate someone else we are lying. We can't love God and hate at the same time. To follow Jesus means to live a lifestyle that is pleasing to God. Sometimes that is different from what your friends want to do or even what you want to do. To love God means to live the way God wants us to.

Complete the following sentence:

✝ One thing I learned today about love is

UNIT 2 SELF-AWARENESS
Session 4
FIELD TRIP SUGGESTIONS

Visit an Art Museum

Visit an art exhibit that emphasizes self-expression. Prepare a worksheet that has questions to prompt the young men to think about why the artist did what he or she did. Or check with the museum to see if a docent will be available to lead a tour. Talk with the person with whom you are making the arrangements to let him or her know the special emphasis of the group, which you would want the docent or tour leader to take into account.

Go to an Arts Studio

Take the group to a studio or an art class in which the participants may try different art media (clay, papier-mâché, drawing pencils, paints, and so on). Invite the young men to create something.

Visit a Hands-on Science Exhibit

Take the group to a museum that has interactive exhibits, which will engage and stimulate their various senses.

Go Out and About

Visit a sit-down or unusual restaurant and have the young men order their own dishes. Encourage them to try new things. Go to a play, show, or museum exhibit with a self-awareness theme. Check the newspapers and entertainment listings for current and special events in your area.

Keep On Learning

Field trips are wonderful learning experiences in themselves. However, to help the youth get the most from them, do two simple things:

1. **Prepare the youth:** Give them some introductory information; talk about expected behavior; identify a question for them to be thinking about.
2. **Debrief the trip:** Ask the group what surprised them, what was interesting to them, what made them think. Have a group conversation or give the youth paper and pencils and have them write a journal page about the trip—or do both. Gather the journal pages and add them to the individuals' folders.

UNIT 2 SELF-AWARENESS
Optional
ACTIVITIES AND SESSIONS

Self-Portrait

This activity (page 114) encourages the boys to identify and affirm personal characteristics and likes. The goal is to help young persons look at themselves introspectively and gain self-knowledge in order to learn self-appreciation.

The Story of My Life

The boys are to write about or draw in their circles (page 115) significant events in their life from birth to the present, and dream about the future. Using the sheet, they then tell their life stories to the group.

Self-Image/Self-Esteem Bag

Give each person a brown paper sack, scissors, glue, and some magazines. The boys are to cut out pictures that symbolize how others see them and to glue the pictures on the outside of their bag. This "outside portrait" represents how they think others perceive them (self-image). Then have them cut out magazine pictures that represent how they feel about themselves. Have them drop these pictures inside their bag. These "inside pictures" represent their how they perceive themselves (self-esteem).

Discuss the importance of having a positive and strong sense of self-esteem and how that affects self-image. Then read aloud Psalm 139 and discuss how special, unique, and important each of them is to God. Finish the activity by distributing slips of paper with *Jesus* written on them and invite the boys to put the slips inside their bags. Give the boys an opportunity to invite Jesus into their hearts, reminding them that if Jesus is at the center of their lives, everything else will fall into place. If God loves them and God is for them, nothing can stand against them (Romans 8:31-39).

Personal Credo

Each of the Young Lions must stand up in front of the group and make a statement of his own personal worth. This may be in the form of a mantra, rap chorus, song, speech, drawing, or reading what he has written. The young person should begin with his name, and then tell what he likes about himself, what he is good at, what he is proud of, and so forth. As the person presents, the group may clap rhythmically, hum ,or keep silent, according to the presenter's wishes. When each boy is finished the group should respond with an affirmation such as applause, shouting "amen" or "all right!"

SELF-PORTRAIT

Inner Person
Things That Describe Me on the Inside (How I Feel About Me)

_____

_____

Outer Person
Things That Describe Me on the Outside (What People See About Me)

_____

_____

4 Things I Like About Me:

_____

_____

_____

_____

Self-Portrait

3 Most Important Things in My Life:

_____

_____

_____

The Person
I Admire Most

3 Things I Enjoy Doing: _____

_____

_____

THE STORY OF MY LIFE

Use pictures or words to fill in the circles with special events of your life.

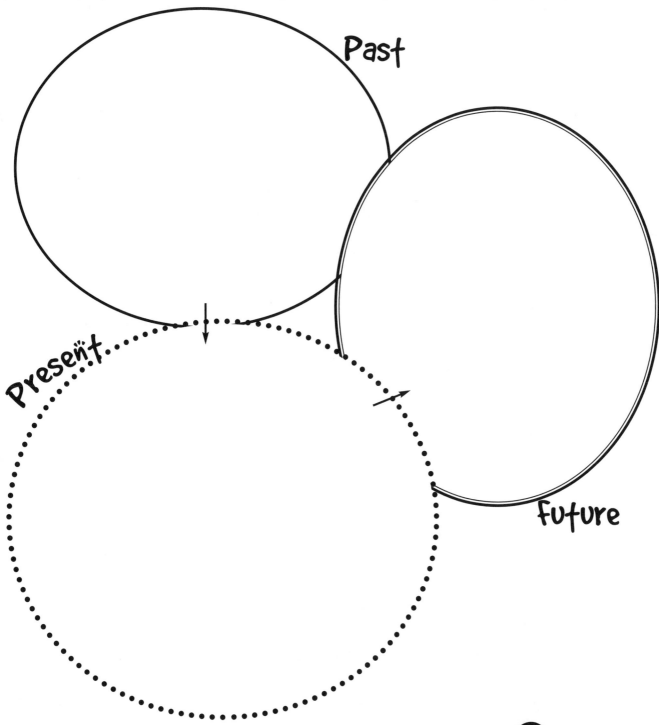

Past

Present

Future

HERITAGE AND CULTURE

The opportunity for young Black male children to learn and appreciate their culture and heritage is of paramount importance in Young Lions. For many African-American children, the earliest memory of learning about their people in public school was about slavery. If they had to go just by most public education, they would think that Blacks (Africans) as a people had no history or experience in the world until they were enslaved by Europeans.

Black children are not often given the opportunity to learn about African history and culture in traditional school curriculum. Consequently, they miss the value of this learning and have little sense of its fundamental connection to their being African Americans. This experience is common to many African-American youth.

A basic knowledge of the complete history of Africans and African Americans in the world (not just North America) is a significant piece of the puzzle in strengthening the self-esteem and self-image of Black males. Self-knowledge will promote self-love among African-American children in contrast to the self-hate cultivated by ignorance and lack of awareness. Unless young persons are taught to love and respect themselves for who they are, we cannot expect them to love and respect others.

UNIT OVERVIEW

This unit seeks to teach the boys their cultural origins and how their heritage has an impact upon their lives today. One of the primary goals of Young Lions is to explore what it means to be African American and to develop a sense of pride in our cultural heritage. This is an excellent time to supplement the boys' history education by teaching African history. For crafts, your group may work together on a cultural project, which will help them explore their heritage. Consider crafts such as making African masks or drums, playing African games, and so forth.

UNIT LEARNING GOALS

The young men will

+ Develop an understanding of the roots of African-American culture in African heritage;,

+ Gain knowledge of the history, geography, and peoples of Africa;

+ Develop a stronger sense of self-identity through their African heritage;

+ Explore and experience African tribal customs and traditions.

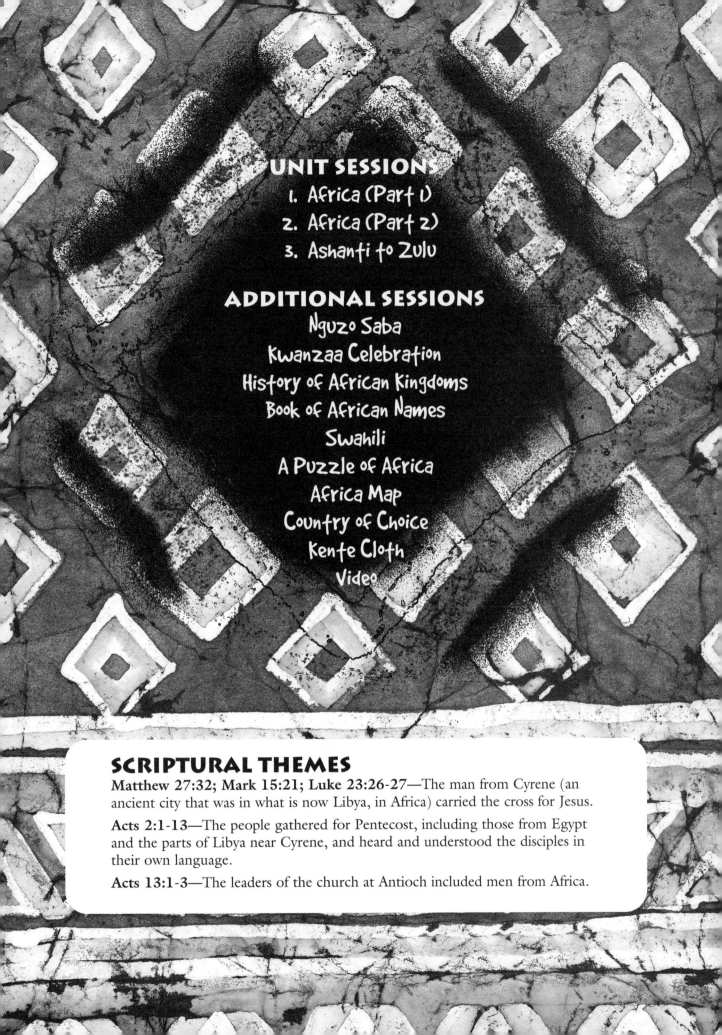

UNIT SESSIONS
1. Africa (Part 1)
2. Africa (Part 2)
3. Ashanti to Zulu

ADDITIONAL SESSIONS
Nguzo Saba
Kwanzaa Celebration
History of African Kingdoms
Book of African Names
Swahili
A Puzzle of Africa
Africa Map
Country of Choice
Kente Cloth
Video

SCRIPTURAL THEMES
Matthew 27:32; Mark 15:21; Luke 23:26-27—The man from Cyrene (an ancient city that was in what is now Libya, in Africa) carried the cross for Jesus.

Acts 2:1-13—The people gathered for Pentecost, including those from Egypt and the parts of Libya near Cyrene, and heard and understood the disciples in their own language.

Acts 13:1-3—The leaders of the church at Antioch included men from Africa.

UNIT 3 HERITAGE AND CULTURE
Session 1
AFRICA (PART 1)

FOCUS: To familiarize the young men with the geography of Africa, the politics of its countries, and its prominence in world history.

Meeting Outline

		Notes
OPENING ACTIVITY & LIBATION	*15 minutes*	
AFRICAN-AMERICAN HEROES	*15 minutes*	
ACHIEVEMENT ACTIVITY	*30 minutes*	
GAME/CRAFT	*20 minutes*	
STORYTELLING	*15 minutes*	
GOD TIME & HARAMBEE CIRCLE	*15 minutes*	

Preparation

 Assign a mentor to review the life of Queen Makeda (page 270) and make a presentation to the young men.

 Have on hand a blanket for the opening activity.

 Photocopy session activity sheets and collect pencils.

 Gather markers, a sheet of posterboard for each boy, rulers, and pencils.

 Assign one or more mentors to do storytelling.

 Gather Bibles and journals for the God Time devotional.

 Have a world globe or map available.

Session 1

OPENING ACTIVITY *(15 minutes)*

Name Game: Divide the group into two teams and ask them to sit on either side of a blanket divider held up by two men. While hidden from the other team, each team will select a person to stand before the blanket. On the count of three, drop the blanket. Whichever of the two players first says the other's name wins a point for his team. Continue until everyone has had a chance to stand and guess.

LIBATION/PRAYER

AFRICAN-AMERICAN HEROES *(15 minutes)*

Queen Makeda: Listen to the presentation about Queen Makeda (see page 270). Discuss these questions, and invite the Young Lions to ask their own questions as well:

- ✚ Who was Queen Makeda?
- ✚ Where did she reign? (Point it out on a map.)
- ✚ By what name is she usually referred to?
- ✚ What contributions did she make to her country?
- ✚ Why should she be considered a hero?
- ✚ For what is she famous?

Note the life of Queen Makeda on the African-American history timeline.

ACHIEVEMENT ACTIVITY *(30 minutes)*

Africa Quiz: Give the boys the quiz about African knowledge. When finished, begin a discussion about Africa by going through the questions. Help for answering the quiz is on page 121. After each question and discussion, affirm all of the young persons who contributed right answers and who added to the discussion.

CRAFT *(20 minutes)*

Achi Board: Achi is a Ghanian game similar to Tic-Tac-Toe. Here are the instructions for having the boys make the gameboard. They will play the game next week:

Draw a border around the posterboard in pencil, about 4½ inches from the edge. Draw a small circle in the center of the gameboard. Draw the lines as shown in the diagram from corner to corner and edge to edge, all going to the center circle. Draw small circles at each of the intersections of the lines (see the diagram, page 120). Trace over the design with a color marker. Decorate and color the outside edge of the gameboard.

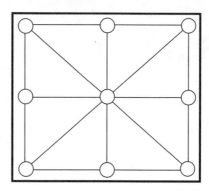

ACHI DIAGRAM

STORYTELLING *(15 minutes)*

My Africa Connection: Ask the chosen mentors to tell a personal story about their African heritage. Perhaps you know a native of African who could come and speak to the group during this session. Review the guidelines for storytelling:

1. Everyone must be silent while the mentor is telling the story.
2. After the mentor is finished, the listeners may ask questions.
3. Each young man should be prepared to ask at least one question about the story.

GOD TIME *(15 minutes)*

Matthew 27:32; Mark 15:21; Luke 23:26–27: Before having three of the boys read aloud the Scripture passages and the devotional message from the God Time activity sheet, ask the group the first question below. Then set the context of the Crucifixion for the listeners and have the boys find and read the passage in their Bibles. Then follow up with the remaining discussion questions:

+ Are there Black/African people in the Bible? Where? (Matthew 12:42; 27:32; Mark 15:21; Luke 11:31; 23:26-27; Acts 2:9-10; 8:27-38; 13:1; and other references)
+ Who was Simon of Cyrene? What was his ethnic background?
+ In what modern country was the ancient city of Cyrene located? *(Point out on a map the location of Cyrene, in Libya.)*
+ What did Simon of Cyrene do? Why did he do it?
+ Was what Simon did important? Why?
+ Why is it important to realize that Blacks/Africans played a significant role in biblical history?

After the discussion, have each boy record his personal response to the lesson in his journal.

HARAMBEE CIRCLE

AFRICA INFORMATION

1. Where do Black people come from?

Point out Africa on the world map.

2. Where in the world do Blacks live today? (Name three places.)

Africans and people of African descent live in many different regions today, including the United States, Europe, the Caribbean and West Indies, South America, the Middle East.

3. How did African culture spread around the world?

Slave trade helped spread African culture throughout the world: Blacks in Israel, Puerto Rico, Jamaica, Haiti, Bermuda, Cuba, Brazil, and so on. Africa was also colonized early by English, French, and Spanish peoples (explaining African presence in those cultures).

4. What place in Africa is referred to as "the cradle of civilization"?

Egypt, an African nation, was the seed of civilization, preceding Greece and Rome.

5. Name five nations in Africa.

Africa is composed of many nations/countries just like the U.S. has many states. Point out and briefly describe some African countries on the map. See list on page 124.

6. What African nations do we hear about regularly in the news?

Talk about why they are getting coverage.

7. Where were the earliest traces of humanity found?

Fossil remains identified as human and prehuman have been found in South Africa (three million years old), in Tanzania (2.5 million years old), and in Ethiopia ("Lucy," 1.8 million years old). These are the oldest indicators of human life.

8. What are the natural resources of Africa?

Africa's resources include oil, diamonds, animal life, alloys for steel and aluminum, clay.

9. Name three different geographical regions in Africa.

Africa has many different geographical regions: deserts, jungle, industrialized areas, bush, mountains, wildlife preserves, grasslands, rain forests, plateaus, and valleys (Rift).

10. Africans have different tribal backgrounds, similar to the different types of Caucasians in Europe (Britains, Germans, Spaniards, and so forth). What are two African tribes?

To review some of the different African tribes, use the book *Ashanti to Zulu: African Traditions,* by Margaret Musgrove, or the list on page 133. (See page 130 and Reading Resources for information about the book.)

MORE ABOUT AFRICA

Africa is

The second largest continent, after Asia. It covers one-fifth of the total land surface of the Earth.

11,724,000 square miles. It is 5,000 miles north to south and 4,600 miles east to west.

Underpopulated. Although Africa is the second largest continent, it contains only ten percent of the world's population.

A
Algeria
Angola
Ascension Island

B
Benin
Botswana
Burkina Faso
Burundi

C
Cameroon
Cape Verde
Central African Republic
Chad
Comoros
Congo
Cote D'Ivoire

D
Dem. Rep. of the Congo
Djibouti

E
Egypt
Equatorial Guinea
Eritrea
Ethiopia

G
Gabon
Gambia
Ghana
Guinea
Guinea-Bissau

K
Kenya

L
Lesotho
Liberia
Libya

M
Madagascar
Malawi
Mali
Mauritania
Mauritius
Morocco
Mozambique

N
Namibia
Niger
Nigeria

R
Reunion
Rwanda

S
Sao Tome And Principe
Senegal
Seychelles
Sierra Leone
Somalia
South Africa
St.Helena
Sudan
Swaziland

T
Tanzania
Togo
Tunisia

U
Uganda

W
Western Sahara

Z
Zambia
Zimbabwe

For a fun quiz to test your knowledge of the locations of countries in Africa, check out the following website: www.lizardpoint.com/fun/geoquiz/afrquiz.html.

AFRICA

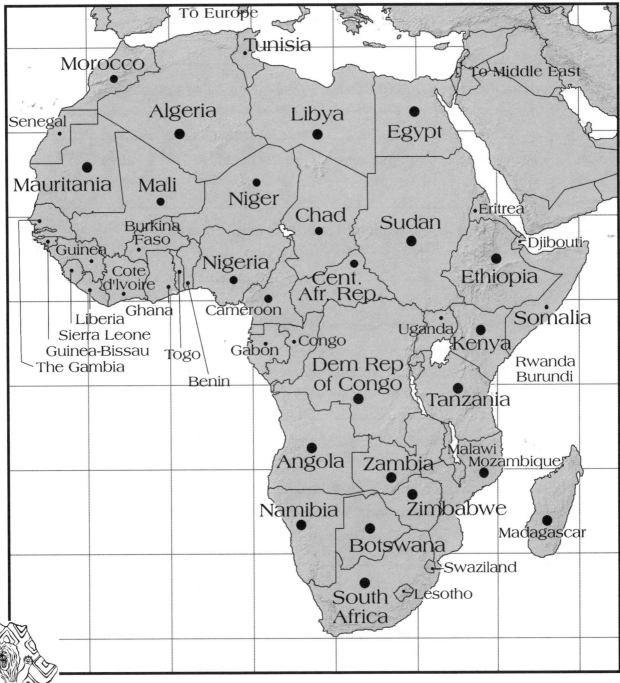

To Europe

Tunisia

Morocco

To Middle East

Senegal

Algeria

Libya

Egypt

Mauritania

Mali

Niger

Chad

Sudan

Eritrea

Burkina
Faso

Djibouti

Guinea

Nigeria

Cent.
Afr. Rep.

Ethiopia

Cote
d'Ivoire

Somalia

Liberia

Ghana

Cameroon

Congo

Uganda

Kenya

Sierra Leone

Gabon

Rwanda
Burundi

Guinea-Bissau

Togo

The Gambia

Benin

Dem Rep
of Congo

Tanzania

Malawi

Angola

Zambia

Mozambique

Namibia

Zimbabwe

Madagascar

Botswana

Swaziland

South
Africa

Lesotho

AFRICA QUIZ

What do you know about Africa?

1. Where do Black people come from?

_____

2. Where in the world do Blacks live today? (Name three places.)

_____

3. How did African culture spread around the world?

_____

4. What place in Africa is referred to as "the cradle of civilization"? Why?

_____

5. Name five nations in Africa.

_____

6. What African nations do we hear about regularly in the news?

_____

7. Where were the earliest traces of humanity found?

_____

8. What are the natural resources of Africa?

_____

9. Name three different geographical regions in Africa.

_____

10. Africans have different tribal backgrounds, similar to the different types of Caucasians in Europe (Britains, Germans, Spaniards, and so forth). What are two African tribes?

_____

GOD TIME

READ MATTHEW 27:32; MARK 15:21; LUKE 23:26-27.

Many times when you watch movies, TV shows, or even read magazines, Black people are not represented. In American society, which is predominantly white right now, Black people sometimes get lost in the shuffle. Even when representing Christianity, the images put forth are often European, when, in reality, many events of the Bible took place in a part of the world in which almost everyone was brown-skinned.

African people and people of other cultures played significant roles in biblical history. In this passage, we read about a man from Cyrene, a city in North Africa.

✠ What do you think Simon from Cyrene did after he carried Jesus' cross? What would you have done?

✠ How does it make you feel to know that Blacks/Africans played a significant role in the Bible?

UNIT 3 HERITAGE AND CULTURE
Session 2
AFRICA (PART 2)

FOCUS: To help the young men become familiar with the nations and cultures of the African continent.

Meeting Outline

		Notes
OPENING ACTIVITY & LIBATION	*15 minutes*	
AFRICAN-AMERICAN HEROES	*15 minutes*	
ACHIEVEMENT ACTIVITY	*30 minutes*	
GAME/CRAFT	*20 minutes*	
STORYTELLING	*15 minutes*	
GOD TIME & HARAMBEE CIRCLE	*15 minutes*	

Preparation

◇ Assign a mentor to review the life of King Shaka (page 271) and make a presentation to the young men.

◇ Have on hand a posterboard or flip chart and marker for the opening activity.

◇ Prepare a map of Africa for the achievement activity. Copy or draw on a large posterboard a big map of Africa that shows the national boundaries. Attach the map to a wall. Bring two dictionaries or encyclopedias and prepare some pins with ribbons of Afrocentric colors (see page 17) attached.

◇ Gather materials for the game: Achi boards made last week, milk-jug caps or checkers for game pieces.

◇ Assign a mentor to do storytelling.

◇ Gather Bibles and journals for the God Time devotional.

◇ Have a world globe or map available.

Session 2

OPENING ACTIVITY *(15 minutes)*

African Numbers Game: Draw five symbols (square, triangle, circle, and so forth) on a chart that everyone can see. Tell the group that they are going to play the African numbers game. Begin by pointing to each of the symbols in order of its position on the chart, and ask the boys what number it represents. The boys do not know that the key to the exercise is that the number of fingers you are pointing with is the clue to the number in question. (If you point to the second symbol with three fingers, the symbol would mean 3 even though you pointed to it second.) After each boy guesses at the number, tell him if he is right or wrong. Point to the symbols in different order each time. Keep going over the numbers (giving them the secret hint) until they all guess the clue.

LIBATION/PRAYER

AFRICAN-AMERICAN HEROES *(15 minutes)*

King Shaka: Listen to the presentation about King Shaka (see page 271). Discuss these questions, and invite the Young Lions to ask their own questions as well:

✚ Who was King Shaka? Where did he reign? (Point it out on a map.)

✚ What is he usually remembered for?

✚ What were his goals as a ruler?

✚ Of what significance was his reign in Africa at that period?

✚ Should he be considered a hero? Why, or why not?

Note the life of King Shaka on the African-American history timeline.

ACHIEVEMENT ACTIVITY *(30 minutes)*

Pin the Flag on Africa: Divide the group into two teams. Taking turns, one member from each group is selected and blindfolded, given a pin, spun around, and pointed in the direction of the Africa map. The blindfolded person must then stick the pin to the map of Africa. The leader identifies the country where the pin has landed and then the two groups race to find information about that country's characteristics in a dictionary or an encyclopedia. The first group that gives information wins a point. Play for as long as time allows.

GAME *(20 minutes)*

Achi: Play Achi with the Ghanian gameboards the boys made last week. Divide the group into teams of two (one boy and one mentor), and hold an Achi tournament. Each team must play another on one board. Each team gets three game pieces (use milk-jug caps, coins, and so on). Teams take turns placing a game piece on any circle they want. Once all of the pieces are on the board, the teams take turns moving one piece at a time to an empty circle. No jumping over empty circles or game pieces is allowed. The object of the game is to get all three of your team's pieces in a straight line before your opponent can. One of the pieces in the line must be in the center circle on the board.

STORYTELLING (OPTIONAL)

My Africa Connection: Ask the chosen mentors to tell a personal story about their African heritage.

GOD TIME *(15 minutes)*

Acts 2:1-13 Read aloud or tell the story of Acts 2. Then have a boy read aloud the God Time devotional. Then discuss:

✠ **What happened?**
✠ **What is the significance of this event in the history of Christianity?**
✠ **What cultures were present at the coming of the Holy Spirit?**

Have the boys read verses 9-11 in their own Bibles and then locate those places mentioned in the Bible on the map or globe as they are able. Some places may not be evident on contemporary maps. Look for a Bible that has maps of that era.

✠ **What cultures do these nations represent?**
✠ **Why do you think it is important to point out that Africans were at the miracle of Pentecost?**

After the discussion, have each boy record his personal response to the lesson in his journal.

HARAMBEE CIRCLE

GOD TIME

READ ACTS 2:1-13.

The coming of the Holy Spirit in Acts 2 is the first important event in the history of Christianity after Jesus' resurrection. This was the beginning of the Church, when the disciples were empowered by God to take the message of Christ throughout the world. The good news began in their own neighborhood, Jerusalem, and spread throughout the whole world. The message wasn't just for Jews. The significance of the event is that people from many cultures and nations were there, and they each heard the gospel message in their own native language at the same time. This is the miracle of Pentecost.

Complete the following sentence:

✚ One thing I have learned today is

✚ God is the author of your African heritage.
How can you honor God in expressing your culture?

UNIT 3 HERITAGE AND CULTURE
Session 3
ASHANTI TO ZULU

FOCUS: To introduce the young men to various tribal groups in Africa: their environment, traditions, and customs.

Meeting Outline

		Notes
OPENING ACTIVITY & LIBATION	*15 minutes*	
AFRICAN-AMERICAN HEROES	*15 minutes*	
ACHIEVEMENT ACTIVITY	*30 minutes*	
GAME/CRAFT	*20 minutes*	
STORYTELLING	*15 minutes*	
GOD TIME & HARAMBEE CIRCLE	*15 minutes*	

Preparation

 Assign a mentor to review the life of Nelson Mandela (page 272) and make a presentation to the young men.

Bring props for the opening activity.

Acquire the children's book *Ashanti to Zulu: African Traditions*, by Margaret Musgrove (1977 Caldecott Award Winner, Dial Books for Young Readers, 1992; ISBN: 0140546049), available at most pubic libraries or bookstores.

Photocopy session activity sheets and collect pencils.

Assign a mentor to do storytelling.

Gather Bibles and journals for the God Time devotional.

Session 3

OPENING ACTIVITY (15 minutes)

Grandma's Grapes: The group leader takes a broom, stick, or some other prop; stands before the group; clears his throat; and says in a loud voice: "Grandma's grapes are the very best grapes. In fact, they're the best grapes around." As he says this, the leader does a series of motions with the prop (twirling the stick, banging the stick on the ground, and so forth). Then he sits down. The object of the game is for the boys to repeat what he does. Everyone takes turns, repeating his words and motions—but no one gets it right unless he clears his throat first. Keep playing until everyone figures out the clue (if there is time to do so).

LIBATION/PRAYER

AFRICAN-AMERICAN HEROES (15 minutes)

Nelson Mandela: Listen to the presentation about this African leader (see page 272). Discuss these questions, and invite the Young Lions to ask their own questions as well:

- ✚ Who is Nelson Mandela?
- ✚ Why is his life noteworthy?
- ✚ What great sacrifice did he make for his people and his country?
- ✚ Why should he be considered a hero?

Note the life of Nelson Mandela on the African-American history timeline.

ACHIEVEMENT ACTIVITY (30 minutes)

Ashanti to Zulu: Hand out the "Ashanti to Zulu" activity sheets and pencils. Read aloud the book *Ashanti to Zulu: African Traditions,* by Margaret Musgrove. If possible, show the pictures as well. Ask the youth to record on their activity sheets each tribe's characteristics or customs. Then divide into groups and discuss which tribes or characteristics of tribes they like or identify with.

If you cannot locate the book, look up tribes in an encyclopedia or search for them by name on reputable websites on the Internet. Bring photocopies or printouts of the information you find. If you are familiar with African tribes other than those listed on page 133, you may locate information about those tribes as well.

GAME *(20 minutes)*

Challenge: Have the boys and men form a circle. Two contestants stand in the middle, right feet in front, toe to toe. While looking each other in the eye, each must attempt to make the other smile or look away without using physical contact. The contestants can tell jokes, make insulting remarks (as long as there is no bad language or personal attacks), or make faces. When one of them wins, he may challenge someone else or two more people may play. African children play this game to build resolution and mental toughness.

STORYTELLING *(15 minutes)*

My Africa Connection: Have the chosen mentor tell a personal story about his African heritage.

GOD TIME *(15 minutes)*

Acts 13:1-3: Ask one of the boys in the group to read aloud the Scripture passage, and ask another to read aloud the God Time devotional. Ask these questions:

+ **Who were these men?**
+ **Why do you think they were leaders in this influential Christian community?**
+ **What do you think is significant about Simeon (called Niger) and Lucius of Cyrene?** (*Niger* **means "black," and Cyrene was in Africa. They were Black men.)**

Point out that Black people played a significant role as leaders in the development of the early Christian church.

After the discussion, have each boy record his personal response to the lesson in his journal.

HARAMBEE CIRCLE

ASHANTI TO ZULU

Under each tribe, note a particular characteristic or custom of that people.

Ashanti (uh-SHAHNT-ee)	**Masai** (mah-SIGH)
Baule (BAH-oo-lay)	**Ndaka** (n-DAH-kuh)
Chagga (CHAH-guh)	**Ouadai** (wah-DY)
Dogon (daw-GAWN)	**Pondo** (PAHN-doh)
Ewe (EH-vay)	**Quimbande** (keem-BAHN-deh)
Fanti (FAHN-tee)	**Rendille** (rehn-DEEL-lay)
Ga (GAH)	**Sotho** (SOO-too)
Hausa (HOW-suh)	**Tuareg** (TWAH-reg)
Ikoma (ik-OH-muh)	**Uge** (OO-gay)
Jie (JEE-yuh)	**Vai** (VY)
Kung (KOOHNG)	**Wagenia** (wuh-GEHN-ee-uh)
Lozi (LOW-zee)	**Xhosa** (KOE-suh)
	Yoruba (YAHWR-uh-buh)
	Zulu (ZOO-loo)

GOD TIME

READ ACTS 13:1-3.

We continue to see the presence of Africans in biblical history in significant ways. In this passage, we have a gathering of church elders in the city of Antioch. Antioch was an influential place in the early Christian church. It replaced Jerusalem as the most important and largest Christian community of those days. Followers of Christ were first called *Christians,* which means "little Christs," in Antioch.

In these verses, we see that Black people played an important part in the development of the early Christian church. In fact, they prayed for and sent off Saul, who is also called Paul, the author of most of the New Testament and the person most responsible for spreading Christianity throughout the world.

✤ Did you know that Black men were leaders of the early Christian church? Does it make a difference to you? If so, in what way?

✤ Is race important to God? Explain your answer.

UNIT 3 HERITAGE AND CULTURE
Session 4
FIELD TRIP SUGGESTIONS

Visit an Art Museum

Visit an art exhibit displaying African art. Prepare some questions to prompt the boys to think about what the art represents. Consider arranging for a knowledgeable guide.

Take a Personal Field Trip

Take your group on a visit to someone in your community who is African or who is knowledgeable about African heritage. Hear the person's stories, look at pictures or artifacts, and ask questions. Afterward, take the Young Lions for a treat. If possible, take your guest along as well. In the informal time, the boys may feel comfortable enough to ask additional questions.

Go Out and About

Take your group to a restaurant that serves African food in a cultural atmosphere. Or go to a play, show, movie, or museum that focuses on some aspect of African life. Check the newspapers and entertainment listings for current and special events in your area. Visit a video rental store to look for movies set in Africa or about Africa. Be sure to preview the video before showing it to the group. Prepare some questions.

Participate in an African Festival

Check local listings for community events or festivals. Find someone from Africa or who has visited Africa and invite him or her to explain or set up a festival.

Visit an African Drum/Dance Studio

Arrange for your group to visit or take a class doing African dance or drums.

Keep On Learning

Field trips are wonderful learning experiences in themselves. However, to help the youth get the most from them, do two simple things:

1. **Prepare the youth:** Give them some introductory information; talk about expected behavior; identify a question for them to be thinking about.
2. **Debrief the trip:** Ask the group what surprised them, what was interesting to them, what made them think. Have a group conversation or give the youth paper and pencils and have them write a journal page about the trip—or do both. Gather the journal pages and add them to the individuals' folders.

UNIT 3 HERITAGE AND CULTURE
Optional
ACTIVITIES AND SESSIONS

Nguzo Saba

Use the "Nguzo Saba" activity sheets (pages 138–139) to teach the boys the Nguzo Saba value system (the seven principles of Kwanzaa). Review with the boys each value and challenge them to think of practical applications of that principle in their lives. Included with each value is a scriptural comparison.

Kwanzaa Celebration

Celebrating Kwanzaa should be an annual event in your Young Lions group. Page 140 provides a brief explanation of the holiday and a description of the various symbols. Pages 141–142 are a suggested format for celebrating Kwanzaa with the Young Lions families in December. You may also wish to purchase a book on celebrating Kwanzaa for regular use by your group.

History of African Kingdoms

Use the "Salute to Black History" series by Empak Publishing (see Reading Resources) to put together a presentation about African kings, queens, and nations. Put together a timeline showing prominent African kingdoms and other world events occurring at the same time. Display it with your timeline of African-American heroes.

Book of African Names

Locate a book of African names. Discuss the importance and significance of naming in African tribal culture. Have the boys choose a name from the book.

Swahili

Teach a few words of Swahili. Remind the group that *Harambee* is a Swahili word they already know. Purchase or borrow the book *Jambo Means Hello*, by Muriel Feelings (Dial Books for Young Readers, 1992; ISBN: 0140546529). It may be found in the children's section at bookstores or in the public library. Use the book to introduce Swahili, the language most widely spoken in eastern Africa, to the Young Lions group. The book is also an excellent tool for exploring African culture. The Internet is another source for learning Swahili. Type *swahili* in the search field.

A Puzzle of Africa

As a group or in small groups work on a puzzle of Africa. As each nation is put into place read from an encyclopedia about that nation's history, resources, people, and so on.

Africa Map

Consider painting a map of Africa for the meeting space. Find out if painting a wall or the floor would be acceptable. If not, get a large sheet of paper or poster board. This project could be done over an extended period by a small group.

Country of Choice

Invite the Young Lions to choose an African country and research it. Have them work in pairs with their mentors or as a team of four or so. The researchers can choose from what they find out about the country and focus on finding a way to present to the whole group what interests them most. The presentations can be as creative and as varied as the teams themselves. This experience of researching, working cooperatively, and making some sort of presentation will also give the boys valuable experience for doing similar tasks successfully in school.

Kente Cloth

Bring a kente scarf or piece of cloth to the meeting. Allow the boys to touch and feel it. Tell them how it is made. Tell them the story of kente cloth: how it is made by the Ashanti tribe of West Africa and historically only kings and queens could wear it. What is its significance today?

Video

Watch the beginning of the first segment of *Roots,* by Alex Haley. The story begins with tribal life in Africa and Kunta Kente's initiation into manhood before he is captured and enslaved. This viewing will lead to positive discussion about life in African tribes and families before slavery.

NGUZO SABA

by Maulana Karenga with additions by Chris McNair

Nguzo Saba (en-GOO-zoh sah-BAH)

THE SEVEN PRINCIPLES OF KWANZAA

Discuss these seven principles and under each one write an application of the principle in daily life. _____

Umoja (oo-MOH-jah)

UNITY

To strive for and maintain togetherness in my family, my community, my nation, and my race.

Try your best to let God's Spirit keep your hearts united. Do this by living in peace. (Ephesians 4:3, Contemporary English Version)

Kujichagulia (koo-jee-CHAH-goo-LEE-ah)

SELF-DETERMINATION

To believe in myself, to be strong in mind and body, and to do things that will not destroy me, but will strengthen me.

Christ gives me the strength to face anything. (Philippians 4:13, Contemporary English Version)

Ujima (oo-JEE-mah)

COLLECTIVE WORK AND RESPONSIBILITY

To build and maintain our community together, to make our sisters' and brothers' problems our problems, and to solve them together.

Bear one another's burdens, and in this way you will fulfill the law of Christ. (Galatians 6:2)

Ujamaa (oo-JAH-mah)

COOPERATIVE ECONOMICS

To build and maintain our own stores, shops, and businesses and to profit from them together.

"For surely I know the plans I have for you" says the LORD, "plans for your welfare and not for harm, to give you a future of hope." (Jeremiah 29:11)

Nia (nee-AH)

PURPOSE

To always remember our ancestors and the struggles they went through to make a better world for us. To work with my brothers and sisters to make a better life for our people.

But you are a chosen race, a royal priesthood, a holy nation, God's own people, in order that you may proclaim the mighty acts of God who called you out of darkness into God's marvelous light. (1 Peter 2:9)

Kuumba (koo-OOM-bah)

CREATIVITY

To use my God-given talents in ways that will leave our community more beautiful and beneficial than we inherited it.

The gifts God gave were that some would be apostles, some prophets, some evangelists, some pastors and teachers, to equip the saints for the work of ministry for building up the body of Christ. (Ephesians 4:11-12)

Imani (ee-MAH-nee)

FAITH

To believe in God my Creator, my parents and all my family, teachers and leaders. To believe in the righteousness and victory of our struggle.

Jesus answered them, "This is the work of God, that you believe in him whom God has sent." (John 6:29)

KWANZAA

The only non-religious, non-heroic, non-political African-American holiday was founded in 1966 by Dr. Maulana Karenga. Kwanzaa is a unique American holiday that pays tribute to the rich cultural roots of Americans of African ancestry. *Kwanzaa* is an East African Kiswahili word that means "the first fruits of the harvest." The celebration begins on December 26th and continues through January 1. A simple celebration can be prepared with a placemat (*mketa*), a candle holder (*kinara*), seven candles (*mishumaa saba*), a variety of fruit (*mazao*), ears of corn (*vibunzi* or *muhindi*), gifts (*zawadi*), and a unity cup (*kikombe cha umoja*). Each day a candle is lit beginning with the Black candle, which is placed in the center of the kinara. The Mishumaa saba are then lit alternately from left to right with three green on the left and three red on the right. Each day one of the seven principles (Nguzo Saba) should be recited as a candle is lit.

SYMBOLS OF KWANZAA

Mazao (mah-ZOW-oh)—fruits and vegetables, which symbolize the rewards of collective labor at harvest time.

Mkeka (Mmm-KAY-kah)—a mat or placemat, which symbolizes tradition and history. "If you know the beginning well, the end will not trouble you."

Kinara (kee-NAH-rah)—a candleholder, which symbolizes our ancestors as a collective whole.

Vibunzi (vee-BOON-zee) or Muhindi (moo-HEEN-dee)—an ear of corn, which represents the produce of the stalk and the potential of the children to become producers themselves. The children are our hope for the future. (Use one ear of corn for each child in the family. Some families consider that each person, no matter what age, is someone's child.)

Zawadi (zah-WAH-dee or sah-WAH-dee)—a gift, which is given as a reward for commitments that have been made and kept.

Kikombe Cha Umoja (kee-KOM-bay CHAH oo-MOH-jah)—the communal unity cup, which honors the ancestors and promotes the spirit of oneness.

Mishumaa Saba (mee-SHOO-mah SAH-bah)—seven candles (one black, three green, and three red), which represent the value system that is the foundation of Kwanzaa.

Bendera ya Taifa (bayn-DEH-rah YAH tah-EE-fah)—the red, black, and green flag used by Marcus Garvey to symbolize the blood (red), the people (black), and the land (green).

A KWANZAA FAMILY CELEBRATION

Welcome and Prayer

Dinner (optional)

Introduction to Young Lions Progam (by the program coordinator)
"Young Lions is a Christian rites-of-passage program for African-American boys that teaches them what it means to be a man—spiritually, culturally, and physically. The goal of Young Lions is to teach African-American boys who they are in Christ."

Presentation of Young Lions
Recite the Young Lions Principles (standards, pledge, symbol, and colors).

Introduction to Kwanzaa
Kwanzaa is a non-religious, non-heroic, non-political African-American holiday founded in 1966 by Dr. Maulana Karenga. It is a unique American holiday that pays tribute to the rich cultural roots of Americans of African ancestry. The core meaning of Kwanzaa is the affirmation of African-American values, culture, and history. *Kwanzaa* is an East African Kiswahili word that means "the first fruits of the harvest." Kwanzaa is a celebration of harvest and community.

Description of the Kwanzaa Symbols (Use a table setting.)
1. Mazao (fruits and vegetables)—represents harvest, the reward of labor
2. Mkeka (mat)—tradition and history, "if you know the beginning well, the end will not trouble you"
3. Kinara (candleholder)—African ancestors, remembering and honoring their suffering
4. Vibunzi or Muhindi (ears of corn)—children, the hope of the future; the kernels of corn are both the produce of the stalk and the potential for reproduction (like children)
5. Zawadi (gifts)—reward for commitments made and kept, gifts represent personal growth and achievement (Young Lions shirts, cards for men)
6. Kikombe Ya Umoja (cup of unity)—Pour libation from four directions and give thanks for ancestors and family.
7. Mishumaa Saba (seven candles)—the seven principles of the Nguzo Saba

Nguzo Saba Ceremony (see the Responsive Reading handout, page 142)
Typically, Kwanzaa begins on December 26 and continues through January 1. A simple celebration can be prepared with a placemat (*mketa*), a candleholder (*kinara*), seven candles (*mishumaa saba*), a variety of fruit (mazao), ears of corn (*vibunzi* or *muhindi*), gifts (*zawadi*) and a unity cup (*kikombe cha umoja*). Each day, a candle is lit, beginning with the Black candle, which is placed in the center of the kinara. The mishumaa saba are then lit alternately from left to right, with three green on the left and three red on the right. Each day, one of the seven principles (*nguzo saba*) is recited as a candle is lit. Today we will participate in a condensed ceremony, lighting all of the candles at once.

Presentation of Gifts
(Present the boys with Young Lions shirts.)

Closing Prayer

RESPONSIVE READING

Read responsively. After each principle has been read, light one of the candles, beginning with the Black candle, then alternating between red and green.

LEADER: Habari gani! (hah-BAH-ree GAH-nee) Umoja! (oo-MOH-jah)

PEOPLE: Umoja! (oo-MOH-jah)

LEADER: *Umoja* means "unity." To strive for and maintain togetherness in my family, my community, my nation, and my race.

PEOPLE: Try your best to let God's Spirit keep your hearts united. Do this by living in peace.

LEADER: Habari gani! Kujichagulia! (koo-jee-cHAH-goo-LEE-ah)

PEOPLE: Kujichagulia! (koo-jee-cHAH-goo-LEE-ah)

LEADER: *Kujichagulia* means "self-determination." To believe in myself, to be strong in mind and body, and to do things that will not destroy me, but will strengthen me.

PEOPLE: Christ gives me the strength to face anything.

LEADER: Habari gani! Ujima! (oo-JEE-mah)

PEOPLE: Ujima! (oo-JEE-mah)

LEADER: *Ujima* means "collective work and responsibility." To build and maintain our community together, to make our sisters' and brothers' problems our problems, and to solve them together.

PEOPLE: Bear one another's burdens, and in this way you will fulfill the law of Christ.

LEADER: Habari gani! Ujamaa! (oo-JAH-mah)

PEOPLE: Ujamaa! (oo-JAH-mah)

LEADER: *Ujamaa* means "cooperative economics." To build and maintain our own stores, shops and businesses and to profit from them together.

PEOPLE: "For surely I know the plans I have for you" says the LORD, "plans for your welfare and not for harm, to give you a future of hope."

LEADER: Habari gani! Nia! (nee-AH)

PEOPLE: Nia! (nee-AH)

LEADER: *Nia* means "purpose." To always remember our ancestors and the struggles they went through to make a better world for us. To work with my brothers and sisters to make a better life for our people.

PEOPLE: But you are a chosen race, a royal priesthood, a holy nation, God's own people, in order that you may proclaim the mighty acts of God who called you out of darkness into God's marvelous light.

LEADER: Habari gani! Kuumba! (koo-OOM-bah)

PEOPLE: Kuumba! (koo-OOM-bah)

LEADER: Kuumba means "creativity." To use my God given talents in ways that will leave our community more beautiful and beneficial than we inherited it.

PEOPLE: The gifts he gave were that some would be apostles, some prophets, some evangelists, some pastors and teachers, to equip the saints for the work of ministry for building up the body of Christ.

LEADER: Habari gani! Imani! (ee-MAH-nee)

PEOPLE: Imani! (ee-MAH-nee)

LEADER: Imani means "faith." To believe in God my creator, my parents and all my family, teachers and leaders. To believe in the righteousness and victory of our struggle.

PEOPLE: Jesus answered them, "This is the work of God, that you believe in him whom God has sent."

* Scripture responses taken from Ephesians 4:3 (CEV); Philippians 4:13 (CEV); Galatians 6:2; Jeremiah 29:11; 1 Peter 2:9; Ephesians 4:11-12; John 6:29.

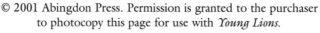

THE BLACK EXPERIENCE

The history of Black people in America is a great epic of a people surviving through tremendous struggles, enduring the persecution and struggle of their enslavement as Africans, the institution of slavery itself, the civil rights movement, and the post-civil rights era. This history has the deepest significance not only for African Americans but for all Americans.

The pivotal social issues of discrimination and racism in American society continue to cause prominent dysfunction in the lives of Black and white Americans. The timeless debate represented by Booker T. Washington and W.E.B. DuBois as to how Blacks were to live and thrive in America still rages today: Should African Americans work hard to establish themselves within the mainstream culture through the traditional and accepted means of commerce and capitalism, or should African Americans forge a new path and destiny for themselves through rising above white mainstream values intellectually and spiritually?

Young Black boys have a unique opportunity in American history to take leadership in healing and providing solutions for the nation. They must know where their people have been before they can take leadership in plotting the course for the future.

UNIT OVERVIEW

This unit focuses on exploring Black history in the United States, particularly slavery and the civil rights period. The purpose of this unit is for the boys to understand what has happened in the past to Blacks as a people in order to gain a proper perspective of the present. Young Lions boys are led to consider the future of Blacks in the United States and how they as individuals will play a part. An understanding of their history will help the boys address racism, prejudice, and discrimination in contemporary society and also help them deal with personal adverse experiences in a self-affirming manner. It is by design that this section is not planned during Black History Month. The youth must know that their history is a significant part of American history as a whole and not simply relegated to one month out of the year.

UNIT LEARNING GOALS

The young men will

- ✚ Examine the development of Blacks in America as a people through slavery, through the civil rights movement, and into contemporary times;
- ✚ Explore the issues of racism in society and its effect on African-American people;
- ✚ Come to an understanding of their own investment in and contribution to African-American history.

UNIT SESSIONS
1. Before the Mayflower
2. Civil Rights
3. Endangered in America

ADDITIONAL SESSIONS AND ACTIVITIES
Being Black
Video Series
The Black Experience
A Salute to Black History
Black History Monuments

SCRIPTURAL THEMES

Genesis 1:26-31—God created humans in God's own image.

Psalm 33:12-15, 18-22—The Lord sees all humankind and watches over those whose faith is in the Lord.

Revelation 1:9-18—John sees a vision of Christ returning.

UNIT 4 - THE BLACK EXPERIENCE
Session 1
BEFORE THE MAYFLOWER

FOCUS: To teach the young men the origins of and circumstances around the African-American presence in America.

Meeting Outline

		Notes
OPENING ACTIVITY & LIBATION	*15 minutes*	
AFRICAN-AMERICAN HEROES	*15 minutes*	
ACHIEVEMENT ACTIVITY	*30 minutes*	
GAME/CRAFT	*20 minutes*	
STORYTELLING	*15 minutes*	
GOD TIME & HARAMBEE CIRCLE	*15 minutes*	

Preparation

 Assign a mentor to review the life of Crispus Attucks (page 273) and make a presentation to the young men.

Gather materials for the opening activity: toilet paper rolls.

Photocopy session activity sheets and collect pencils.

Ask four or five of the mentors to bring an old set of clothing (pants, shirt, shoes, and so forth).

Assign a mentor to do storytelling.

Gather Bibles and journals for the God Time devotional.

Session 1

OPENING ACTIVITY *(15 minutes.)*

Toilet Paper Relay: Have the men and boys gather in small groups. Give each group a roll of toilet paper. Instruct the groups to stand in the tightest circle they can. They are to take the roll of toilet paper and wrap it around and around the group until the entire roll is used up. If the sheets break apart, someone must hold it and continue unrolling. The first group to finish wins.

LIBATION/PRAYER

AFRICAN-AMERICAN HEROES *(15 minutes)*

Crispus Attucks: Listen to the presentation about Crispus Attucks (see page 273). Discuss these questions, and invite the Young Lions to ask their own questions as well:

+ How and why did he die?
+ Why is his death significant for the experience of Black people in America?
+ The American Revolutionary War was fought for freedom, and the Constitution guarantees equal rights for all. But Blacks and other groups of people have often been denied those rights in American history. What do you think Crispus Attucks would have to say about this country?

Note the life of Crispus Attuck on the African-American history timeline.

ACHIEVEMENT ACTIVITY *(30 minutes)*

Before the Mayflower: Have the boys and men gather in small groups. Have them read the "Before the Mayflower" activity sheet (page 148) and go through the discussion questions (page 149).

GAME *(20 minutes)*

Clothes Relay: Collect the clothes the mentors brought to the meeting and put the clothes in four separate piles at the end of the room. Have the boys form four teams. Have the teams stand on the other end of the room, each team opposite a clothes pile. When the leader calls "Go!" The first person in each team must run to the clothes pile and put on each article of clothing, do ten jumping jacks, and run back to his group. He then removes the clothes and helps the next person put them on, who returns to the other end of the room, does ten jumping jacks, and then removes the clothes and runs back to his group to tag the next person. Repeat this activity for each person on the team. The group whose members have all put on the clothes and returned first wins.

STORYTELLING (15 MINUTES)

Being Black: Have the chosen mentor tell a personal story about his experience of being Black. Review with the group the guidelines for storytelling:

1. **Everyone must be silent while the mentor is telling the story.**
2. **After the mentor is finished, the listeners may ask questions.**
3. **Each young man should be prepared to ask at least one question about the story.**

GOD TIME (15 MINUTES)

Genesis 1:26–31: Ask one of the boys to read aloud the passage; then reread Genesis 1:27. Then have one of the boys read the devotional on the God Time activity page. Ask:

✢ What do you think the following statement means?

   "It takes God to be a Black man."—Tom Skinner

✢ What does it mean to be made in God's image?

✢ Why do you think there are so many different kinds of people in the world?

✢ If we are all made in God's image, shouldn't we all look the same? Explain your answer.

✢ Why do you think God made you an African American?

✢ If you are an African American and you are made in God's image, and other people are different from you but are also made in God's image, what does that say about God?

After the discussion, have each boy record in his journal his personal response to the lesson.

HARAMBEE CIRCLE

BEFORE THE MAYFLOWER

In August 1619, a year before the *Mayflower* landed, an unnamed ship, manned by pirates and thieves, sailed into the small Virginia settlement of Jamestown. The captain bartered his cargo for food and supplies. The deal was struck, and he sailed away leaving behind twenty Africans, whom he had captured earlier from a Spanish vessel bound for the sugar industry of the West Indies.

When Antoney, Isabella, Pedro, and the seventeen other unnamed Africans stepped ashore that day, it was not as slaves. They had been sold by the captain; but rather than as slaves, they, like many white new arrivals, came as indentured servants.

Indentured servants hired themselves out for a period of time (usually years!) in order to pay off a debt. Often people who came to America were very poor (many from debtors' prisons); this system of debt repayment was socially acceptable and widely used. After the agreed-upon period of time was over, the person went about the business of his or her life with no shame for having been a servant.

The first generation of African Americans benefitted from this system and were able to gain freedom. For the first forty years or so, the Black settlers could accumulate land, vote, testify in court, and mingle with whites equally. Some held positions of leadership in the communities. Some even owned other indentured servants, both white and Black.

Soon, however, because of greed, attitudes shifted and opportunities closed. Slavery came about in America because the growing cotton industry needed cheap labor in order to thrive. And a whole system of trade in human beings grew up to supply the demand for workers.

Slavery was different from indentured servitude because servants had rights—slaves did not. Servants were given basic human respect; Black slaves were considered less than human. Servants could work their way out of their servitude, but slaves were slaves for life.

Cotton growers enslaved Native Americans for a time, but soon moved to Africans, whom the slave masters perceived to be stronger. Also, because Africans were dark-skinned, they were easy to identify as slaves and be denied their humanity. Soon the growing demand for slave labor for the cotton industry resulted in ships going to Africa to bring back more Africans to enslave.

Based on *Before the Mayflower: A History of Black America*, by Lerone Bennett (Johnson Publishing Company, Inc., 1982).

BEFORE THE MAYFLOWER

When did Black people first come to North America?

Why do you think they came?

Why do you think they were headed for the West Indies?

What happened to them when they got to America?

What is the difference between an indentured servant and a slave?

If you had to choose, which would you rather be?

How did Blacks end up being enslaved in America?

What makes one group of people try to enslave another?

Were the first Blacks in America slaves?

Explain your answer. What does this fact mean you?

GOD TIME

READ GENESIS 1:26-31.

Urban Christian evangelist, ex-gang leader, and author Tom Skinner proclaimed, "It takes God to be a Black man!" Many African Americans today are celebrating and rediscovering their heritage in different ways; but if they are leaving out God, they are not being true to their African-American heritage.

God is the author of Blackness. In the same way, God is the author of every ethnic heritage: Native American, Hispanic and Latino, European, and Asian. Your spiritual connection to God is a fundamental part of who you are as a person and as an African American.

Some people have negative images of what it means to be Black. They think White is good and Black is bad. Some African Americans in urban communities believe this themselves and live negative lifestyles. But God created Blackness, and God created it good. So live your life in a way that is true to your ethnic and spiritual heritage and true to God.

✚ What does it mean to you to be made in the image of God?

UNIT 4 - THE BLACK EXPERIENCE
Session 2
CIVIL RIGHTS

FOCUS: To expose the young men to some of the issues surrounding the civil rights movement during the 1950s and '60s.

Meeting Outline

		Notes
OPENING ACTIVITY & LIBATION	*15 minutes*	
AFRICAN-AMERICAN HEROES	*15 minutes*	
ACHIEVEMENT ACTIVITY	*30 minutes*	
GAME/CRAFT	*20 minutes*	
STORYTELLING	*15 minutes*	
GOD TIME & HARAMBEE CIRCLE	*15 minutes*	

Preparation

◇ Assign a mentor to review the life of Medgar Evers (page 274) and make a presentation to the young men.

◇ Prepare stickers with the names of African-American historical or public figures for the opening activity.

◇ Photocopy session activity sheets and collect pencils.

◇ Gather materials for the craft: a large sheet of newsprint or an old bedsheet, pencils, and markers.

◇ Assign a mentor to do storytelling.

◇ Gather Bibles and journals for the God Time devotional.

Session 2

OPENING ACTIVITY *(15 minutes)*

Guess Who: As each of the boys and men come into the room, place a sticker on his back with the name of an African-American historical or public figure. The object of the game is for each person to guess whose name is on his back by going around the room and asking people questions. Only yes or no questions may be asked.

LIBATION/PRAYER

AFRICAN-AMERICAN HEROES *(15 minutes)*

Medgar Evers: Listen to the presentation about this African-American civil rights worker (see page 274). Discuss these questions, and invite the Young Lions to ask their own questions as well:

- ✚ Why is he a hero?
- ✚ Why do you think he was assassinated?
- ✚ What was he doing that was promoting civil rights for Blacks?
- ✚ What key event for civil rights occurred after his assassination?

Note the life of Medgar Evers on the African-American history timeline.

ACHIEVEMENT ACTIVITY *(30 minutes)*

Word Puzzle: Have the men and boys gather in small groups, and distribute copies of the "Marching to Freedom" word puzzle (page 154). As they solve the puzzle in their small groups, have the participants discuss each word about the civil rights movement, using the accompanying definition sheet (page 155).

CRAFT *(20 minutes)*

Black Experience Mural: The group will create a mural on a large sheet of paper, on several sheets of paper, or on a large bedsheet. Indicate on the paper(s) different sections for depicting the Black experience in America (for example, slavery, segregation, civil rights, racism, discrimination). Have the boys and men gather around and draw scenes from African-American history. Continue the project next week.

STORYTELLING *(15 minutes)*

My Civil Rights Efforts: Ask one of the mentors to tell a personal story about his experience with civil rights issues.

GOD TIME *(15 minutes)*

Psalm 33:12–15, 18–22: Invite one or two boys to read aloud this passage. Discuss these questions:

✠ How important is it to have hope? How important is it to have hope in God? What's the difference between these two?

✠ How has having hope in God made a difference for Black people throughout our history?

✠ How can African Americans, as a people, follow God?

✠ What are some ways you see African-American culture affirming God? (art, music, and so on)

✠ What are some ways you see African-American culture turning away from God?

Scripture has been wrongly used at times in order to justify slavery and discrimination (Genesis 9:25 and 1 Peter 2:18, for example). But these Scriptures were taken out of context and twisted in meaning. Our Blackness comes from God, and what God has created is good! African Americans must keep God first in order to be the people and individuals God created us to be.

After the discussion, have each boy record in his journal his personal response to the lesson.

HARAMBEE CIRCLE

MARCHING TO FREEDOM

The following word puzzle focuses on the subject of the civil rights movement. As you do the puzzle read and discuss the meaning of each term or the history-shaping contribution of the person or event.

```
N A A C P S R E F R E E D O M R I D E R S
O O N O Y D H W D R N D I E T R A T J M E
I B N L I S R E V E R A G D E M U G E R L
T D Q V P T R C S E J N A I T S N E H C M
A I N D I S C R I M I N A T I I C L D E A
R S H W A O M H O L K O G N K I I T E S T
T C L S A N L T H A N E L R D A R E V L O
S R S I C T I E N M O V E U M E O N O T M
I I S S N I I C N K L H J I W Y S R S R O
G M R A L T V T I T T E S E G R A T I O N
E I N C A P P I N U R M A R T I P N N Y T
R N R O Y S N C L P I E C R E G A I T W G
R A C I S M S N T R R L S A T I R O I I O
E T N V I O I L E N I T R I B O K Y S L M
T I C O T T M N G M R G C I S D S B A K E
O O J V R S I S N C C M H B G T A M E I R
V N N A T O R I N G P R O T G H A R A N Y
M P M B U S B O Y C O T T A S R K N A S E
N R U E C H U S E G R E G A T I O N C R H
D C E C N E I D E B O S I D L I V I C E H
```

bus boycott	prejudice
civil disobedience	racism
civil rights	Rosa Parks
discrimination	Roy Wilkins
Dr. Martin Luther King, Jr.	segregation
Freedom Riders	Selma to Montgomery
Medgar Evers	sit-ins
NAACP	SNCC
non-violent resistance	voter registration

DEFINITION OF TERMS

bus boycott (Montgomery)—Staged to protest segregated bus seating in the South. Catalyst of civil rights movement and Dr. King's leadership.

civil disobedience—Refusal to obey unjust civil laws, characterized by nonviolent protest. .

civil rights—Equal privileges in society for all people regardless of race, color, sex or religious beliefs.

discrimination—Acting on prejudice to treat people unfairly.

Dr. Martin Luther King, Jr.—Baptist minister, leader of civil rights movement, advocate for non-violent resistance. Assassinated in 1968.

Freedom Riders—Volunteers (white and Black) who rode through the South on buses to protest segregation enduring threats and violence.

Medgar Evers—NAACP secretary. Worked for desegregation and Black voter registration in Mississippi. Assassinated on his front lawn in 1963.

NAACP—National Association for the Advancement of Colored People.

non-violent resistance—Successful method of protest adopted by civil rights leaders of the 1950's and 60's.

prejudice—An opinion formed about someone or something before the facts are known.

racism—Discrimination, unjust and unfair treatment based on racial differences.

Rosa Parks—"Mother of civil rights movement" Woman who sparked Montgomery bus boycott by refusing to give up her seat on the bus for a white passenger.

Roy Wilkins—Executive director of NAACP during civil rights movement.

segregation—Policy of separating Blacks and whites in social settings with separate facilities.

Selma to Montgomery—Historic march from Selma to Montgomery, Alabama, by civil rights protesters.

sit-ins—Protest movement begun by Black students at segregated lunch counters in North Carolina to protest segregation and discrimination.

SNCC—Student Non-violent Coordinating Committee, organized by college students to protest segregation (Freedom Riders/voter registration).

voter registration—Strategy to get political power for Blacks in the South by registering them to vote.

ANSWER KEY

Answer Key
TO "MARCH TO FREEDOM" WORD FIND PUZZLE

```
N A A C P S R E F R E E D O M R I D E R S
O O N O Y D H W D R N D I E T R A T J M E
I B N L I S R E V E R A G D E M U G E R L
T D Q V P T R C S E J N A I T S N E H C M
A I N D I S C R I M I N A T I I C L D E A
R S H W A O M H O L K O G N K I I T E S T
T C L S A N L T H A N E L R D A R E V L O
S R S I C T I E N M O V E U M E O N O T M
I I S S N I I C N K L H J I W Y S R S R O
G M R A L T V T I T T E S E G R A T I O N
E I N C A P P I N U R M A R T I P N N Y T
R N R O Y S N C L P I E C R E G A I T W G
R A C I S M S N T R R L S A T I R O I I O
E T N V I O I L E N I T R I B O K Y S L M
T I C O T T M N G M R G C I S D S B A K E
O O J V R S I S N C C M H B G T A M E I R
V N N A T O R I N G P R O T G H A R A N Y
M P M B U S B O Y C O T T A S R K N A S E
N R U E C H U S E G R E G A T I O N C R H
D C E C N E I D E B O S I D L I V I C E H
```

GOD TIME

READ PSALM 33:12-15, 18-22.

From the days of slavery through the civil rights era, Christian spirituality has played a significant role in the struggle of Blacks in America. The Christian faith of slaves allowed them to endure untold suffering by trusting in God for a better future. Many slaves worshiped the true God and rose above their circumstances and so-called "masters." During the civil rights movement, the Black church lent spiritual strength and integrity to the protests.

Some whites tried to keep Black people down by teaching that according to the Bible they were cursed by God. Slaveholders also found justification for slavery in the Bible. Those claims, however, were a misuse of the Scriptures and not representative of the Christian faith.

On the other hand, godly people such as the Quakers (who were white) helped slaves along the Underground Railroad. Others, like some of the Freedom Riders, marched, rode, and stood alongside Blacks in the protests for civil rights.

Our Blackness comes from God; it is something to be honored. African Americans must keep God first to be the people and individuals God created us to be.

✚ How is following God a part of your African-American heritage?

UNIT 4-THE BLACK EXPERIENCE
Session 3
ENDANGERED IN AMERICA

FOCUS: To explore with the young men racism in America and its effects among African-American people.

Meeting Outline

		Notes
OPENING ACTIVITY & LIBATION	*15 minutes*	
AFRICAN-AMERICAN HEROES	*15 minutes*	
ACHIEVEMENT ACTIVITY	*30 minutes*	
GAME/CRAFT	*20 minutes*	
STORYTELLING	*15 minutes*	
GOD TIME & HARAMBEE CIRCLE	*15 minutes*	

Preparation

 Assign a mentor to review the life of Shirley Chisholm (page 275) and make a presentation to the young men.

 Gather paper and pencils for icebreaker game.

 Photocopy session activity sheets and collect pencils.

 Gather materials for the craft: mural from last week, markers, paint, and paintbrushes.

 Assign a mentor to do storytelling.

 Gather Bibles, and God Time journals for the devotional. Also gather pictures of Jesus from Sunday school curriculum or the library, if possible.

Session 3

OPENING ACTIVITY *(15 minutes)*

African-American List It: Have the men and boys gather into teams and give everyone a pencil and paper. The game leader will announce the subject of one of the lists on page 161. The teams get one minute to write down as many responses as they can think of. Each team can work collaboratively to create one list. At the end of the minute the teams must stop writing and the leader reads aloud his list. For each response on the teams' list that is on the leader's list, the team gets one point.

LIBATION/PRAYER

AFRICAN-AMERICAN HEROES *(15 minutes)*

Shirley Chisholm: Listen to the presentation about Shirley Chisholm (see page 275). Discuss these questions and invite the Young Lions to ask their own questions as well:

+ Who is she?
+ What was her unique dream in politics?
+ What were her obstacles to success in American politics?
+ Why should she be considered a hero?

Note the life of Shirley Chisholm on the African-American history timeline.

ACHIEVEMENT ACTIVITY *(30 minutes)*

Hmmm?: As a group, read the activity sheet (page 162) and discuss each statistic.

+ What is your response to these statistics?
+ How do they make you feel?
+ Do any of them affect you personally?
+ How do you think they reflect on African-American manhood?
+ What do people mean when they say that the African-American male is an endangered species?

CRAFT *(20 minutes)*

Mural: Finish the mural the group began last week. This week have the boys color with markers or paint the scenes they have drawn on the mural. When finished, display the mural in the room or the building.

STORYTELLING

Looked Down On: Ask one of the men to tell a personal story about experiencing racism or discrimination.

GOD TIME *(15 minutes)*

Revelation 1:9-18: If possible, gather various depictions of Jesus from children's Sunday school curriculum and teaching pictures, from books of art at the library, and from other sources. Do not yet show them to the boys. Ask:

✚ **Have you ever heard anyone say that Christianity is a white religion? Why do they say that?**

Show the pictures to the boys.

✚ **What do you see as you look at all of these pictures of Jesus? (Or if you do not have any pictures, ask: "Have you seen any pictures of Jesus? What does he look like in them?")**

✚ **What do you think Jesus looked like and why?**

✚ **What does the variety of ethnic depictions of Jesus say about the people who worship Christ?**

Tell the boys that Jesus Christ was both human and divine. As a human being, he lived in an area we today call the Middle East. Israel was both part of the continent of Asia and a very important trade route for people traveling from Africa and Europe to other regions of the world. In this area where peoples from various continents came together, many people were of mixed race. Most of the people who lived in Israel then, as well as now, were dark-skinned with dark hair. Jesus, as a Jew living in the Middle East at that time, was not white. He too would have had dark skin and dark hair.

Have a volunteer read aloud Revelation 1:12-16. Tell the Young Lions that the Book of Revelation was written to encourage Christians long ago who were being persecuted and discriminated against. The book gives a vision of how the new world will be when Christ comes again, when God ultimately triumphs over the evils of this world, including persecution and discrimination. John, the writer, describes the heavenly Christ in his vision as having skin like burnished bronze and hair like lamb's wool.

The point of the matter isn't that Jesus was Black or white or whatever ethnic background but that he was the true Son of God who loves and saves peoples of all races and cultures of all time, and every ethnic culture can identify with him.

After the discussion, have each boy record in his journal his response to the lesson.

HARAMBEE CIRCLE

AFRICAN-AMERICAN LIST IT

List 1—Black History Figures

Martin Luther King, Jr.
Medgar Evers
Harriet Tubman
Mary McLeod Bethune
Nat Turner
Rosa Parks
Crispus Attucks
Malcolm X

List 2—Civil Rights Issues

Voting Rights
Desegregation
Bus Segregation
Education
Boycotts
Protest Marches
Discrimination
Non-violence

List 3—African-American Culture

Food
Music
Family
Art
Clothes
Literature
Religion
Dance

List 4—Historic Events

Civil Rights Act
Emancipation Proclamation
First Blacks in America
Assassination of MLK, Jr.
Brown vs. Board of Education
Black migration
Juneteenth
March on Washington

List 5—Affected by Segregation

Public Facilities
Schools
Buses
Jobs
Neighborhoods
Politics
Relationships
Sports

List 6—Institutions of Black Culture

Families
Colleges
Churches
Communities
Barbershops
The South
Magazines
Newspapers

HMMM?

Did you know that

1. The life expectancy for a Black man is 67.6 years while the average life expectancy for a white man is 74.5 years? **Why is that?**

2. The number one cause of death among young Black males ages 15–24 is homicide? **Why is that?**

3. Black men are 18 times more likely to be jailed than white men? **Why is that?**

4. While Black people make up 12.7% of the nation's population, they account for 37% of all AIDS cases in this country? The rate of infection is growing: 50% of all new AIDS cases are African Americans. One in 50 African American males is infected compared with one in 160 females. **Why is that?**

5. In 1999 African Americans were 7 times more likely than whites to commit murders? Blacks were also 6 times more likely than whites to be murdered. **Why is that?**

6. Every day 500 Black teenagers drop out of school? More than one in eight (12%) Black youth are drop-outs. **Why is that?**

7. More than one in three (33%) African-American children live in poverty? **Why is that?**

8. Most Black homicide victims (94%) are killed by Blacks? **Why is that?**

9. The most common cause (66.6%) for Black murders is drug related? **Why is that?**

10. Only 14% of all African Americans are college educated, compared with 25% of the white population and 42% of Asian Americans? **Why is that?**

11. One in four (25%) of all African-American men will have spent some time in prison during his lifetime? **Why is that?**

12. The probability that a 15-year-old African-American male will be murdered before the age of 45 is nationally one in 45; for white males the probability is one in 345. **Why is that?**

* 1. Centers for Disease Control and Prevention, 1998; 2. Center for the Study and Prevention of Violence; 3. prisoners.com/minority.html; 4. CDC National Center for HIV, STD, and TB Prevention, 1999; 5. Bureau of Justice Statistics; 6. Children's Defense Fund and National Center for Policy Analysis, 1997; 7. Children's Defense Fund; 8. Bureau of Justice Statistics, 1976–1999; 9. Bureau of Justice Statistics, 1976–1999; 10. US Census Bureau, 1998; 11. prisoners.com/minority.html; 12. Heritage Center for Data Analysis, No. 00-05, 2000.

GOD TIME

READ REVELATION 1:9-18.

Have you ever heard anyone say that Christianity is a "white" religion? You may have seen pictures showing Jesus as being white. These pictures are an inaccurate representation of what people looked like in that part of the world where Jesus lived. All the people native to that region (what is known today as the Middle East) enjoyed an African-Asian heritage. Jesus was not a white man.

Jesus Christ was a human being with a particular culture and ethnicity (Jewish) in a particular time (2000+ years ago), but Jesus Christ is also divine, the Son of God. As the Son of God, he is not limited to a particular culture or ethnicity or time. As the Son of God, Jesus rose from the dead and lives forever, and through him every man, woman, and child whoever lives can know God and God's love.

John, the writer of the Book of Revelation, describes Jesus in his vision as having skin like burnished bronze and hair like lamb's wool. The point of the matter isn't that Jesus was Black or white or whatever ethnic background, but that he was the true Son of God and reflects God's love for all and every ethnic culture can identify with him.

✚ Do you think that Christianity is a "white" religion? Why, or why not?

Complete this sentence:
✚ I see my ethnic culture affirmed in the Bible because

UNIT 4 - THE BLACK EXPERIENCE
Session 4
FIELD TRIP SUGGESTIONS

Visit an Art Museum

Visit an art exhibit by an African-American artist. Prepare a worksheet that has questions to prompt the boys to think about why the artist did what he or she did and how his or her works express his or her Blackness.

Visit a Historic Landmark

Take the group to a historic landmark in your city that relates to the civil rights movement or some other period in Black history.

Go on a Personal Field Trip

Find someone in your community who has had personal involvement in the civil rights movement or some other historic event (for example, war veterans or athletes). Take your group to visit, hear his or her stories, and ask questions. Afterward, take the group for a treat. Encourage the young men to write a follow-up note of thanks to the person for his or her contribution to their lives.

Visit an African-American Celebrity

Arrange a visit with some local public figures. Invite them to come to a group meeting or go to meet them. Ask them to tell their stories to your group.

Go Out and About

Take your group to a restaurant that specializes in "soul food." Or go to a play, show, or movie that focuses on some aspect of African-American life. Check the newspapers and entertainment listings for current and special events in your city.

Keep On Learning

Field trips are wonderful learning experiences in themselves. However, to help the youth get the most from them, do two simple things:

1. **Prepare the youth:** Give them some introductory information; talk about expected behavior; identify a question for them to be thinking about.
2. **Debrief the trip:** Ask the group what surprised them, what was interesting to them, what made them think. Have a group conversation or give the youth paper and pencils and have them write a journal page about the trip—or do both. Gather the journal pages and add them to the individuals' folders.

UNIT 4 THE BLACK EXPERIENCE
Optional
ACTIVITIES AND SESSIONS

Being Black

The goals of this activity sheet (page 166) are to 1) increase awareness of what it means to each group member to be Black, and 2) gain a new awareness and appreciation of being Black. Discuss goals with the group. Ask them to divide into small groups (one or two men to two boys). Have the groups review the activity sheet and discuss the statements. When they are finished, return to the large group and ask people to talk about what they have learned.

Video Series

Bring a presentation to the group about the content covered by the *Eyes on the Prize* video series. (Check www.shop.pbs.org for more information. The videos may also be available at the public library or nearest video store.) Allow the group to vote on which segment to watch. After watching the video, lead a discussion or stage a roleplay or reenactment of significant events.

The Black Experience

Lead your group in a discussion about what it is like to be Black in their everyday settings. Talk about experiences at home, at school, with their friends, in the community. Use questions such as: Have you ever experienced discrimination? racism? Where and how? What is discrimination? racism? Divide the Young Lions into smaller groups and have each group choose an incident common to their experience or a recent event that says something about being Black in contemporary American society. Have them roleplay these situations in the larger group.

A Salute to Black History

Use the books of A Salute to Black History series (see the Reading Resources section) to spark group discussions about contemporary music and art and their roots in Black culture. Assign booklets on Black musicians and Blacks in fine arts and ask the boys to bring back a report to the group. You could also ask the boys to do some research on their favorite African-American musician or artist and give an oral report to the group.

Black History Monuments

Does your city have a tribute (birthplace, house, gravesite, monument) to some aspect of African-American history? Make plans for a field trip to the site and spend time studying the person or event in the meeting before the trip.

BEING BLACK

FINISH THESE STATEMENTS:

As a Black person, I feel _____

_____

One thing I have to offer as a Black person is _____

_____

One problem I see in my being Black is _____

_____

One thing I value about my Blackness is _____

_____

I feel most powerful when I _____

_____

I feel powerless when I _____

_____

I feel good about myself when I _____

_____

I feel bad about myself when I _____

_____

My Blackness has cost me _____

_____

The benefits of being Black are _____

_____

Right now I feel _____

_____

FAMILY AWARENESS

The welfare of the Black family is a central issue in addressing the problems facing youth in the Black community. Arguments range from demonstrating the total disintegration of the family unit to praising its enduring strength through extended family networks. One sees both ends of the spectrum when working with children in inner-city communities.

The significance of the family unit is that it is an emotional cradle for each person. All persons need someplace to feel they belong. This desire to belong is fundamental. God created families to meet this need. Many youth who are suffering from the lack of a nurturing network seek to have this need met in self-destructive, non-traditional ways. This drive is the impetus behind the growth of gangs in urban communities.

Youth crave someplace to belong and people who care about them. Many youth weave positive networks of support around themselves involving neighbors, schools, and churches. Tragically, many other youth simply slip through the cracks and waste away—their lives unnoticed and unmourned.

An awareness of the role and function of family and of individual roles as males is critical, helping young Black males appreciate and support their families and draw strength from the resources families can provide. The restoration of traditional African values such as respect for the wisdom of elders, the extended family network, and a return to spiritual values is needed to reweave the fabric of support for Black youth in urban communities.

UNIT OVERVIEW

This section attempts to foster within the boys a sense of value and respect towards their families, whether they are traditional, single-parent, or extended families. The activities are designed not only to help the boys appreciate their families, but also to start them thinking about the families they may have in the future. They will consider the type of family they will have, the kind of person they might choose for a wife, whether they will have children, and what their familial relationships might be like. The devotionals in this section affirm that the family unit is a creation of God and that each family is unique and special.

UNIT LEARNING GOALS

The young men will

✚ Gain an appreciation for family history and traditions;

✚ Learn the value and importance of the family unit and their own places in it as sons and brothers, potential fathers and husbands;

✚ Develop appreciation for various family structures, particularly the extended family, which is a cultural value;

✚ Experience personally a positive family environment and observe positive familial relationships.

UNIT SESSIONS
1. Your Family Shield
2. Understanding Family
3. In My House

ADDITIONAL SESSIONS AND ACTIVITIES
Your Family Tree
The Ideal Family
Family Roleplay
A Letter to Me
The Perfect Father/Husband
Color Your Family

SCRIPTURAL THEMES

Ephesians 5:21–6:4—Here is guidance for living as a Christian household.

Ephesians 3:14-15—Families are from God.

Acts 16:25-34—The faith of the head of the household can be a saving grace for the whole family.

John 3:16, 36—God invites us to accept the gift of salvation and eternal life.

UNIT 5 FAMILY AWARENESS
Session 1
YOUR FAMILY SHIELD

FOCUS: To help the young men articulate positive characteristics of their family.

Meeting Outline

		Notes
OPENING ACTIVITY & LIBATION	*15 minutes*	
AFRICAN-AMERICAN HEROES	*15 minutes*	
ACHIEVEMENT ACTIVITY	*30 minutes*	
GAME/CRAFT	*20 minutes*	
STORYTELLING	*15 minutes*	
GOD TIME & HARAMBEE CIRCLE	*15 minutes*	

Preparation

 Assign a mentor to review the life of Ida B. Wells Barnett (page 276) and make a presentation to the young men.

 Bring rubber bands for the opening activity.

 Photocopy session activity sheets and collect pencils and markers.

 Gather materials for the craft: wooden plaques (purchase from a craft shop), pencils, paper, paint, paintbrushes, and a woodburning kit.

 Assign a mentor to do storytelling.

 Gather Bibles and journals for the God Time devotional.

Session 1

OPENING ACTIVITY *(15 minutes.)*

Family Bonding: Beforehand, hide a treat (food is good!) somewhere in the room. Divide into teams of at least five. Give each team member two medium-sized rubber bands. Each person is to connect the rubber bands and put one around his ankle and the other around the ankle of another person on the team. When the team is banded together, each person should be connected to two other people. Give a clue for finding the treat. As soon as a team thinks they know were the treat is hidden, they should start moving toward it. If any rubber band breaks, the whole team must stop and replace it. The team that finds the treat first wins. You may want to use this game in your discussions as a reference point for being part of a family.

LIBATION/PRAYER

AFRICAN-AMERICAN HEROES (15 MINUTES)

Ida B. Wells Barnett: Listen to the presentation about Ida B. Wells Barnett (see page 276). Discuss these questions and invite the Young Lions to ask their own questions as well:

+ How did she grow up?
+ How did her family influence her?
+ What issue did she commit herself to?
+ What were some of her accomplishments?

Note the life of Ida B. Wells Barnett on the African-American history timeline.

ACHIEVEMENT ACTIVITY *(30 minutes)*

Family Shield: In small groups have the boys work with the mentors on their Family Shield activity sheets (page 172). When they are finished, let them present their shields to the group and tell why they chose the symbols that they did. You may choose to have the boys draw their shields on larger sheets of paper allowing more space for artwork.

CRAFT (30 minutes)

Family Crest: Give each boy a wooden plaque and instruct him to begin thinking about what kind of family crest or shield he wants to make. The boys should first sketch their family name at the top of the crest, and then sketch a design, symbol, or drawing representing their family in the center of it. (For example: graffiti art of family name, an animal representing family attributes, the state or country the family is from.) Refer them to the previous activity, creating the family shield, as a starter.

Instruct the boys to draw their crest on a sheet of paper for a mentor to approve before they begin on the wood. Give them the options then of either painting their crest or etching it with a woodburning kit. When they finish, have them paint over their plaque with clear lacquer to protect and finish their crest. This activity will continue in the next session.

STORYTELLING (15 minutes)

My Family: Have the chosen mentor tell a personal story either about growing up in his family or about the family he has now.

GOD TIME (15 minutes)

Ephesians 5:21–6:4. Have one of the boys read aloud Ephesians 5:21–6:4, and have another boy read aloud the devotional on the God Time page. Ask:

- ✠ What is the main idea of this Scripture passage?
- ✠ According to this passage, what are various members of the family to do in relationship to one another?
- ✠ How do these instructions compare with roles in your family for parents, children, husband, and wife?
- ✠ What are your father's responsibilities?
  —your mom's?
  —your siblings'?
  —yours?
- ✠ What example is the husband/wife relationship supposed to follow?

After the discussion, have each boy record in his journal his personal response to the lesson.

HARAMBEE CIRCLE

FAMILY SHIELD

Draw a picture
of Your family.

Draw something
your family does
together.

Draw one thing
you would Change
about your family.

Draw one
thing you like
about your family.

GOD TIME

READ EPHESIANS 5:21–6:4.

Families are the building blocks of society and human community. If the family unit is weak, then the result is a weak society. Families are critical to the development of the individual. It is within the family that a person learns basic values for living and attitudes toward self. Families provide support, self-identity, and a sense of belonging.

The tragic truth in our society is that many families are sick and weak. Some families are not doing the jobs God created them to do. Many youth turn to negative sources, such as gangs, for the support, love, and caring that they are not receiving from their families.

Persons represent both the family they were born into and the family they have the potential to become. Every girl is someone's daughter, perhaps a sister, and potentially someone's wife or mother. Every boy is someone's son, perhaps a brother, and potentially someone's husband or father. It is important to know the purpose for which God created families so that you can begin to prepare yourself to be the brother, son, husband, and father God wants you to be.

✚ Describe God's ideas for the family.

✚ Do you want a family when you grow up? Why, or why not?

UNIT 5 FAMILY AWARENESS
Session 2
UNDERSTANDING FAMILY

FOCUS: To help the young men understand different family dynamics and explore their personal feelings about family.

Meeting Outline

OPENING ACTIVITY & LIBATION	*15 minutes*	
AFRICAN-AMERICAN HEROES	*15 minutes*	
ACHIEVEMENT ACTIVITY	*30 minutes*	
GAME/CRAFT	*20 minutes*	
STORYTELLING	*15 minutes*	
GOD TIME & HARAMBEE CIRCLE	*15 minutes*	

Preparation

◇ Assign a mentor to review the life of James Weldon Johnson (page 277) and make a presentation to the young men.

◇ Ask various mentors to be familiar with and able to tell briefly the Bible stories listed in the God Time section on page 176.

◇ Photocopy session activity sheets and collect pencils.

◇ Materials for the craft: wooden plaques from last week, pencils, paper, paint, paintbrushes, and a woodburning kit.

◇ Assign a mentor to do storytelling.

◇ Gather Bibles and journals for the God Time devotional.

Session 2

OPENING ACTIVITY (15 minutes)

Guess Who? The purpose of this game is to test how well members of the group know one another. Choose one person to be "It," and send him out of the room. While he is gone, the group must choose one person to be the object of the search. When "It" returns, he is allowed ten questions to determine who the group has chosen. The questions must be addressed to a particular individual, not to the whole group. "It" must ask only yes-or-no questions that cannot be about physical characteristics. When that person is finished, choose another to be "It."

LIBATION/PRAYER

AFRICAN-AMERICAN HEROES (15 minutes)

James Weldon Johnson: Listen to the presentation about James Weldon Johnson (see page 277). Discuss these questions and invite the Young Lions to ask their own questions as well:

- ✦ What is James Weldon Johnson famous for?
- ✦ Do you know the "Negro National Anthem"?
- ✦ Why is it called that?
- ✦ What was Johnson's profession?
- ✦ What were some of his other accomplishments?

Note the life of James Weldon Johnson on the African-American history timeline.

ACHIEVEMENT ACTIVITY (30 minutes)

Understanding My Family: Have the boys and mentors work in small groups to complete the "Understanding My Family" activity sheets with the mentors (page 177). If possible, match the boys, one on one, with a mentor to encourage open discussion.

CRAFT (20 minutes)

Family Crests: Have the boys continue their craft project (family crests) from last week. They should be either at the painting or the woodburning stage. If they have finished that, they may begin applying the clear lacquer or shellac to their wooden plaques.

STORYTELLING (15 minutes)

My Family: Ask one of the men to tell a personal story either about growing up in his family or about the family he has now.

GOD TIME (15 minutes)

Ephesians 3:14–15. Ask one of the boys to read aloud the Scripture passage and another to read the devotional from the God Time page. Ask these questions and then have the assigned mentors briefly tell the stories listed:

⬦ How many in the group have parents who are divorced or separated?
(Tell the story of Abraham and Hagar [Genesis 16].)

⬦ How many have fathers who are not at home?
(Tell the story of Hagar and Ishmael [Genesis 21:9-21].)

⬦ How many in the group know of teenage girls who are pregnant or who have had children?
(Mary was a pregnant teenager. She was pregnant with Jesus at a young age before she was married [Matthew 1:18].)

⬦ How many come from interracial families?
(Tell the story of Moses and Zipporah [African] [Numbers 12; Exodus 2:21-22].)

⬦ How many have two parents at home?
(Tell the story of Adam and Eve [Genesis 2:18-25].)

⬦ How many in the group were adopted?
(Use God's relationship with us through Jesus Christ to represent the adoptive family [Ephesians 1:4-6].)

After the discussion, have each boy record in his journal his personal response to the lesson.

HARAMBEE CIRCLE

UNDERSTANDING MY FAMILY

Complete the following sentences:

I feel loved in my family when—

My position (oldest/youngest/middle) in my family is—

One thing my family likes to do together is—

One thing I wish could happen in my family is—

One word I would use to describe my family is—

One thing to pray for my family right now is—

What I like best about my family is—

One thing I would change about my family is—

My favorite place in my house is—

When I grow up I want/do not want (*circle one*) to have a family because—

GOD TIME

READ EPHESIANS 3:14-15.

All families come from God, the author of families. Every family, no matter what size or shape, belongs to God. Every kind of family you see in society is represented in the Bible. Genesis 16 tells the story of Abraham and Hagar, representing families who are divorced or separated. The same story about Hagar and her son Ishmael tells about God's faithfulness toward families whose fathers are not there. Mary, the mother of Jesus, was for a time a single pregnant teenager before she married Joseph (Matthew 1:18). The story in Numbers 12. of Moses and Zipporah tells of an interracial family, Hebrew and African. Adam and Eve (Genesis 2:18-25) represent a traditional two-parent family. Finally, the story of Jesus Christ's sacrifice for us represents adoptive families as we have *all* been adopted into the family of God (Ephesians 1:4-6). All families come from God; families that follow God experience God's blessings.

✚ How do you see God in your family?

✚ If your family does not reflect God, how can you help it change?

UNIT 5 FAMILY AWARENESS
Session 3
IN MY HOUSE

FOCUS: To invite the young men to identify themselves as part of the family of God.

Meeting Outline

OPENING ACTIVITY & LIBATION	*15 minutes*	*Notes*
AFRICAN-AMERICAN HEROES	*15 minutes*	
ACHIEVEMENT ACTIVITY	*30 minutes*	
GAME/CRAFT	*20 minutes*	
STORYTELLING	*15 minutes*	
GOD TIME & HARAMBEE CIRCLE	*15 minutes*	

Preparation

◇ Assign a mentor to review the life of Bill Cosby (page 278) and make a presentation to the young men.

◇ Photocopy session activity sheets and collect pencils.

◇ Gather materials: plaques from previous sessions, pencils, paper, paint, paintbrushes, a woodburning kit, shellac, scissors.

◇ Assign a mentor to do storytelling.

◇ Gather Bibles and journals for the God Time devotional.

◇ Talk with the mentors about the invitation to Christian commitment and possible follow-up with the boys during the week. Ask them to be in prayer for the young men.

Session 3

OPENING ACTIVITY *(15 minutes)*

Scissor Twister: Have everyone sit on chairs in a circle. The leader of the activity begins by handing to the person next to him a pair of scissors (safety scissors, if possible) and announcing whether they are closed or open. (For example, "My name is Chris, and I'm giving these scissors to Jerry closed.") The next person passes the scissors to the next person, making a similar statement about whether "they" are open or closed. The object of the game is for people to guess the clue, which is that it does not matter if the scissors are closed or open, it is the position of the legs of the person holding the scissors that determines "open" or "closed" (crossed). A person may receive the scissors open; but if his own legs are crossed, he will pass the scissors closed. Each time the scissors are passed, the leader announces whether the statement is correct or not. The game continues until everyone catches on to the secret.

LIBATION/PRAYER

AFRICAN-AMERICAN HEROES *(15 minutes)*

Bill Cosby: Listen to the presentation about Bill Cosby (see page 278). Discuss these questions and invite the Young Lions to ask their own questions as well:

- ✚ Who is Bill Cosby, and what is his profession?
- ✚ What contributions has he made or is he making to African-American history and contemporary Black experience?
- ✚ What are some things that separate him from other Black comedians?

Note the life of Bill Cosby on the African-American history timeline.

ACHIEVEMENT ACTIVITY *(30 minutes)*

Who Lives in Your House: Distribute the "Who Lives in Your House" activity sheets (page 182). Divide the group into small teams of boys and mentors and have them work on the sheets. The mentors should encourage discussion with the boys about who lives in their house, and who is related to whom and so forth. Get them to talk about their feelings about each family member and try to discover others who may or may not be related to them but who are a part of the boys' extended family network. You may choose to have them draw houses on larger sheets of paper to allow more space for their work.

CRAFT (20 minutes)

Family Crests: The boys should finish their family crests today, applying clear shellac as a finish. If some have already finished, you may occupy them with a game of "Family List It" (page 186) or some other game.

STORYTELLING (15 minutes)

My Family: Ask one of the men to tell a personal story either about growing up in his family or about the family he has now.

GOD TIME (15 minutes)

Acts 16:25–34. This story is very dramatic. As a change of pace, invite three of the men ahead of time to work out and then present the story as simple drama. Or have one or two of them tell or read the story with a lot of energy, using their voices to convey the drama. Then ask one of the boys to read aloud Acts 16:30-31. Ask:

- ✤ **How did the jailer change in this story? (He washed the wounds of the prisoners; he was baptized, he took the prisoners home and fed them; he and his family rejoiced.)**
- ✤ **What does it mean to be a part of God's family?**
- ✤ **What is the difference between belonging to God's family and being a part of your earthly family that God gave you?**
- ✤ **Have you ever committed your life to Christ?**

Talk about God's desire for us to be in relationship with God and the fact that God gave us a way through Jesus Christ. Jesus' death on the cross and his resurrection mean that our sin that separates us from being with God can be forgiven. Have the boys read John 3:16, 36, and the devotional prayer in their God Time journal.

After the discussion, have each boy record in his journal his personal response to the lesson. Invite the boys to talk with a mentor or the group leader after the meeting about making that commitment to God. You may also want mentors to follow up during the week with the boys about this invitation to become a Christian.

HARAMBEE CIRCLE

WHO LIVES IN YOUR HOUSE?

Write the names or draw pictures of the members of your family (or everyone who lives in your house) inside the house. List their names, their relationship to you (mother, brother, and so forth), and their ages. If you have immediate family members who do not live in your house, list them outside the house.

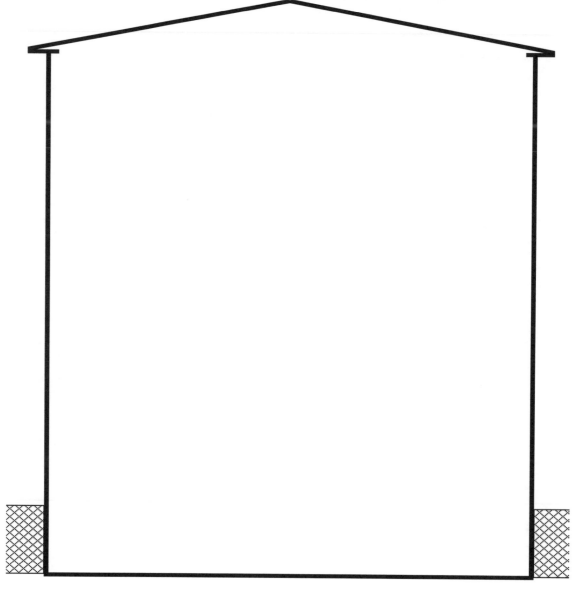

GOD TIME

READ ACTS 16:25-34.

We all have a family to belong to. The writer of Psalms said: "If my mother and father forsake me, then God will take me up." God is our Father and Mother; and if we believe in Christ, we are one another's family. You are not alone. God said, I will never leave you nor forsake you (Hebrews 13:5). You have a family!

If your biological family is loving and supportive, give thanks to God and remember that you belong to God. If your family is not loving or supportive, ask God for what you need and remember that you belong to God. God doesn't love anyone more than God loves you.

READ JOHN 3:16, 36.

Belonging to God's family means inviting Christ into your life. It is as simple as praying: "Dear Jesus, I need you in my life. Thank you for dying on the cross for me. Please forgive my sins and live through me. Help me to be the person you created me to be; in Jesus' name. Amen."

✚ Are you in God's family? (Explain your answer.)

If you want to pray this prayer inviting Christ into your life,
talk to your mentor or group leader after the meeting.

UNIT 5 FAMILY AWARENESS
Session 4
FIELD TRIP SUGGESTIONS

Visit a Mentor's House

Get one of the mentors to sponsor a field trip to his house for breakfast or a barbecue and to meet his family.

Sponsor a Family Outing

Sponsor a family outing day in which boys may bring their families for a picnic, bowling, skating, or other fun activity.

Have an Open House

Stage a Young Lions open house to demonstrate to parents what their boys have been doing at Young Lions. Serve refreshments.

Family Dinner

Have the boys prepare a family dinner and invite their parents for dinner and a show.

Have a Family Camp/Retreat

Invite the boys and their families on a retreat that will focus on fun and family nurture.

Go to Church

Invite the boys' families to attend a local church (if not your own), and take them to lunch afterward.

Watch Some Families in Action

Go to a play, show, or movie with a family theme. Check the newspapers and entertainment listings for current and special events in your area.

Keep On Learning

Field trips are wonderful learning experiences in themselves. However, to help the youth get the most from them, do two simple things:

1. **Prepare the youth:** Give them some introductory information; talk about expected behavior; identify a question for them to be thinking about.

2. **Debrief the trip:** Ask the group what surprised them, what was interesting to them, what made them think. Have a group conversation or give the youth paper and pencils and have them write a journal page about the trip—or do both. Gather the journal pages and add them to the individuals' folders.

UNIT 5 FAMILY AWARENESS
Optional
ACTIVITIES AND SESSIONS

Your Family Tree

Hand out copies of page 187 for the boys to take home to fill out and return the following week. Talk about what they learned. Use this worksheet to discuss the concept of an extended family and its importance in society and in their own lives.

The Ideal Family

Follow the directions on the activity sheet (page 188). In the discussions affirm that no family is perfect and all families have problems; point out the scriptural family values.

Family Roleplay

Choose volunteers to act out the following situations in an impromptu roleplay:

1. A mother and father reacting to their son's bad report card.
2. An unmarried couple at home after a long and busy day and irritating each other.
3. A child attempting to break up a terrible fight between his mother and father.
4. An older brother attempting to get his younger brother to join a gang when their single parent (mother or father) walks in.

Bring clothes and props to help your volunteers get into these roles. After each roleplay, discuss the issues that arose and the pros and cons of solutions or choices made.

A Letter to Me

Have the boys write a letter to themselves fifteen years into the future. They should write about if they are married or have children, what kind of woman they married, what kind of job they have, where they live. Then in small groups have the boys and mentors discuss what they want their lives to be like in fifteen years.

The Perfect Father/Husband

Brainstorm a list describing the perfect father, then one describing the perfect husband. Pair the boys with men to talk about how well their fathers fit their lists, how they hope to measure up in the future, and whether they know any men who come close to their lists.

Color Your Family

Instruct the boys to draw a portrait of their family using a different color for each person. When they are finished, discuss in small groups why they chose the colors they did for their family members. This activity encourages children to talk about their family relationships, and the strong feelings they may have for various family members.

FAMILY LIST IT

For directions on how to play, see African-American List It (page 159).

List 1—Members of a Family
parents
grandparents
sister
brother
baby
great-grandparents
aunt
uncle
step-parents
cousins

List 2—Family Chores
take out garbage
wash dishes
clean room
do yard work
baby-sit
cook dinner
feed pets
dust furniture
vacuum
clean bathroom

List 3—Family Activities
bowl
roller skate
go to park
go to church
go to movies/shows
watch TV
eat dinner
visit relatives
take a vacation
celebrate special occasions

List 4—Family Problems
sickness
school
divorce
parents fighting
chemical abuse
delinquency
financial difficulties
death
physical abuse
teen pregnancy

List 5—Rooms in Your House
your bedroom
bathroom
living room
kitchen
TV room/den
dining room
play room
nursery/baby's room
parent's room
porch

List 6—Family Rules
no fighting
no foul language
respect parents
observe curfew
do your homework
bedtime
don't cut up in public
do chores
don't run in the house
no feet on the furniture

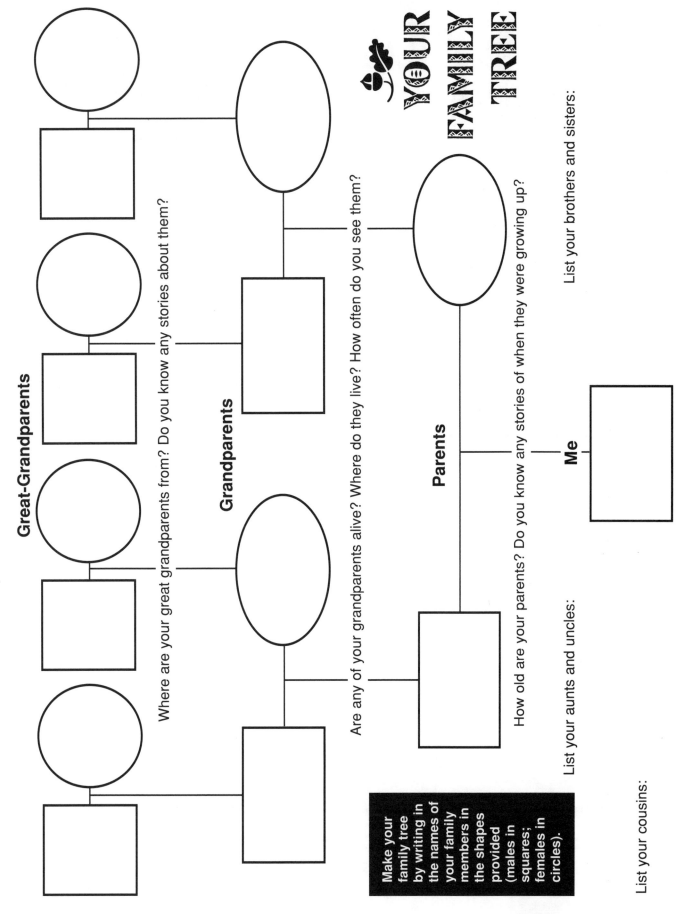

YOUR FAMILY TREE

Great-Grandparents

Grandparents

Parents

Me

Where are your great grandparents from? Do you know any stories about them?

Are any of your grandparents alive? Where do they live? How often do you see them?

How old are your parents? Do you know any stories of when they were growing up?

List your brothers and sisters:

List your aunts and uncles:

List your cousins:

Make your family tree by writing in the names of your family members in the shapes provided (males in squares; females in circles).

THE IDEAL FAMILY

No family is perfect or without problems. But if you could create the perfect family what would it look like? In the diagram below describe or draw your idea of the perfect family. Then in each corner write what you think of these different aspects of the family: children, marriage, fatherhood, and home life..

Fatherhood

Marriage

Children

Home

Read Ephesians 5:21–6:4.
Discuss the concepts of family in this passage and compare them to your ideas.

GROWING UP

A basic need of youth is a physically and emotionally safe environment. At this age girls are becoming mothers, and young men are fathering children, with no clue or thought as to the emotional responsibility involved. Children are growing up by themselves. Boys are buying into false standards for manhood, defined by negative characteristics such as material possessions, violence, physical and sexual abuse, or drug or alcohol abuse.

African-American boys in the inner city coming from fatherless homes need positive attention of a caring adult Black male. The emotional and physical changes experienced in adolescence and puberty are intimidating for any young male. Seemingly simple tasks like grooming and personal hygiene take on a special significance if no one is around to model good habits.

Young Black boys need a safe and structured environment to learn what it means to be men in every sense. They need to be able to ask the uncomfortable and embarrassing questions and know they won't be ridiculed or even abused for their ignorance. Young Lions provides a setting where boys can be boys and ask any question at all. Nothing is off-limits and every concern or issue is examined with the utmost seriousness.

UNIT OVERVIEW

At every meeting the boys should be encouraged to speak their minds. Nothing is off-limits for discussion at Young Lions as long as it is done in a respectful manner. Throughout the year strive to create an environment in which the boys will feel comfortable discussing issues and situations they might be embarrassed speaking about in mixed-gender company or in a less supportive group of men. A goal of this section is to openly discuss and address some changes boys go through during puberty and adolescence. This section addresses human sexuality and personal hygiene. This is a time to discuss with the boys the practical things they should know about their bodies as they grow up into young men. Field trips should be some sort of event that promotes male bonding and socialization such as a father-and-son outing, project, or camping experience.

UNIT LEARNING GOALS

The young men will

+ Engage in open discussion about human sexuality in order to erase misconceptions and myths and promote responsibility;

+ Examine the physical and emotional changes of puberty;

+ Develop a regimen of personal hygiene that is culturally affirming;

+ Participate in and experience appropriate cultural and social rites of passage leading to adulthood.

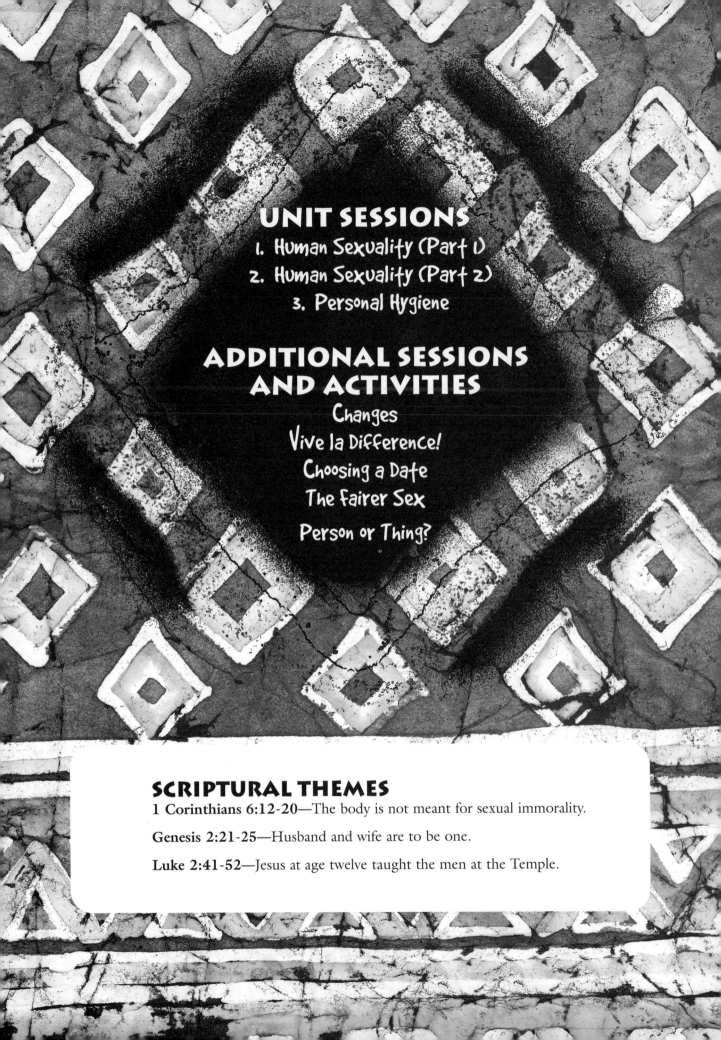

UNIT SESSIONS
1. Human Sexuality (Part 1)
2. Human Sexuality (Part 2)
3. Personal Hygiene

ADDITIONAL SESSIONS AND ACTIVITIES
Changes
Vive la Difference!
Choosing a Date
The Fairer Sex

Person or Thing?

SCRIPTURAL THEMES

1 Corinthians 6:12-20—The body is not meant for sexual immorality.

Genesis 2:21-25—Husband and wife are to be one.

Luke 2:41-52—Jesus at age twelve taught the men at the Temple.

UNIT 6 GROWING UP
Session 1
(PART 1)
HUMAN SEXUALITY

FOCUS: To encourage the young men to explore and talk openly about issues of human sexuality in order to promote clear and healthy understanding and respect for themselves and for women.

Meeting Outline

		Notes
OPENING ACTIVITY & LIBATION	*15 minutes*	
AFRICAN-AMERICAN HEROES	*15 minutes*	
ACHIEVEMENT ACTIVITY	*30 minutes*	
GAME/CRAFT	*20 minutes*	
STORYTELLING	*15 minutes*	
GOD TIME & HARAMBEE CIRCLE	*15 minutes*	

Preparation

◇ Assign a mentor to review the life of Richard Wright (page 279) and make a presentation to the young men.(Wright's autobiography, *Black Boy,* is available at public libraries and bookstores.)

◇ Bring some balloons for the opening activity.

◇ Photocopy session activity sheets and collect pencils.

◇ Meet with mentors to discuss the session and deal in advance with questions about the content.

◇ Assign a mentor to do storytelling.

◇ Gather Bibles and journals for the God Time devotional.

Session 1

OPENING ACTIVITY *(15 minutes.)*

Balloon Relay: Have everyone in the group grab a partner and then gather the pairs into teams. Give each team an inflated balloon. The object of the game is to carry the balloon to the designated finish line and back. The teams must carry the balloon by having two people press it between their bodies (without using hands) and shuffle down to the finish line and back without dropping it. They hand off the balloon to the next two people on their team, and they do the same thing. The first team that has everyone complete the course successfully wins.

LIBATION/PRAYER

AFRICAN-AMERICAN HEROES *(15 minutes)*

Richard Wright: Listen to the African-American hero presentation about Richard Wright's *Black Boy* (see page 279). Discuss these questions, and invite the Young Lions to ask their own questions as well:

- ✠ What are your impressions of what it was like for Wright growing up?
- ✠ What were the facts of life for him growing up? Who taught him?
- ✠ Were there any adults he trusted or looked up to when he was a boy?
- ✠ What were his biggest fears as a young boy?
- ✠ How did his childhood affect who he became in adulthood? What did he become?

Note the life of Richard Wright on the African-American hero timeline.

ACHIEVEMENT ACTIVITY *(30 minutes)*

Human Sexuality Quiz (Part 1): Have the boys gather in small groups with the mentors. There should be no more than two boys per mentor (ideally one per mentor). Hand out the Human Sexuality Quiz (pages 194–195). Instruct the groups to respond to the first page of the statements individually, then go back and discuss them as a group. (They will work on the second page next week.) Give them twenty minutes to do this in small groups and then discuss answers in the larger group.

GAME *(20 minutes)*

Brother, If You Love Me, Smile: Have the men and boys sit in a circle, with the person who is "It" standing in the middle. The object of the game is to get one of the people sitting down to give up his chair by making him smile or laugh. The person who is "It" may do anything short of actually tickling a person. He may choose anyone sitting in the circle to work on. If that person cracks a smile, he must give up the seat and he becomes "It."

STORYTELLING *(15 minutes)*

Growing Up Male: Ask your chosen mentor tell a personal story about growing up. Review the guidelines for storytelling:

1. **Everyone must be silent while the mentor is telling the story.**
2. **After the mentor is finished, the listeners may ask questions.**
3. **Each young man should be prepared to ask at least one question about the story.**

GOD TIME *(15 minutes)*

1 Corinthians 6:12–20: Have the group read 1 Corinthians 6:12-20.

Ask each one to tell what he thinks the main idea of the passage is.

+ **What does the author mean when he says that the body is made for the Lord?**
+ **If your body is a temple, how should you treat it? (Give examples.)**
+ **What forms may sexual immorality take?**
+ **How can you honor God with your body?**

After the discussion, have each boy record in his journal his personal response to the lesson.

HARAMBEE CIRCLE

HUMAN SEXUALITY QUIZ

Directions: Read each statement. Write "A" if you agree, "D" if you disagree, and "W" if you want to discuss it further. Ask about words you do not understand.

1. _____ It is wrong for boys and girls to discuss sex with each other.

2. _____ It is all right for boys to tell dirty jokes but not for girls to do so.

3. _____ Teenage boys are naturally clumsy.

4. _____ Girls reach puberty at a younger age than boys do.

5. _____ Boys should decide where to go and what to do on a date.

6. _____ Nice girls don't ask boys out on dates.

7. _____ Girls are more graceful than boys are.

8. _____ Kissing is sexual communication.

9. _____ Girls like boys to be rough and tough.

10. _____ Girls like boys who readily fondle them.

11. _____ Since a girl can stop sexual activity if she wants to, it is her fault if she gets pregnant.

12. _____ After a few dates, a boy has a right to expect sexual favors from a girl.

13. _____ Using derogatory terms to refer to women is not degrading, it's just cultural slang.

14. _____ A man has a right to hit a woman if she keeps irritating him.

15. _____ It is natural to want to engage in petting.

16. _____ All sexual excitement should be avoided until after marriage.

17. _____ When a person feels excited around someone of the opposite sex, it is a good sign that he or she is in love.

18. _____ When you meet the right person, "you'll know."

19. _____ Modern contraceptive measures guarantee prevention of conception during sexual intercourse.

20. _____ A person should check out the sexual history of a partner in order to prevent getting a sexually-transmitted disease (STD).

21. _____ A person can get AIDS from physical contact with someone who is HIV positive.

22. _____ Girls are "sick" during menstruation.

23. _____ If a boy has a nocturnal emission, or "wet dream," it means he thinks too much about sex.

24. _____ Masturbation can cause insanity.

25. _____ Most boys and girls practice masturbation at some time.

26. _____ There is no relation between the size or length of a man's penis and his sexual power.

27. _____ Dating women for sexual conquest is socially acceptable.

28. _____ The only way a man can get respect from a woman is to physically dominate her.

29. _____ Menopause marks the end of a woman's sexual life.

30. _____ Sexual intercourse involves not just two bodies, but also the persons' thoughts and emotions.

31. _____ "Having sex" and "making love" are the same thing.

32. _____ Sex between a man and a woman is no different basically from two animals mating.

33. _____ God gave humans the gift of sex for the purpose of enjoying it.

34. _____ Sex is safest in a monogamous relationship.

35. _____ Sex is best in the context of a marriage relationship.

GOD TIME

READ 1 CORINTHIANS 6:12-20.

You are valuable and precious to God. You are valuable and precious because God made you, and because God gave God's own Son to die on the cross for you. Since you are precious and valuable to God, do not treat your body like garbage. Some people mistreat their bodies through drugs or alcohol abuse; others, through sexual immorality.

"Sexual immorality" means using your body for sexual pleasure in ways that God did not intend. The Bible teaches that adultery (sleeping with someone else's husband or wife or sleeping with someone other than your spouse) and fornication (having sex with someone you are not married to) are sins. This kind of behavior puts your body at risk for sexually-transmitted diseases (STDs) such as gonorrhea, syphilis, and AIDS. Another possible consequence of sexual immorality that can forever change your life—and the lives of others—is an unexpected pregnancy.

So fellas, honor God with your body! Your body belongs to God. God gave it to you as a gift. So take care of it!

✚ Your body is a temple. How will you treat it? (Give examples.)

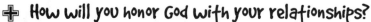

✚ How will you honor God with your relationships?

UNIT 6 GROWING UP
Session 2
(PART 2)
HUMAN SEXUALITY

FOCUS: To encourage the young men to explore and talk openly about issues of human sexuality in order to promote clear and healthy understanding of and respect for themselves and women.

Meeting Outline

		Notes
OPENING ACTIVITY & LIBATION	*15 minutes*	
AFRICAN-AMERICAN HEROES	*15 minutes*	
ACHIEVEMENT ACTIVITY	*30 minutes*	
GAME/CRAFT	*20 minutes*	
STORYTELLING	*15 minutes*	
GOD TIME & HARAMBEE CIRCLE	*15 minutes*	

Preparation

 Assign a mentor to review the life of Claude Brown (page 279), and make a presentation to the young men. (Brown's autobiographical novel, *Manchild in the Promised Land*, is available at public libraries and bookstores.)

◇ Prepare for the opening activity by bringing paper cups and spoons.

◇ Bring human sexuality quiz sheets from last week and pencils.

◇ Gather materials for the game: hacky sacks or beanbags.

◇ Assign a mentor to do storytelling.

◇ Gather Bibles and journals for the God Time devotional.

Session 2

OPENING ACTIVITY *(15 minutes)*

Water Relay: Divide the group into equal teams, and line the teams up to race. Each team must fill an empty cup with water. Each team member takes a spoonful of water from the cup and carries it along the designated route to an empty cup and empties the spoonful of water into it. The team with the most water in their cup at the end of the designated time period wins.

LIBATION/PRAYER

AFRICAN-AMERICAN HEROES *(15 minutes)*

Claude Brown: Listen to the African-American hero presentation about Claude Brown's book, *Manchild in the Promised Land* (see page 279). Discuss these questions, and invite the Young Lions to ask their own questions as well:

- ✠ What are your impressions of what it was like for Claude Brown growing up?
- ✠ Are there any similarities with life in your neighborhood?
- ✠ What were the facts of life for him growing up? Who taught him?
- ✠ Were there any adults whom he trusted or looked up to when he was a boy?
- ✠ What were his biggest fears as a young boy?
- ✠ How did his childhood affect who he became in adulthood? What did he become?

Note the life of Claude Brown on the African-American hero timeline.

ACHIEVEMENT ACTIVITY *(30 minutes)*

Human Sexuality Quiz (part 2): Have the boys gather into the same groups they did last week. Instruct them to finish working on their Human Sexuality Quiz (pages 194–195) individually, and then discuss their responses in their group. Have each participant choose one issue to bring to the small group to discuss. Bring them back together in a large group after fifteen or twenty minutes to finish the discussion. You may also wish to spend more time on this information if it seems needed.

GAME *(20 minutes)*

Hacky Sack: You will need adequate room to do this activity. Tell everyone to gather into groups of six and stand in a circle. Each group needs a hacky sack. The object of the game is for each group to keep the hacky sack in the air and not let it touch the ground. You cannot use your hands or arms to do this but you can use other parts of your body. The group that can keep it going the longest wins.

STORYTELLING *(15 minutes)*

Growing Up Male: Ask your chosen mentor to tell a personal story about growing up.

GOD TIME *(15 minutes)*

Genesis 2:21-25: Have one of the boys read aloud the Scripture and another read the devotional on the God Time page.

✚ Ask each person to tell what he thinks the main idea of the passage is.

✚ Why do the man and woman become "one flesh"? What does this mean?

✚ What happens to a person if he or she has sex with a lot of people?

✚ God created sex for two reasons; what do you think those reasons are?

✚ God created sex good; but if people abuse it, there are consequences. Name some consequences for abusing the privilege of sex.

✚ If people use sex the way God intended, there are benefits. Name some benefits of sex.

After the discussion, have each boy record in his journal his personal response to the lesson.

HARAMBEE CIRCLE

GOD TIME

READ GENESIS 2:21-25.

Sex is good! It is a gift from God. God created sex for two reasons: 1) for reproduction of the human species, and 2) for pleasure between a husband and wife. If you take God's gift and misuse it, it becomes spoiled and a barrier between you and God.

God created sex as part of a special and unique relationship between two people. Sex is a lot more than physical pleasure. It involves caring for another person, love, and commitment. As husband and wife, coming together as "one flesh," Adam and Eve had a relationship of partnership and mutual respect. God was the center of their relationship.

Sleeping around and having sex with a lot of people before you are married is like taking a piece of tape and sticking it on a lot of different surfaces. Before long, what happens? The tape loses its stickiness. If you waste this gift from God through misuse, when the time comes and you want to share it with that special person in your life, it is no longer special. Sex is good; it is a gift from God; so use it the way God intended.

✚ Name some of the benefits of enjoying sex as God intended it:

Complete the following sentence:

✚ God, I thank you for the gift of sex because

UNIT 6 GROWING UP
Session 3
PERSONAL HYGIENE

FOCUS: To challenge the young men to develop good habits of personal hygiene and grooming.

Meeting Outline

OPENING ACTIVITY & LIBATION	*15 minutes*	*Notes*
AFRICAN-AMERICAN HEROES	*15 minutes*	
ACHIEVEMENT ACTIVITY	*30 minutes*	
GAME/CRAFT	*20 minutes*	
STORYTELLING	*15 minutes*	
GOD TIME & HARAMBEE CIRCLE	*15 minutes*	

Preparation

 Assign a mentor to review the life of Nathan McCall (page 279) and make a presentation to the young men. (McCall's autobiography, *Makes Me Wanna Holler,* is available at public libraries and bookstores.)

◇ Bring sets of dominoes for the opening activity.

◇ Photocopy session activity sheets and collect pencils.

◇ Prepare materials for the game: a list of topics for playing charades.

◇ Assign a mentor to do storytelling.

◇ Gather Bibles and journals for the God Time devotional.

Session 3

OPENING ACTIVITY *(15 minutes)*

Dominoes: Teach the boys how to play dominoes, using a standard set of Western double-six dominoes (28 tiles in all) and the instructions for the games below or any other instructions that you know. Place all of the dominoes face-down on a table. To deal, slide dominoes to each player. Players keep the pips (the dots) concealed from other players. To start, players look over their dominoes for doublets (dominoes with the same number of pips on both ends. The player with the largest doublet begins the layout. The winner is the first player to run out of dominoes or who has the least pips when no one can place a domino.

Draw Dominoes: If there are 2 players, deal 7 dominoes each; if there are 3 or 4 players, deal 5 each. The remaining dominoes are left face-down to form a boneyard from which extra dominoes are drawn by a player unable to play to the layout. Players match up ends with the same number of pips.

Block Dominoes: Distribute all of the dominoes. (There is no boneyard.) Players match up ends with pips that add up to 7.

LIBATION/PRAYER

AFRICAN-AMERICAN HEROES *(15 minutes)*

Nathan McCall: Listen to the African-American hero presentation about Nathan McCall's memoir, *Makes Me Wanna Holler* (see page 279). Discuss these questions, and invite the Young Lions to ask their own questions as well:

✚ What are your impressions of what it was like for McCall growing up?

✚ What were the "facts of life" for him growing up? Who taught him?

✚ Were there any adults that he trusted or looked up to when he was a boy?

✚ What were his biggest fears as a young boy?

✚ How did his childhood affect who he became in adulthood? What did he become?

Note the life of Nathan McCall on the African-American hero timeline.

ACHIEVEMENT ACTIVITY *(30 minutes)*

Personal Hygiene & Grooming: Divide the boys into small groups with the men and hand out the "Personal Hygiene & Grooming" activity sheets (page 204). Have them fill out the sheets and discuss the questions about daily hygiene. If you prefer, play Charades (below) as a fun teaser for a few minutes before starting the activity sheet. If there is still time, the charades can continue after the achievement activity is completed.

GAME *(20 minutes)*

Charades: Begin with the group divided into two teams, and give each team a list of subjects to play charades. The subjects should be related to personal hygiene and grooming, such as: "brushing your teeth" or "taking a shower." Include some funny ones like: "shaving your armpits," or "you're funky." Taking turns, have each person act out the subject for his own group. Record the time it takes for the groups to guess the subject. The group that guesses their subjects in the least amount of time wins.

STORYTELLING *(15 minutes)*

Growing Up Looking Good: Ask your chosen mentor to tell a personal story about growing up.

GOD TIME *(15 minutes)*

Luke 2:52: Have someone in the group read aloud the Scripture. Then tell the story of Jesus leaving his parents to speak with the elders when he was twelve years old (Luke 2:41-52). If your group enjoys acting out scenes, invite some of the mentors and a boy ahead of time to prepare a dramatic presentation of the story. Then lead the discussion. Ask:

- ✤ What kind of boy do you think Jesus was?
- ✤ Do you think he had any problems as a child and teenager? Explain.
- ✤ Name some problems or struggles you have that Jesus probably had at your age (with peers, parents, school, fighting, and so on).
- ✤ Did Jesus go through puberty?
- ✤ How do you think he grew as a person: mentally? physically? spiritually? socially?

After the discussion, have each boy record in his journal his personal response to the lesson.

HARAMBEE CIRCLE

PERSONAL HYGIENE & GROOMING

TASK	HOW OFTEN?
Brushing your teeth	_____
Combing your hair	_____
Putting conditioner in your hair	_____
Taking a shower/bath	_____
Putting on deodorant	_____
Changing clothes	_____
Changing underwear and socks	_____
Flossing your teeth	_____
Gargling with mouthwash	_____
Putting on lotion	_____
Putting on lip balm	_____
Cleaning out ear wax	_____
Trimming nails	_____

What is the difference between grooming and hygiene?

Can you tell when people do not keep up good grooming or hygiene? How?

Why is keeping a clean appearance important?

How do you feel after you take a bath or shower? When you put on clean clothes?

What is important to you about how you look?

GOD TIME

READ LUKE 2:41-52.

Other than Jesus' birth, we do not know very many particulars of Jesus' life before he turned thirty. This is one story in his life when he was twelve. Do you ever stop to think Jesus was once your age?

Hebrews 4:15 says Jesus went through the same temptations and struggles of life as everyone else. If we accept the prophet Isaiah's description of a suffering servant as a reference to Jesus, then Jesus was a man like any other man to look at, nothing special. In a lot of ways Jesus was an ordinary guy, even though he was the Son of God.

Because we know Jesus was a human being as well as the Son of God, we know he understands us. He experienced life as a baby, a child, a teenager, and a young adult. We can tell him how we feel, and he can help us. Jesus knows the troubles you might be experiencing today. Trust him and tell him how you feel, because he cares for you.

✜ If Jesus were here today and he was your age, would you hang out with him? Why, or why not?

✜ Does knowing that Jesus was a boy just like you change your thinking about him? How?

UNIT 6 GROWING UP
Session 4
FIELD TRIP SUGGESTIONS

Go to a Sports Club or Gym

Spend time playing basketball, swimming, and so on. Afterward, use showers to emphasize the importance of personal hygiene.

Visit a Dance Club or Some Hangout Popular With Youth

Dress up nicely. Use the opportunity to spark discussion about youth culture and habits.

Visit a Hospital

Arrange a field trip to the maternity ward of a hospital or have a childbirth educator talk to the boys about the experience of birth.

Go to a Restaurant

Take your group to a restaurant and discuss public manners, behavior, and appearance.

Check Out Special Events

Attend a play, show, or movie that deals with young people growing up. Check the newspapers and entertainment listings for current and special events in your area.

Attend a Concert

Attend the concert of a rap group or rapper popular among youth and discuss the messages of the music. Talk also about behavior the group observed that was inappropriate and why it was so.

Keep On Learning

Field trips are wonderful learning experiences in themselves. However, to help the youth get the most from them, do two simple things:

1. **Prepare the youth:** Give them some introductory information; talk about expected behavior; identify a question for them to be thinking about.
2. **Debrief the trip:** Ask the group what surprised them, what was interesting to them, what made them think. Have a group conversation or give the youth paper and pencils and have them write a journal page about the trip—or do both. Gather the journal pages and add them to the individuals' folders.

UNIT 6 GROWING UP
Optional
ACTIVITIES AND SESSIONS

Changes

Use the Growing Up Means Changes activity sheet (page 208) to lead a frank discussion with the boys about going through puberty and adolescence. This is a unique opportunity for the boys to learn from positive, mature men in the area of sexual growth and changes. The purpose is to focus on the emotional and physical changes that accompany puberty. Small groups work best in dealing with this material.

Vive la Difference!

These activity sheets (pages 209–210) explore male and female anatomy. The material prompts discussion on how babies are made, emotional maturity, and sexual responsibility. The material is factual and frank, yet very useful for educating boys about body parts and functions in a safe environment. Encourage questions. Create an atmosphere in which any question may be asked and dealt with. Work in small groups. Answers: Male Sex Organs: 1-D, 2-C, 3-G, 4-A, 5-H, 6-I, 7-B, 8-E, 9-F; Female Sex Organs: 1-D, 2-E, 3-B, 4-F, 5-G, 6-C, 7-A. Consider also using human sexuality resources, such as *Let's Be Real: Honest Discussions About Faith and Sexuality* (Abingdon Press, 1998; ISBN: 0687721997).

Choosing a Date

This activity sheet (page 211) encourages the boys to examine the qualities that are important in a mate. It also opens the door for discussing male/female relationships at whatever stage the boys happen to be. Have them fill out and discuss the sheet in small groups. Have the boys take turns roleplaying the dating situations.

The Fairer Sex

Gather a panel of women to visit your group and ask them to make brief presentations about their thoughts on masculinity and on what they like and dislike in a man. Then let the boys ask questions of them.

Person or Thing?

Invite the Young Lions to bring some CDs that have lyrics about women. Listen with the group to the words and ask if the words reflect the view that a woman is a "person" to be respected and loved or that a woman is a "thing" to be used and abused. Talk about music choices, especially in relationship to the Christian faith. Then have the group make a list of words that are used to talk about women. Ask the same question: "Person or thing?" Point out the power of our words to shape our thinking.

GROWING UP MEANS CHANGES

PHYSICAL

Size—A sudden "growth spurt" occurs. At first, girls grow faster; but then boys catch up and usually grow taller than girls.

Body Contours—Your body changes and begins to look like that of an adult. Boys' shoulders broaden and muscles develop; girls develop breasts and rounded hips.

Sweat glands—Sweat glands become more active, making you perspire more.

Hair—Hair grows in your armpits and around your genitals (pubic hair). Boys grow whiskers; some girls develop fine hair on the upper lip and legs.

Voice—Both girls' and boys' voices change and become deeper (more noticeable in boys).

Skin—Acne (pimples) appears on face, chest, and back. (Bathe frequently and eat nutritious meals to lessen breakouts.)

EMOTIONAL

Puberty—This time of changes in your life (beginning sometime between nine and about fourteen years of age) is called puberty. These changes are caused by hormones (special chemicals affecting body functions) that are beginning to work in your body. The fundamental changes during puberty are sexual; but they influence your whole being, especially your emotions.

Moods—You may feel down and depressed one day, and happy the next day for no apparent reason.

Family tensions—You and your parents may clash over how ready you are for new responsibilities. Be patient and work toward compromise. Consider others' opinions and feelings.

Ideas, emotions—Feelings about people and issues all become stronger and deeper. You begin to form very close friendships.

Activities—Adolescence is a time to experiment with new hobbies and fads. Most are fun, but be careful not to be pressured to try harmful ones.

MALE SEX ORGANS

Match the term to the correct definition:

___1. Bladder

___2. Seminal vesicles

___3. Prostate gland

___4. Vas deferens

___5. Urethra

___6. Penis

___7. Testes

___8. Scrotum

___9. Foreskin

A Tube that carries semen to penis

B Produce and store sperm

C Gives sperm nutrients and fluid

D Holds urine

E Pouch of skin holding testes

F Flap of skin at end of penis, often removed by surgery (circumcision)

G Makes whitish fluid that combines with sperm to form semen

H Tube through which sperm and urine pass

I Delivers semen to female's vagina; varies in size from person to person and, at different times, in same person

At puberty, the male sex organs begin producing sperm and continue for the rest of your life. Sperm are male sex cells (tadpole-shaped) that fertilize the female egg. They are so small that 400–500 million could fit on the head of a pin. At puberty, males are physically able to become fathers but are not emotionally or financially ready for the lifelong responsibilities of a family.

Additional Facts

Erection—hardening of the penis. One sign of sexual maturity; an erection is usually the result of sexual stimulation; but it can also be caused at any age by having to urinate.

"Wet Dreams"—nocturnal emissions. This discharge of extra semen while you sleep is common during adolescence. These emissions are not bad or harmful to your health.

Masturbation—handling your sex organs. This is a common practice during adolescence. Masturbation won't cause physical harm; but if you feel worried or guilty about it or any of the thoughts that accompany it, talk it over with an adult you like and trust.

FEMALE SEX ORGANS

Match the term to the correct definition:

___1. Bladder   A Passageway from uterus to outside of body

___2. Clitoris   B Contain egg cells

___3. Ovaries   C Opening at bottom of uterus

___4. Fallopian tubes   D Holds urine

___5. Uterus (womb)   E Very sensitive organ near opening of the vagina

___6. Cervix   F Connect ovaries and uterus; eggs travel through them once a month

___7. Vagina   G Stretchable container where fertilized egg develops into baby

At puberty, the female sex organs begin making available ripe eggs for meeting with a sperm. The female sex cells develop into a baby when fertilized. Thousands of them are present in the ovaries at birth; but usually, beginning at puberty, only one ripens per month. At puberty, females are physically able to become mothers, but they are not ready emotionally or financially for lifelong family responsibilities.

Additional facts

Ovulation—ripening of an egg cell and its passage from ovary through fallopian tube to uterus. Begins at puberty and continues until a woman is about 45 or 50 years old. Ovulation usually happens once a month. Shortly before ovulation, the uterus builds up an extra lining to nourish a fertilized egg becoming a baby.

Menstruation—happens when the egg isn't fertilized. No baby will develop, so the nourishing lining isn't needed. The lining peels away with some bleeding and leaves the body during a period of three to six days. A new lining builds up every month. At first, periods will be irregular; but in about a year, the pattern will become fairly regular (26–33 days between the starting times of periods). Sanitary napkins (pads) or tampons may be used to absorb the flow.

Masturbation—handling your own sex organs. This is a common practice during adolescence. It won't cause physical harm.

CHOOSING A DATE

Read the list of personal qualities below and rank them in terms
of how important they are to you in choosing a companion of the opposite sex.
Rank the items from 1–10, with 1 being the most important to you. In the other
column, check the qualities you feel that you possess and have to offer someone else.

Girlfriend	Qualities	Myself
_____	Christian	_____
_____	intelligent	_____
_____	athletic	_____
_____	fun to be around	_____
_____	good-looking	_____
_____	easy to talk to	_____
_____	sense of humor	_____
_____	common interests	_____
_____	from "good" family	_____
_____	positive attitude	_____
_____	a good friend	_____
_____	_____	_____
_____	_____	_____

"Practice Makes Perfect"

Build your confidence. Roleplay the following scenes:

- introducing yourself to a girl you like
- asking a girl out
- going on your first date
- meeting her parents
- having the first kiss

PERSONAL RESPONSIBILITY

Many children lack a simple moral or spiritual code of behavior. Instead of having had appropriate behavior and relationships modeled to them, young persons often see unhealthy conduct glorified. Young Black boys need a strong moral and spiritual code to live by to combat the lure of negative behavior. They must be infused with a sense of right and wrong—not based on the injustices they see and experience in the world, but one that comes from above and dwells deep within.

Young Lions attempts to instill moral and spiritual values. A primary goal is to help the boys internalize beliefs that are self-affirming and that give them the self-respect to respect others.

This kind of spiritual strength is absolutely necessary in order to survive in the hardened environments in which many of them live. They need the spiritual strength to resist negative peer pressure as well as the negative messages society sends young Black males. Such a personal code enables them to maintain a strong self-image and offers internal guidance for every situation they encounter.

UNIT OVERVIEW

The focus of this section is to teach the boys responsibility in their everyday lives. They will examine their conduct and behavior at home, school, and in their neighborhoods with their friends. Issues such as violence, expression of anger, and attitudes toward women will be brought out and challenged. This section also provides a setting for examining how a young man conducts himself in different situations such as interviewing for a job, being on a date with a girl, or experiencing conflict with his teacher. Respect, which is a huge issue with urban Black boys, should be a major theme this month. How does a person give and earn respect? Your field trip for this month may be to a prison, chemical dependency treatment center, or even a homeless shelter in order to graphically illustrate the consequences for uncontrolled and irresponsible behavior in our society.

UNIT LEARNING GOALS

The young men will

- ✚ Build self-respect through examining personal responsibility in relationships, behavior, and self-image;
- ✚ Realize the impact of personal behavior and conduct on self, family, and society;
- ✚ Explore how to make positive choices and decisions for daily living;
- ✚ Observe the effect of both positive and negative choices in the lives of African-American men.

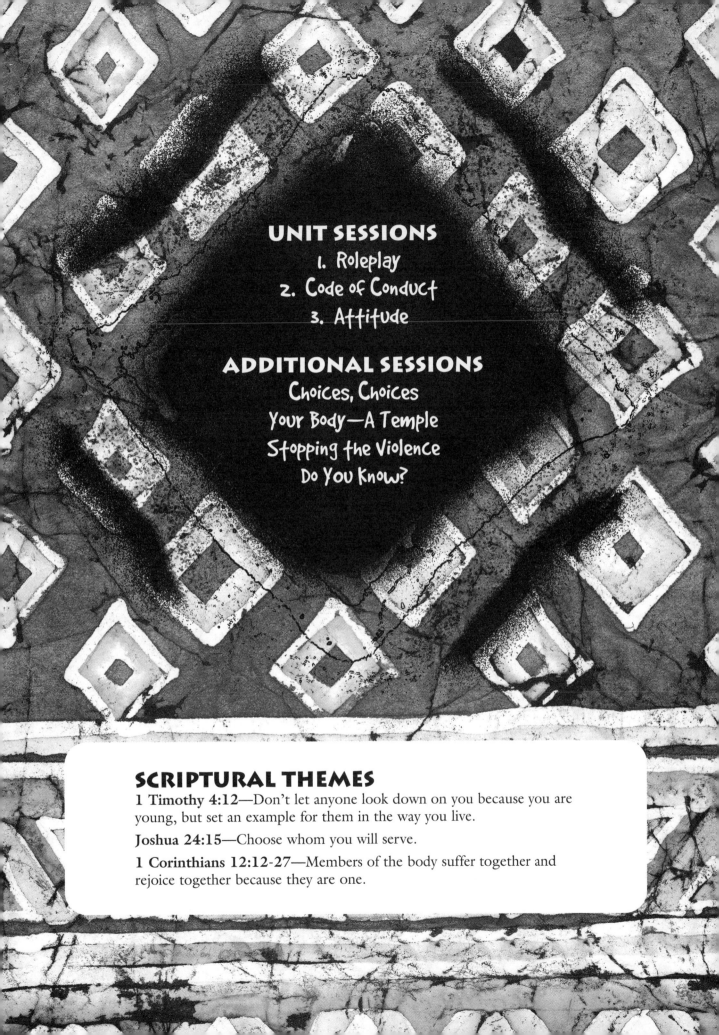

UNIT SESSIONS
1. Roleplay
2. Code of Conduct
3. Attitude

ADDITIONAL SESSIONS
Choices, Choices
Your Body—A Temple
Stopping the Violence
Do You Know?

SCRIPTURAL THEMES

1 Timothy 4:12—Don't let anyone look down on you because you are young, but set an example for them in the way you live.

Joshua 24:15—Choose whom you will serve.

1 Corinthians 12:12-27—Members of the body suffer together and rejoice together because they are one.

UNIT 7 PERSONAL RESPONSIBILITY
Session 1
ROLEPLAY

FOCUS: To help the young men examine everyday situations that have the potential to become problems and discover how a person may behave responsibly in these circumstances.

Meeting Outline

OPENING ACTIVITY & LIBATION	15 minutes	*Notes*
AFRICAN-AMERICAN HEROES	15 minutes	
ACHIEVEMENT ACTIVITY	30 minutes	
GAME/CRAFT	20 minutes	
STORYTELLING	15 minutes	
GOD TIME & HARAMBEE CIRCLE	15 minutes	

Preparation

◇ Assign a mentor to review the life of Thurgood Marshall page 280) and make a presentation to the young men.

◇ Bring a few decks of cards for the opening activity.

◇ Bring props and ideas for roleplaying.

◇ Gather materials for the craft: paper egg cartons, paint, paintbrushes, glue, scissors, and modeling clay.

◇ Assign a mentor to do storytelling.

◇ Gather Bibles and journals for the God Time devotional.

Session 1

OPENING ACTIVITY *(15 minutes)*

Play Spades: As the boys and men arrive, have them gather in groups. Give each group a deck of cards to play spades (or some other game of your choice). Distribute pencils and paper for keeping score.

LIBATION/PRAYER

AFRICAN-AMERICAN HEROES *(15 minutes)*

Thurgood Marshall: Listen to the African-American hero presentation about Thurgood Marshall (see page 280). Discuss these questions, and invite the Young Lions to ask their own questions as well:

✚ Who was Thurgood Marshall?
✚ What significant achievements did his career include?
✚ Describe the legal case for which he is most well known.
✚ What does his life say about personal responsibility?

Note the life of Thurgood Marshall on the African-American hero timeline.

ACHIEVEMENT ACTIVITY *(30 minutes)*

Roleplay: Ask for volunteers to act out one of the roleplaying situations before the group (see page 217). Describe the situation. Give everyone a chance to participate. When each roleplay is finished, have the group discuss the situation. Use questions such as these:

✚ Was this situation realistic?
✚ Have you ever been in a situation like that?
✚ What did you do?
✚ Was your action right or wrong?
✚ What else could you do in this situation?

When the discussion is exhausted, go on to the next roleplay situation.

CRAFT *(20 minutes)*

Mancala: Assemble the materials for Mancala, an African game of strategy. Give each boy an empty egg carton. Have the boys cut the bottom part with the cups from the top part and save it. Cut out two sections from the top part of the carton and glue or tape one section on each end of the big piece. (see diagram below). This is the Mancala board. Have the boys decorate it with paint and make playing pieces out of modeling clay. After molding the playing pieces, they need to place them in a dry place until next week to allow them to harden. (As an alternative, use stones as playing pieces and paint them too.) Next week the group will learn how to play Mancala.

STORYTELLING *(15 minutes)*

What I Learned: Ask the chosen mentor to tell a personal story about learning responsibility. Review the guidelines for storytelling:

1. **Everyone must be silent while the mentor is telling the story.**
2. **After the mentor is finished, the listeners may ask questions.**
3. **Each young man should be prepared to ask at least one question about the story.**

GOD TIME *(15 minutes)*

1 Timothy 4:12: Ask someone to read aloud the Scripture passage and someone else to read the devotional on the God Time page. Explain the background of the relationship between Paul and Timothy. Ask:

✚ Why do you think Paul gave Timothy these instructions?
✚ Do you think people ever look down on you because of your age?
✚ Do people look down on you for other reasons?
✚ Are you an example to others? How?
✚ What are some other ways you can set an example for others?
✚ How can following Christ set an example for others?

After the discussion, have each boy record in his journal his personal response to the lesson.

HARAMBEE CIRCLE

PERSONAL RESPONSIBILITY

ROLEPLAYING SITUATIONS

Situation 1

You are walking home with a group of friends. Everything is cool until someone brings up the idea of going down to the discount store and shoplifting some items. Everyone else seems to think that it is a good idea. What do you think? What do you say or do?

Situation 2

For some reason you don't get along with one of your teachers at school. The teacher is very strict and usually you argue over little things, and your anger gets you sent to the office or suspended. Today you walk into class and say hi to your friend. Your teacher hollers at you for disrupting the class. What do you do?

Situation 3

You are telling your friends about a girl you met last night at a party. You didn't know her, but she was being extra friendly and wouldn't leave you alone. Everyone else at the party paired up and went someplace private. Finally, she said that she wanted you to go upstairs with her. What did you do? What will you tell your friends?

Situation 4

You are walking along the sidewalk with your friends and you pass a group of boys. One of them bumps you accidentally and you drop your books. Your friends say he "dissed" you and you should fight. What do you do?

GOD TIME

READ 1 TIMOTHY 4:12.

In this passage, Paul is giving Timothy instructions for living a godly life. The apostle Paul was a role model and mentor for Timothy. Paul helped Timothy develop strong spiritual and personal values.

Spiritual and personal values are important because they give you guidance and direction through life's situations. The first place children learn values is in the home and from parents, but it is also beneficial to have other positive adult relationships in your life as well.

The challenge for you is to choose who will be your model. Many youth are surrounded by negative role models such as people abusing drugs or alcohol, men who sleep around and leave babies everywhere they go, or people involved in gangs and crime. Don't make foolish choices just because you are young. Be careful about who you choose as friends and models in your life. Find someone who demonstrates positive behavior and values that you appreciate, and learn from him or her.

Recognize also that you too are a role model. Although you are young, there are people, especially younger children, who look up to you. Be an example for others by how you live.

✚ Whom do you have as a role model in your life? How is this person a role model for you?

Complete the following sentence:

✚ I will set an example for others in these ways:

UNIT 7 PERSONAL RESPONSIBILITY
Session 2
CODE OF CONDUCT

FOCUS: To challenge the young men to develop a code of behavior and personal standards that will serve as guides to conduct in any situation.

Meeting Outline

OPENING ACTIVITY & LIBATION	*15 minutes*	*Notes*
AFRICAN-AMERICAN HEROES	*15 minutes*	
ACHIEVEMENT ACTIVITY	*30 minutes*	
GAME/CRAFT	*20 minutes*	
STORYTELLING	*15 minutes*	
GOD TIME & HARAMBEE CIRCLE	*15 minutes*	

Preparation

◇ Assign a mentor to review the life of Marian Wright Edelman (page 281) and make a presentation to the young men.

◇ Bring a sack of old newspapers, garbage bags, masking tape, and a snack for the opening activity.

◇ Photocopy session activity sheets and collect pencils.

◇ Bring instructions for playing Mancala and gameboards made last week.

◇ Assign a mentor to do storytelling.

◇ Gather Bibles and journals for the God Time devotional.

Session 2

OPENING ACTIVITY (*15 minutes*)

Cleanup Relay: As the boys enter the room, give them a bunch of newspapers. Instruct them to crumple up the newspaper pages and throw them on the floor. Choose a dividing line down the middle of the room (mark with masking tape), and gather the boys and men into two teams. The object of the game is for each team to clear their area of newspaper within the appointed time (1–2 minutes) by pushing the paper into the other team's area. When the time is up, the team with the cleanest area wins. When you are finished, offer an extra snack to the team that puts all of the paper on their side in garbage bags the fastest.

LIBATION/PRAYER (*5 minutes*)

AFRICAN-AMERICAN HEROES (*15 minutes*)

Marian Wright Edelman: Listen to the African-American hero presentation about Marian Wright Edelman (see page 281). Discuss these questions, and invite the Young Lions to ask their own questions as well:

- ✚ What is she well known for?
- ✚ What is the purpose of the Children's Defense Fund?
- ✚ In the civil rights movement, Edelman served with the NAACP and SNCC. What are these organizations?
- ✚ What does her life say about personal responsibility?

Note the life of Marian Wright Edelman on the African-American hero timeline.

ACHIEVEMENT ACTIVITY (*30 minutes*)

Code of Conduct: Using the Code of Conduct activity sheet (page 222) as a model, make a chart and use it to lead a discussion with the group on standards of behavior and consequences of conduct. (Or allow the boys to work on the standards individually.) Ask them to describe the "rules of acceptable behavior" in each setting listed. Address the topics of language, behavior, dress, and so on. Talk about why accepted standards seem to change in each setting.

GAME *(20 minutes)*

Mancala: Setup: Boys should pair up with men and use one playing board for Mancala, an African game of strategy. Each player receives twenty-four playing pieces. They then place four pieces in each of the six cups on their side of the playing board. The two large slots *(kahalas)* on the ends of the board remain empty. The goal of the game is to have the most pieces in your *kalaha* at the end of the game.

How to play: The first player takes all of the pieces from one of the slots on his side of the board. He then drops one piece into each slot moving counterclockwise (to his right), including his *kahala* and continuing onto his opponent's side of the board. If he comes to his opponent's *kahala*, he skips it. If the last piece falls into his own *kahala*, he gets to take another turn. If the last piece falls into an empty slot on his side of the board, he then "captures" the pieces in his opponent's slot directly across. He takes all of the opponent's pieces in that slot, plus his own single piece, and places them in his *kahala*. It is then the opponent's turn.

The game is over when all six slots on one side of the board are empty. The player who still has pieces in his slots gets to place them in his *kahala*. It is better not to be the one with the empty slots, so try to keep pieces in one of your slots throughout the game. The winner is the player with the most pieces in his *kahala*. When you win you say, "*Nashinda*!" which means "I win!" in Swahili.

STORYTELLING *(15 minutes)*

What I Learned: Ask one of the men whom you have chosen before the meeting to tell a personal story about learning responsibility.

GOD TIME *(15 minutes)*

Joshua 24:15: Ask someone to read aloud the Scripture and another one to read the devotional on the God Time page. Then tell the history of Joshua as the leader of the Hebrew people. Ask:

✚ Why did he make this statement?
✚ Do other people affect what decisions you make or how you conduct yourself? How?

Say: "No one else can decide for you the kind of person you will be. Only you can make that decision and only you can act on it. You have to choose." Ask:

✚ Do you have a principle or code that you live your life by? What is it?
✚ Can serving the Lord help you to live a satisfying life? How?

After the discussion, have each boy record in his journal his personal response to the lesson.

HARAMBEE CIRCLE

CODE OF CONDUCT

A person often encounters different expectations, or rules in different settings. What is acceptable when you are with your friends may not be acceptable at home. Think about the expectations you are faced with in these different areas, and list them to compare with one another:

	At Home	At School	At Work	With Friends
Language				
Friends				
Dress				
Behavior				
Respect				
Other:				

✚ How do you gain respect in these various settings?

✚ Are you ever compelled to do anything that compromises your principles?

✚ How important is it to you to satisfy other people's expectations of you?

✚ What are the consequences in these various areas for not following the rules of conduct?

GOD TIME

READ JOSHUA 24:15.

How do you make decisions in life? Some people let their feelings guide them. But feelings aren't always reliable. Some people make pleasure their goal in life. Their attitude is that "If it feels good, then do it." But, there's more to life than "feeling good." Other people live by the motto, "Look out for number one." The only thing that matters to them is what they need and want.

On the other hand, some people let their conscience be their guide. They pay attention to their inner sense of right and wrong. God gave each of us a conscience, and God also gave us the Word (the Bible) to guide us in how to live.

You must decide for yourself how you will live and what kind of person you will be. You can choose whether you will live for yourself or God. As a young person, it is important for you to develop a set of personal values and an inner sense of right and wrong. If you don't develop your own values and convictions, then you will always be following others. Model your values after God's Word. God made you; God knows who you are inside.

✚ Do you have personal values that you live by? Describe them.

✚ Describe the kind of person you would like to be and tell some things that you can do to be the kind of person you want to be.

UNIT 7 PERSONAL RESPONSIBILITY
Session 3
ATTITUDE

FoCUS: To help the young men see how one's attitude affects a person's potential for success and positive interaction with others.

Meeting Outline

		Notes
OPENING ACTIVITY & LIBATION	*15 minutes*	
AFRICAN-AMERICAN HEROES	*15 minutes*	
ACHIEVEMENT ACTIVITY	*30 minutes*	
GAME/CRAFT	*20 minutes*	
STORYTELLING	*15 minutes*	
GOD TIME & HARAMBEE CIRCLE	*15 minutes*	

Preparation

◇ Assign a mentor to review the life of Jesse Jackson (page 282) and make a presentation to the young men.

◇ Bring several copies of a current newspaper edition for the opening activity.

◇ Photocopy session activity sheets and collect pencils.

◇ Gather materials for the game: Nerf® basketball set.

◇ Assign a mentor to do storytelling.

◇ Gather Bibles and journals for the God Time devotional.

Session 3

OPENING ACTIVITY *(15 minutes)*

Newspaper Relay: Have the boys and men form teams and give each team a copy of the same edition of the newspaper. Stand at the other end of the room and ask questions that can be answered only by looking through the newspaper. The first team that races a person to you across the room with the answer gets a point. Ask questions that will direct the participants through different parts of the newspaper (sports, business, comics, front page, and so on). The team with the most points when you have gone through all your questions wins.

LIBATION/PRAYER

AFRICAN-AMERICAN HEROES *(15 minutes)*

Jesse Jackson: Listen to the African-American hero presentation about Jesse Jackson (see page 282). Discuss these questions and invite the Young Lions to ask their own questions as well:

- ✚ **What is he most known for?**
- ✚ **What is the Rainbow Coalition?**
- ✚ **What do you think is the most significant accomplishment of Jesse Jackson in modern history? Why?**
- ✚ **What does his life say about personal responsibility?**

Note the life of Jesse Jackson on the African-American history timeline.

ACHIEVEMENT ACTIVITY *(30 minutes)*

Attitude Poem: Read the poem about attitude (page 228). Lead a discussion with the group asking the following questions:

- ✚ **Do you agree or disagree with this poem?**
- ✚ **What is your definition of attitude?**
- ✚ **How does a person develop an attitude?**
- ✚ **What are some factors that contribute to whether you have a positive or a negative attitude?**

After this discussion, have the men and boys gather in their small groups and fill out and discuss the "Attitude" activity sheets (page 227) .

GAME (20 minutes)

Basketball: Bring a Nerf® basketball set (the kind you can attach to a door). Set it up and choose teams. Stage a Nerf® basketball tournament. Or shoot paper wads into the wastebasket.

STORYTELLING (15 minutes)

What I Learned: Ask one of the men whom you have chosen before the meeting to share a personal story about learning responsibility.

GOD TIME (15 minutes)

I Corinthians 12:12–27: Have the group take turns reading one or two verses of the Scripture passage and the devotional on the God Time page. Ask:

✚ What is the main idea of this passage?

✚ What does community mean? (someplace to belong)

✚ What are some different communities you belong to? (family, teams, church, school, neighborhood, and so forth)

✚ How does your behavior affect those around you in your community?

✚ How do the behaviors of other people affect you?

✚ Do you agree or disagree with the idea in this Bible passage? Why?

✚ How does the principle of *Ujima (Nguzo Saba*—"collective work and responsibility") relate to the discussion of a person's responsibility to his community?

After the discussion, have each boy record in his journal his personal response to the lesson.

HARAMBEE CIRCLE

A-T-T-I-T-U-D-E

Use the acrostic below to describe your attitude. For each letter, write a word that describes your attitude.
(For example: *A—alone, arrogant, angry, all right!*)

A _____

T _____

T _____

I _____

T _____

U _____

D _____

E _____

✛ How do attitudes differ from emotions?

✛ Can a person control an attitude? How?

✛ What can change or influence an attitude?

✛ What makes an attitude good or bad?

✛ How does your attitude affect you physically? emotionally? spiritually?

✛ How does your attitude affect your relationships? your success at school or work?

ATTITUDE

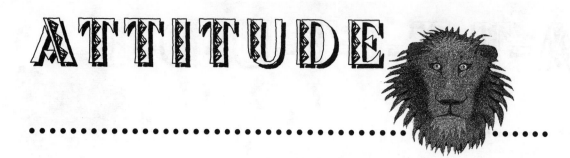

The longer I live the more I realize

the impact of attitude on life.
Attitude, to me, is more important
than facts.

It is more important than the past,
than education, than money,
It is more important than circumstances,
than failure, than successes,
than what other people think or say or do.
It is more important than appearance,
giftedness, or skill.
It will make or break a company,
a church, a home.

The remarkable thing is I have a choice
every day, regarding the attitude I will
embrace for that day.
I cannot change the past,
I cannot change the fact
that people will act in a certain way.
I cannot change the inevitable.
The only thing I can do is
play on the one string I have,
and that is my attitude.

I am convinced that life is 10%
what happens to me and 90%
how I react to it. And so it is with you—

We are in charge of our attitude.

–Author Unknown

GOD TIME

READ 1 CORINTHIANS 12:12-27.

Everyone needs a place to belong and a sense of purpose in life. In fact, if these needs are not met, a person can get really messed up. It is important to know that you can have these needs met in Christ. You are a part of the body of Christ, God's family.

1 Corinthians 3:22-23 says everything belongs to you (believers in Christ), "because you belong to Christ, and Christ belongs to God." If you have Jesus you have everything! Everything belongs to you because he is Lord over everything. Romans 8:31 says that if God is for you, who can be against you? No person and no thing can stand against you and God.

With this blessing comes responsibility. God wants you to live in a way that pleases God and shows other people that you love God. Your attitude and conduct should reflect the fact that you belong to God.

✚ How does your behavior affect those around you?

✚ What does a person's conduct say about him or her? Give examples.

✚ What does your conduct say about you?

Complete the following sentence:

✚ I have a responsibility to others around me to

UNIT 7 PERSONAL RESPONSIBILITY
Session 4
FIELD TRIP SUGGESTIONS

Visit a Jail or Correctional Center

Discuss the consequences of socially unacceptable behavior.

Visit a Court or Judge

Arrange for a visit to juvenile court or with a lawyer or judge. Find out what happens when persons break the law.

Visit a Local Leader

Visit a local civic leader or someone who has excelled in his profession. Talk about the benefits of personal discipline and responsibility.

Check Out Special Events

Attend a play, show, or movie that deals with adolescent behavior and responsibility. Check the newspapers and entertainment listings for current and special events in your area.

Visit a Drug Rehabilitation Center

Discuss the responsibility a person has to take care of himself and his family.

Do a Service Project

Have the group plan and do a community service project together. Talk about the fact that part of personal responsibility involves giving back to the community in ways that are helpful to others.

Keep On Learning

Field trips are wonderful learning experiences in themselves. However, to help the youth get the most from them, do two simple things:

1. **Prepare the youth:** Give them some introductory information; talk about expected behavior; identify a question for them to be thinking about.
2. **Debrief the trip:** Ask the group what surprised them, what was interesting to them, what made them think. Have a group conversation or give the youth paper and pencils and have them write a journal page about the trip—or do both. Gather the journal pages and add them to the individuals' folders.

UNIT 7 PERSONAL RESPONSIBILITY
Optional
ACTIVITIES AND SESSIONS

Choices, Choices

In small groups under the supervision of mentors, have the boys go through this activity sheet (page 232). Use the discussion questions as a basis for dialogue about personal freedom and the responsibility that goes with it. At the end of the activity, help the boys in developing a positive decision-making process.

Your Body—A Temple

This exercise (page 233) uses the scriptural principle of the body as God's temple to help the boys think through the choices they make daily. Personal responsibility involves how a person lives and how a person respects himself physically and spiritually. Discuss and contrast both positive and negative influences. Focus on the goal of internalizing positive values.

Stopping the Violence

Use the material from *Skillstreaming the Adolescent: New Strategies and Perspectives for Teaching Prosocial Skills,* by Arnold P. Goldstein and Ellen McGinnis (Research Press, 1997; ISBN: 087822369X) to bring out issues of anger, aggression, and violence. The series includes:

1. **Using self-control;**
2. **Problem-solving; and**
3. **Accepting consequences.**

Each session involves roleplaying and working through steps to resolution.

Do You Know?

This fact sheet (page 234) engages youth in a discussion of sexual choices, responsibility, and consequences. The discussion of statistics and hypothetical situations will help the boys to visualize how they will deal with similar circumstances if and when they arise.

CHOICES, CHOICES

1. Tell about a major decision you have had to make in the last six months. How did you make your decision?

2. Place an **X** next to the two most difficult choices to make. Place an **O** next to the two easiest ones. Discuss your choices in your small group.

_____ Whether to cheat on tests and homework
_____ Whether to obey parents
_____ Whether to be prejudiced
_____ Whether to attend school
_____ Whether to be a Christian
_____ What to watch on television
_____ Whether to do drugs or alcohol
_____ What to do after school
_____ What clothes to wear
_____ Whether to have sex

_____ Whom to hang out with
_____ What to eat for dinner
_____ What to spend money on
_____ When to pray
_____ Whether to join a gang
_____ Who my friends are
_____ Whether to get into fights
_____ Whether to come to Young Lions
_____ Whether or not to steal or shoplift
_____ What to do on weekends

3. On a scale of 1 to 6, how much freedom do you feel you have to make choices?

| 1 | 2 | 3 | 4 | 5 | 6 |

Others make my
choices for me.

I get to make all
my own choices.

Who makes choices for you? How do you make choices for yourself?

4. Which of the following do you think would be most helpful in making a decision?

_____ Asking your parent(s) for advice
_____ Praying about it
_____ Waiting a few days to decide
_____ Reading your horoscope
_____ Thinking that if it feels good, do it
_____ Asking a friend
_____ Thinking about the consequences

_____ Deciding as quickly as possible
_____ Flipping a coin
_____ Going along with the crowd
_____ Letting someone else decide for you
_____ Finding Scripture that gives direction
_____ Going with what "feels" right
_____ Other _____

5. Make a list of good guidelines for making decisions.

_____

_____

_____

YOUR BODY— A TEMPLE

READ 1 CORINTHIANS 3:16-17.

Persons can affect their attitude or personality by what they expose themselves to spiritually, mentally, and physically. How are you a temple of God?

Use the diagram below to draw two faces—one happy, one sad. On the happy side list five factors (types of music, kinds of friends, environment, and so forth) that influence you positively (build you up). On the sad side list five factors that influence you negatively (tear you down). Discuss the effect of these influences on you.

Positive:

1. _____
2. _____
3. _____
4. _____
5. _____

Negative:

1. _____
2. _____
3. _____
4. _____
5. _____

Personal responsibility involves taking care of yourself, inside and out.

DO YOU KNOW?

Studies show that many unmarried girls who become pregnant:

—will probably not finish high school; only one-third (33%) do;

—will become pregnant again within two years;

—will have an 8-in-10 (80%) chance of living in poverty and being on welfare, even if they finish high school, if they remain single;

—will lessen their chances of a good marriage later on;

—will have low-birthweight babies who often die from a high incidence of illness;

—will have babies who will do poorly in school and will have emotional problems later;

—will have a tendency to abuse or neglect their babies due to their own lack of experience and their frustration with their situation;

—will have daughters who are 22% more likely to become teen mothers themselves;

—will have sons who are 13% more likely to end up in prison.

Visit www.teenpregnancy.org and check out the section on the homepage entitled "Sex Has Consequences . . . A Site for Teens."

MANY YOUNG PEOPLE (8 IN 10 GIRLS AND 6 IN 10 BOYS) SAY THAT THEY WISH THEY HAD WAITED UNTIL THEY WERE OLDER TO HAVE SEX.

Only 20% of the fathers marry the mothers of their first child; the other 80%, on average, pay less than $16 a week child support.

Statistics from National Center for the Prevention of Teen Pregnancy

Although boys and girls are often physically able to have babies by the time they are twelve, they are not emotionally or financially equipped to be fathers and mothers until they are older and have more experience and maturity. Raising a child is a lifelong commitment. God gave human beings the gift of sex for reproduction and for pleasure between a husband and a wife, but the gift carries with it a weight of responsibility.

Any boy can have sex, but it takes a man to be a father.

ECONOMIC RESPONSIBILITY

Economic responsibility is not about making money; it is about values, resources, and goals. The Young Lions curriculum teaches boys to work towards the goals of financial security and personal satisfaction in life.

Young Black boys must be taught to apply the values of their spiritual heritage to economic principles in order to avoid the materialism of American society. Our goal is to teach them the value of irreplaceable resources such as people, time, and education as opposed to the "I want it now" mentality of immediate self-gratification. Cultivating this attitude will in turn create motivated, enterprising, and innovative young men who will go a long way in addressing the crises of inner city neighborhoods and problems of the broader society.

Learning to save money and cultivating good work habits builds self-esteem and personal value. It is not too early for Black boys to learn skills for financial planning and management of resources. Economic responsibility involves looking at the big picture for communal and individual financial health.

UNIT OVERVIEW

This section allows the boys to learn the *Nguzo Saba* principle of *Ujamaa* (cooperative economics), one of the principles celebrated during Kwanzaa (see pages 138–139). The curriculum focuses on financial planning, saving, and management of personal resources. The boys will be encouraged to develop the ability to delay gratification in order to work towards a future goal of more benefit. Boys will learn about earning and saving and spending money through preparing personal budgets. The mentors will assist the boys in developing some kind of business or fundraising event (yard work, washing cars, for example) to earn money towards a special group event or trip. The boys should come away with a fundamental understanding of economics as it applies to their lives and setting and the experience of achieving financial goals. Your field trip may be to one of the mentor's places of business.

UNIT LEARNING GOALS

The young men will

+ **Examine and apply the principle of delayed gratification in order to gain desired goals;**

+ **Discuss the dynamics of employment and job readiness through roleplaying;**

+ **Appreciate the values of hard work and consistent effort to achieve financial goals;**

+ **Explore the principle of cooperative economics (*Ujamaa*) by working together to develop a business.**

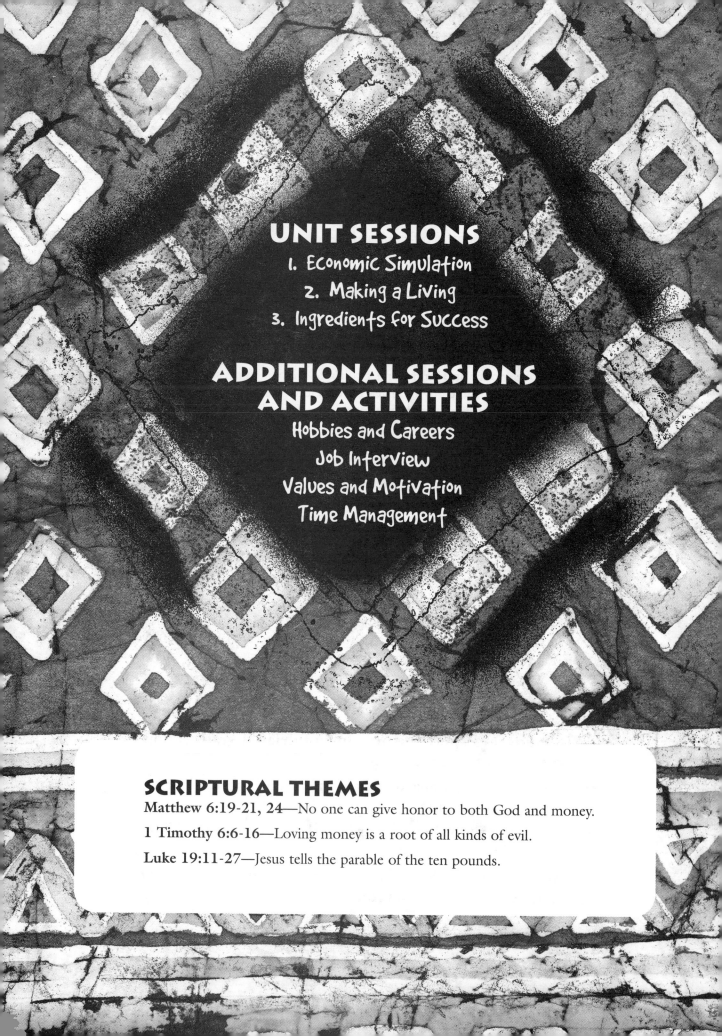

UNIT SESSIONS
1. Economic Simulation
2. Making a Living
3. Ingredients for Success

ADDITIONAL SESSIONS AND ACTIVITIES
Hobbies and Careers
Job Interview
Values and Motivation
Time Management

SCRIPTURAL THEMES
Matthew 6:19-21, 24—No one can give honor to both God and money.

1 Timothy 6:6-16—Loving money is a root of all kinds of evil.

Luke 19:11-27—Jesus tells the parable of the ten pounds.

UNIT 8 ECONOMIC RESPONSIBILITY

Session 1
ECONOMIC SIMULATION

FOCUS: To examine with the young men the economic dynamics of modern society and how those dynamics have an impact on our everyday lives.

Meeting Outline

OPENING ACTIVITY & LIBATION	*15 minutes*	*Notes*
AFRICAN-AMERICAN HEROES	*15 minutes*	
ACHIEVEMENT ACTIVITY	*30 minutes*	
GAME/CRAFT	*20 minutes*	
STORYTELLING	*15 minutes*	
GOD TIME & HARAMBEE CIRCLE	*15 minutes*	

Preparation

◇ Assign a mentor to review the life of Madame C.J. Walker (page 283) and make a presentation to the young men.

◇ Bring a blanket for the opening activity.

◇ Gather props and materials and prepare for the Economic Simulation activity.

◇ Gather materials for the game: a few sets of Monopoly®.

◇ Assign a mentor to do storytelling.

◇ Gather Bibles and journals for the God Time devotional.

Session 1

OPENING ACTIVITY (15 minutes)

Name Game 2: Divide the group into two teams as everyone arrives. Have the teams sit at opposite ends of the room, using a blanket suspended by two men to separate them (be sure the two teams cannot see each other). Each team will send one person up to the blanket. On the count of three have the men drop the blanket; the first boy who says the name of the person facing his team on the other side of the blanket wins. Continue until everyone has had a chance to stand behind the blanket.

LIBATION/PRAYER

AFRICAN-AMERICAN HEROES (15 minutes)

Madame C.J. Walker: Listen to the African-American hero presentation about Madame C.J. Walker (see page 283). Discuss these questions, and invite the Young Lions to ask their own questions as well:

+ Who was she?
+ What was her significant achievement in history?
+ How did she get started in business?
+ What did she do with her resources?
+ What lessons can we learn from her about economic responsibility?

Note the life of Madame C.J. Walker on the African-American hero timeline.

ACHIEVEMENT ACTIVITY (30 minutes)

Economic Simulation: Lead the group through the economic simulation activity. This simulation is an exercise portraying the socioeconomic dynamics in American society. The division of the chips approximates the division of wealth and resources in the United States. The group is divided into three groups of people corresponding to the upper income, middle income, and lower income economic classes in America. The guidelines for bargaining simulate the real-life restrictions people face in society. The activity that follows results in a certain amount of stress and frustration. This frustration is by design to emulate the economic and social circumstances experienced by people in the real world. The goals of the simulation are to experience the frustration and unfairness many people feel and to discuss feelings and observations.

GAME *(20 minutes)*

Monopoly®: Divide the men and boys into groups of four and give them sets of Monopoly® with which to play. Use game situations to discuss real-life financial issues. (There may not be enough time for a game this session.)

STORYTELLING *(15 minutes)*

Money and Me: Ask the chosen mentor to tell a personal story about economic responsibility. Review the guidelines for storytelling:

1. **Everyone must be silent while the mentor is telling the story.**
2. **After the mentor is finished, the listeners may ask questions.**
3. **Each young man should be prepared to ask at least one question about the story.**

GOD TIME *(15 minutes)*

Matthew 6:19–21, 24: Ask someone to read aloud the Scripture passages and someone else to read aloud the devotional from the God Time page.

✚ **What is the meaning of these two passages?**
✚ **What is the difference between serving God and serving money?**
✚ **What place should money and possessions have in the life of a Christian? What should Christians treasure?**

After the discussion, have each boy record in his journal his personal response to the lesson.

HARAMBEE CIRCLE

ECONOMIC SIMULATION

PREPARATION

You will need a bag of game chips in five different colors. You need enough chips so that each person has five. For a group of twenty people (100 chips) you will need: 5 gold or yellow chips, 10 red, 25 green, 25 white, and 40 blue. Assign each color a point value: gold=25 points, red=20 points, green=15 points, white=10 points, and blue=5 points. The object of the game is to get the most points through trading and negotiation in order to end up in the top five percent.

Divide the chips into 3 bags: A, B, and C. Into Bag A, place 3 gold, 6 red, and 6 green chips. In Bag B, place 2 gold, 4 red, 9 green, and 10 white chips. In Bag C, place 5 green, 15 white, and all of the blue chips.

INSTRUCTIONS

1. Distribute the chips around the room, allowing each person to draw five chips from only one of the bags (A, B, or C). Do not tell people the value of the chips until after everyone has drawn.

2. After everyone has his chips, write all the players' names on a point chart (use a markerboard or posterboard) in front of the room where everyone can see. Next to their names record the value of the chips they possess.

3. Seat the top five percent according to the point chart in the front of the room, the next thirty-five percent in the middle of the room, and the last sixty percent in the back of the room.

4. Explain to the group that the object of the game is to move up in their standings through trading and negotiation. The only way to negotiate is to trade chips (one chip for one chip). Negotiation can take place only when the two parties are clasping hands in a handshake.

5. After giving instructions allow people to begin trading. After ten minutes have people return to their seats and tally points again. Allow for some discussion. The role of the game leader and helpers is to keep the game going, not to explain every issue or resolve every complaint.

6. Reshuffle the players' positions according to point changes so that the top five percent are together, and so on. Allow another trading period, and at the end of that time count up points again.

When positioning the groups, make sure that the top five percent are in the most comfortable positions, and make sure the bottom sixty percent are in the most uncomfortable places. Show preferential treatment to the top five while treating the bottom sixty with disdain. Allow for discussion between each trading period. Be sensitive to the complaints and issues of the top five percent and ignore the bottom sixty. The middle group should be treated according to their position—not as well as the top five, but not as badly as the bottom sixty. Make sure the top five have chairs and make the bottom sixty sit on the floor. Give the middle group enough chairs for half their number. Provide refreshments for the top five percent as well. Players may get irritated or angry, but becoming emotionally involved is part of the game.

DISCUSSION

What did you think of the simulation?

Discuss these facts: Five percent of the world's population controls ninety-five percent of the world's wealth and resources. Conversely, the other ninety-five percent of the world's population controls the remaining five percent of the world's wealth and resources.

The three groups correspond with the economic levels in our society: lower income, middle class, and upper income. How did you feel being at the lowest economic level level? the middle level? the upper level?

Did you think the simulation was fair? Was it hard or easy to move up the economic ladder? Why?

How do you think this simulation compares with real life?

How were the different economic levels treated? Why? How does this compare with real life?

Basically, how did the rich get rich and the poor get poor in the simulation? How do you think this compares with real life?

How can a person change his economic circumstances in real life?

The principle of cooperative economics (*Ujamaa*) involves sharing resources so that everyone's situation may improve. How could the application of this principle have changed the game?

How can it work in real life?

GOD TIME

READ MATTHEW 6:19-21, 24.

Someone once said that love makes the world go round, but that's not really true. Love certainly matters, but in our society it is money that makes things go. People's lives are focused on money and possessions. You need money to eat, sleep, and raise a family. You need money for your basic needs, and it seems that all the really fun things to do and have cost money. The world says you have to have money to be somebody. If you believed TV commercials, movies, and magazine ads, you could live your whole life consumed with making money to buy stuff.

But that is not the way God wants you to live. God didn't create you to make acquiring money your goal in life. God wants you to have peace and everlasting joy. Contrary to popular belief, money really doesn't buy happiness. There are a lot more important and fulfilling things to pursue in life besides money.

The attitude you should have about money is that it is a tool for doing good. Money should be used for helping yourself and others, not getting as much stuff as you can. Money and possessions don't last forever, but God's love does.

✚ What place does money have in your life?

✚ Make a list of some things more important in life than money, some things that you treasure.

UNIT 8 ECONOMIC RESPONSIBILITY
Session 2
MAKING A LIVING

FoCUS: To teach the young men what it is like to make and live on a budget.

Meeting Outline

		Notes
OPENING ACTIVITY & LIBATION	*15 minutes*	
AFRICAN-AMERICAN HEROES	*15 minutes*	
ACHIEVEMENT ACTIVITY	*30 minutes*	
GAME/CRAFT	*20 minutes*	
STORYTELLING	*15 minutes*	
GOD TIME & HARAMBEE CIRCLE	*15 minutes*	

Preparation

◇ Assign a mentor to review the life of Booker T. Washington (page 284) and make a presentation to the young men.

◇ Bring toothpicks for the opening activity.

◇ Photocopy session activity sheets and collect pencils.

◇ Gather materials for the game: several decks of cards.

◇ Assign a mentor to do storytelling.

◇ Gather Bibles and journals for the God Time devotional.

Session 2

OPENING ACTIVITY *(15 minutes)*

Earning "Money": Have everyone sit in a circle (or have the participants form two smaller groups sitting in circles). Each person starts with ten toothpicks. The object of the game is for each person think of something that he has done that no one else in the group has. Choose someone to start. If a person is successful in choosing something that no one else has done, each person in the group must give him a toothpick. If he chooses something that at least one other person in the group has done, he must hand the leader a toothpick. Go around the circle until everyone has had a turn. The person with the most toothpicks at the end wins.

LIBATION/PRAYER

AFRICAN-AMERICAN HEROES *(15 minutes)*

Booker T. Washington: Listen to the African-American hero presentation about Booker T. Washington (see page 284). Discuss these questions, and invite the Young Lions to ask their own questions as well:

- ✚ Who was Booker T. Washington?
- ✚ What was the greatest issue facing Blacks in his lifetime?
- ✚ What was his response to that issue?
- ✚ What was his approach to improving the economic well-being of African Americans?

Note the life of Booker T. Washington on the African-American history timeline.

ACHIEVEMENT ACTIVITY *(30 minutes)*

Making a Budget: As a group go through the scenario described on the Making a Budget activity sheet (page 246). Discuss the importance of budgeting money, time, and other resources. After going through the activities on the sheet, have the boys and men pair off and work on "My Monthly Budget" (page 247). Have each group show their budget to the large group.

GAME *(20 minutes)*

Concentration: Divide the group into teams of three or four, and give each team a stack of cards. Each stack should contain half a regular deck with only two of each number or face card. Lay the cards out on a flat surface face down. Each person takes a turn turning up two cards. The object of the game is to turn up two cards that match. When a player finds two that match, he picks them up. If the cards do not match, the player must turn them back over and it is the next player's turn. The player with the most cards when all the cards are picked up wins.

STORYTELLING *(15 minutes)*

Money and Me: Have the chosen mentor tell a personal story about economic responsibility.

GOD TIME *(15 minutes)*

1 Timothy 6:6–16: Ask someone to read aloud the Scripture and someone else to read aloud the devotional on the God Time page. Ask:

- ✚ What is the message of this passage?
- ✚ Do you agree or disagree?
- ✚ How can the love of money be a root of evil?
- ✚ Is money bad? Why or why not?
- ✚ Did God make money? Explain your answer.
- ✚ Can money be used for good? How?
- ✚ Describe a healthy attitude about money.

After the discussion, have each boy record in his journal his personal response to the lesson.

HARAMBEE CIRCLE

MAKING A BUDGET

What is a budget?

In order to be economically responsible, you must live within your means (not spending more than you have) and set aside money for the future. To make your budget work (or balance), follow this simple formula:

$$\underline{\text{Your total expenses} = \text{Your total income}}$$

Why budget?

A budget helps you keep track of your money so that you do not get into debt that is inappropriate. Appropriate debt is for big things such as an education, a house, or a car.

A budget helps you plan for the future. You can save for special events or for items you want. You can set aside money for opportunities and for emergencies that will pop up.

A budget helps you live within your means and saves you from financial worry and stress. Poor money management is one of the biggest causes of family problems and divorce.

How do I budget?

To make a budget, you must distinguish between necessities (needs) and luxuries (wants). Here is a list of items that might be on your budget. Put an *X* next to those items that are necessities and an *O* next to those items that are luxuries (things you want, but could do without). Add anything to the list you think should be there and mark it accordingly.

____ Food	____ Personal needs
____ Housing	____ Contributions
____ Utilities (gas, electricity, phone)	____ Insurance
____ Transportation	
____ Clothes	____ Other:_____
____ Entertainment	
____ Emergencies	____ Other:_____
____ Vacation	
____ School loans	____ Other:_____
____ Savings	

MY MONTHLY BUDGET

Assume you make a yearly salary of $25,000 after taxes.

This breaks down to a twice monthly paycheck of $1041.67. Using this income figure, fill in the amount you will budget for each item below. Ask a mentor to help you look over your figures to make sure they are realistic. What are your total monthly expenses? Figure out your monthly income total. Do your expenses exceed your income? If so, go back and refigure.

MONTHLY INCOME (AFTER TAXES):

1st paycheck of the month   _____
2nd paycheck of the month   _____
Any other income   _____ (from _____)
Total monthly income   _____

MONTHLY EXPENSES:

Food   _____
Housing   _____
Utilities (gas, electricity, phone)   _____
Transportation (car, gas, insurance)   _____
Clothes   _____
Entertainment   _____
Emergencies   _____
Vacation   _____
School loans   _____
Insurance (medical, life)   _____
Personal needs   _____
Savings   _____ (Do you have a goal?)
Contributions (to help others)   _____
Total monthly expenses   _____

My Budget for Now

Make a personal budget for your current circumstances. List your monthly expenses in one column, and your monthly income in another. Does your budget balance?

Income:		Expenses:	
$_____		$_____	
$_____		$_____	
$_____		$_____	
Total income	$_____	Total expenses	$_____

GOD TIME

READ 1 TIMOTHY 6:6-16.

God has a purpose for your life, and that purpose is for you to become a man of God. God wants you to be like Jesus, a strong and godly man who respects himself and others and who honors God in everything he does.

In this passage, Paul is giving Timothy instructions about what it means to be a man of God. Being a man of God is the opposite of what the world wants you to be. If you want to be a man of God, you will be different from other people. A man of the world is self-serving and selfish, greedy, without compassion and love, and cares only for himself. However, when people try to serve only themselves, they end up being worried, sick, jealous, angry, and unhappy.

But if you live your life to serve God, you have peace, love, and joy. A poor Christian has a lot more peace and joy than the man in the world who is not a Christian. God doesn't want you to be poor; but neither does God want you to put your trust in money and riches instead of in God. Besides, God has promised to take care of all your needs (Philippians 4:19). So trust God and make Jesus the center of your life.

Complete the following sentences:

✛ The kind of attitude I want to have about money is

✛ The kind of person I want to be is one who

UNIT 8 ECONOMIC RESPONSIBILITY
Session 3
INGREDIENTS FOR SUCCESS

FOCUS: To help the young men learn personal preferences and dynamics that will contribute to pursuing their goals.

Meeting outline

		Notes
OPENING ACTIVITY & LIBATION	*15 minutes*	
AFRICAN-AMERICAN HEROES	*15 minutes*	
ACHIEVEMENT ACTIVITY	*30 minutes*	
GAME/CRAFT	*20 minutes*	
STORYTELLING	*15 minutes*	
GOD TIME & HARAMBEE!	*15 minutes*	

Preparation

Assign a mentor to make an African-American hero presentation about an African-American CEO or businessperson of their choosing. Or invite a local businessperson or entrepreneur to speak at your meeting.

Bring a small ball or beanbag for the opening activity.

Prepare "Ingredients for Success" activity sheets and bring pencils.

Bring a ball to play outside.

Assign a mentor to do storytelling.

Gather Bibles and God Time journals for devotional.

Session 3

OPENING ACTIVITY (15 minutes)

Look!: Have the group form a circle by stretching arms to their sides. Someone starts passing a beanbag around the group. The object of the game is to pass the bag around the circle to unsuspecting players (in no particular order). If someone drops the bag, he has to sit out. The challenge is to do trick and "no-look" passes to fake out other players. Passes must be "catchable". The group determines what is a good pass and what is not. Keep playing until there are only two players left, then start again.

LIBATION/PRAYER

AFRICAN-AMERICAN HEROES (15 minutes)

Local African-American Success: Listen to the African-American hero presentation about a local African-American CEO, entrepreneur, or businessperson. Invite this person to your group to tell his story.

- ✚ How did he or she get started in business?
- ✚ What words of advice does he or she have for young people?
- ✚ What is important about what he or she does?
- ✚ What lessons can we learn from him or her about economic responsibility?

Note this person's life on the African-American history timeline.

ACHIEVEMENT ACTIVITY (30 minutes)

Ingredients for Success: Have the boys and men gather into small groups. Hand out the "Ingredients for Success" activity sheets and have the boys work on them in their small groups. When they are finished, discuss these questions:

- ✚ What is your definition of *success*?
- ✚ What is the relationship between motivation and success?
- ✚ What are your personal goals for life?

GAME (20 minutes)

Outdoor Game: Take the boys to play an outdoor game of touch football or basketball. If the weather does not permit, play a game of Monopoly.

STORYTELLING (15 minutes)

Money and Me: Have your chosen mentor tell a personal story about economic responsibility.

GOD TIME (15 minutes)

Luke 19:11-27: Ask someone to read Luke 19:11-27.

+ What is the message of this story?
+ Do you agree or disagree?
+ Which servant would you like to be?
+ Which servant do you think you are right now?
+ What talents do you have that God gave you?
+ In what ways are you using them?
+ God wants us to be good stewards of the resources God gives us. How can we do that?

After the discussion have each boy record his personal response to the lesson in his journal.

HARAMBEE CIRCLE

INGREDIENTS FOR SUCCESS

I have little respect for myself and I treat others badly.

I respect myself and demonstrate it by respecting others.

1   2   3   4   5   6

I do not feel any support from my family.

My family supports me and encourages me in everything I do.

1   2   3   4   5   6

I never take responsibility for my actions.

I always take responsibility for my actions.

1   2   3   4   5   6

I dislike school and cannot get along with my teachers.

I like learning and respect my teachers.

1   2   3   4   5   6

I do not think getting good grades at school important.

Getting good grades at school is very is very important to me.

1   2   3   4   5   6

In my spare time I sit around or watch a lot of TV.

I occupy myself with lots of hobbies in my spare time.

1   2   3   4   5   6

I don't have any dreams or goals for my life.

I have specific ideas about what I want to do with my life.

1   2   3   4   5   6

GOD TIME

READ LUKE 19:11-27.

"It's not how much you have, it's what you do with what you have that counts." "Use it or lose it." These statements could describe the moral of this parable. God has given you what you have for a reason. Family support, educational opportunities, friends and relationships, personal talents and skills, and so on. Even if you feel like you have nothing positive in your life, if you look around, you will see that there is always someone worse off than you.

So the point is to not complain about what you don't have, but to use what you do have. Remember, the Bible says with Jesus you can do anything (Philippians 4:13), but without Jesus you can do nothing (John 15:5). Ask God to help you be the best person you can be.

God is like the master who gave away the talents in the story. God wants a return on the investment. Your life is God's gift to you; what are you going to do with it? Will you waste it, or use it to glorify God?

✚ Do a personal inventory; list all the positive resources in your life (things that will help you achieve your goals, including family, education, attitude, and so on):

✚ How can you be a good steward (responsible) in using the "talents" God has given you?

UNIT 8 ECONOMIC RESPONSIBILITY
Session 4
FIELD TRIP SUGGESTIONS

Visit a Local Business or Businessperson

Visit a local merchant or businessperson at his place of work. Allow the boys to ask questions. Give them a taste of what the business world is like.

Plan a Party or Other Event

Set a dollar amount for a special event. Have the boys create a budget and plan the event.

Develop and Plan a Fundraiser

In small groups have the boys brainstorm ideas for fundraising activities. Collect all the ideas and have the whole group choose one to execute. Spend as many weeks as necessary to plan and stage the event. As part of the planning, have the boys create a budget.

Check Out Special Events

Attend a play, show, or movie that deals with economic responsibility. Check the newspapers and entertainment listings for current and special events in your area.

Visit a Charitable Organization

Part of being a good steward of the resources God gives us is giving to others. Choose an organization that will have specific stories or examples of how money given to them is helpful. Or ask the pastor of the church to tell about how the congregation collectively gives to others through their tithes and offerings. Encourage the young men to be contributors to causes they believe in.

Keep On Learning

Field trips are wonderful learning experiences in themselves. However, to help the youth get the most from them, do two simple things:

1. **Prepare the youth:** Give them some introductory information; talk about expected behavior; identify a question for them to be thinking about.
2. **Debrief the trip:** Ask the group what surprised them, what was interesting to them, what made them think. Have a group conversation or give the youth paper and pencils and have them write a journal page about the trip—or do both. Gather the journal pages and add them to the individuals' folders.

UNIT 8 ECONOMIC RESPONSIBILITY
Optional
ACTIVITIES AND SESSIONS

Hobbies and Careers

Use this activity sheet (page 256) in small groups or one large group to help the boys identify areas of interest. Encourage and stimulate dialogue in order to get the participants to talk about their hobbies. Lead them in identifying career choices or vocations that match their interests. Discuss issues of personal satisfaction and enjoyment related to choosing a career or job.

Job Interview

In this activity the boys will roleplay a job interview (page 257). Create a job situation with an interviewer and a job applicant. Let different boys take turns in each role. Have the interviewer ask the applicants the questions on the activity sheet. After each applicant, lead the group in a discussion using the questions listed.

Values and Motivation

Use this activity sheet (page 258) to lead the boys in a discussion of African cultural values and how they contrast with those of mainstream American society. Go through the discussion questions about values and motivation.

Time Management

Assign mentors to help the boys find out exactly how they spend their time by having them fill out this weekly schedule (page 259). Once the schedule has been filled out identify where most of their time goes. Evaluate whether the boys spend their time wisely or not so wisely. Discuss the value of time as a resource.

HOBBIES & CAREERS

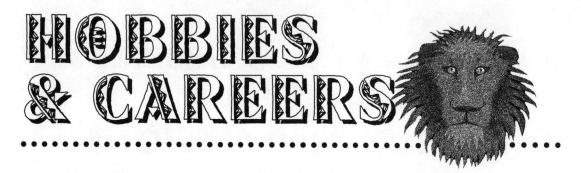

After each hobby listed below, write down as many careers you can think of that are related to that hobby. Add your own hobbies at the bottom of the list.

ANIMALS:

CARPENTRY:

COLLECTING:

COOKING:

DANCE:

DRAWING:

ELECTRONICS:

GAMES:

GARDENING:

MUSIC:

OUTDOORS:

PHOTOGRAPHY:

READING:

SCULPTURE:

SEWING:

SINGING:

SPORTS:

TRAVEL:

WRITING:

OTHER:

INTERVIEW QUESTIONS

Tell me about yourself.

Tell me about one of your major accomplishments.

Tell me about your strengths and weaknesses.

Are you able to take instructions from a supervisor?

Are you unemployed right now? Why?

Why did you leave your last job?

How do you respond to criticism?

Do you consider yourself successful or unsuccessful? Why?

What are your long-term goals?

What was the last book you read? movie you saw?

What do you like to do in your spare time?

What interests do you have?

Are you creative? Explain.

Are you a leader? Explain.

Do you have any questions?

Why do you want this job?

Why should we hire you?

DISCUSSION QUESTIONS:

Was this a successful interview? Why or why not?

What first impression did the interviewee give?

What is the importance of personal appearance?

What advice would you give to the interviewee?

VALUES & MOTIVATION

Discuss the following contrasts in values frequently associated with these cultures. Be aware that individuals within a culture will live out of the the values of that culture to varying degrees—some more than others. Persons can also be influenced by both cultures.

	African	American
self	holistic	fragmented
feelings	expressed	suppressed
survival	communal	individual
communication	oral	written
world perception	harmony	control
sense of worth	contribution	material possession
working with others	cooperation	competition

✚ How much are you influenced by the values taught and "caught" through each of these (Number 1 being "a little"; 6 being "a lot")?

home	1	2	3	4	5	6 _____
school	1	2	3	4	5	6 _____
church/faith	1	2	3	4	5	6 _____
peers	1	2	3	4	5	6 _____
TV/movies	1	2	3	4	5	6 _____

✚ Which culture is predominant in each of these? African or American? Write your assessment in the blanks above.

✚ What are three values that you want to live out?

✚ Which do you believe is the better motivator for work and success: earning lots of money or personal satisfaction? Explain your answer.

WEEKLY SCHEDULE

	Sunday	Monday	Tuesday	Wednesday	Thursday	Friday	Saturday
6:00 a.m.							
7:00 a.m.							
8:00 a.m.							
9:00 a.m.							
10:00 a.m.							
11:00 a.m.							
12:00 p.m.							
1:00 p.m.							
2:00 p.m.							
3:00 p.m.							
4:00 p.m.							
5:00 p.m.							
6:00 p.m.							
7:00 p.m.							
8:00 p.m.							
9:00 p.m.							
10:00 p.m.							
11:00 p.m.							
12:00 a.m.							
1:00 a.m.							
2:00 a.m.							
3:00 a.m.							
4:00 a.m.							
5:00 a.m.							

.... IV. HEROES & RESOURCES

AFRICAN-AMERICAN HISTORY TIMELINE

Materials:
2 cardboard tubes (from the center of paper towel rolls)
4 to 6 sheets of 8½-by-11 paper
a broad-tip marker

Directions:
—Take four to six sheets of paper and attach the 8½ ends together, end to end, using glue or tape.
—Attach each end of this long sheet to a cardboard tube.
—Use a broad-tip marker to make a horizontal line from one end of the long sheet to the other.
—Put hash marks at at regular intervals throughout the line, marking significant events in African-American history.

Example:

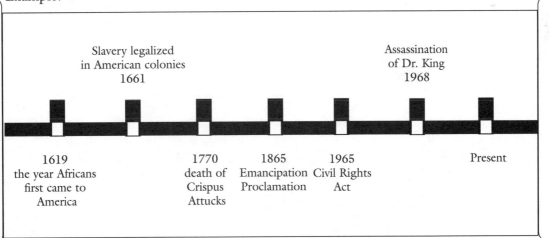

Slavery legalized
in American colonies
1661

Assassination
of Dr. King
1968

1619
the year Africans
first came to
America

1770
death of
Crispus
Attucks

1865
Emancipation
Proclamation

1965
Civil Rights
Act

Present

* Add the birth dates of members of your Young Lions group or other events significant to your group.

DYNAMIC PRESENTATIONS

You've been asked to make the presentation of this week's African-American hero to the Young Lions group. You're not a public speaker; you're not a researcher; you're not sure the boys will pay attention. But you do think that introducing the young men to the ones who have paved the way for their lives is important.

Here are some tips for making your presentation effective:

1. **Start with the one-page biography.** Read the ones given in this book (pages 262–282). Note the information that intrigues you. Mark the places where the information raises new questions for you. But don't stop there.

2. **Look for other biographical information.** Different writers will emphasize different aspects of a person's life, times, and accomplishments. And sources have different amounts of space in which to present the biography, so some will be able to go into more detail than will others. Check the library or search the Internet. Simply type in the person's name in your search field; you will be amazed at the number of sources available to you.

3. **Think about the boys.** What will they find interesting? What will capture their imagination—not just about the past, but also about their present and their future? From what details will they draw inspiration?

4. **Create an outline for your presentation.** Look at the questions in the session plan that the boys will be addressing to give you some guidance. In addition, you may want to cover questions such as these:

   ✚ What was the person's childhood like?
   ✚ What barriers or hardships did this person have to overcome?
   ✚ Were there "mentors" and other helpers?
   ✚ How did the person change?
   ✚ What were the person's contributions?
   ✚ What connection is there between this person's contributions and our lives today?

5. **Tell the story.** Don't read to the boys. It's fine to have notes, but your passion for the person will come through best if you tell the story in your own words. They in turn will respond well to your enthusiasm. Don't worry about perfection.

6. **Ask questions as you tell the story.** Some of the boys will have had exposure to some of the heroes in school or in other settings. Find out what they know. But also find out what they think! Ask questions such as these:

   ✚ What do you think were the person's choices, given those circumstances?
   ✚ How do you think people responded to the person's actions?
   ✚ Why do you think what the person did is significant?
   ✚ If you had been in this person's shoes, what might you have done?

By engaging the boys in this manner, not only are you holding their attention and introducing them to an important person, you are also teaching them to think.

W.E.B. DuBois

William Edward Burghardt DuBois was born in 1868 in Massachusetts. He graduated from Fisk University in 1888 and went on to become the first African American to receive a doctorate from Harvard University. He also studied at the University of Berlin, in Germany.

Throughout his lifetime, DuBois was a strong advocate for education. He was a professor of Latin and Greek at Wilberforce University, in Ohio, and later a professor of economics and history at Atlanta University. He wrote at least eighteen books, which are still highly valued by historians for their insight. His most famous are *The Souls of Black Folk* (1903) and his autobiography (1968).

DuBois was also a student of society. He turned his keen intellect upon racial problems in the United States and in the rest of the world. In the face of such evils as lynching, disfranchisement, Jim Crow segregation laws, and race riots, he saw the need for political action and advocacy for civil rights. He helped found the National Association for the Advancement of Colored People (NAACP) in 1909. He also extended his concern to the conditions of Black people everywhere, advocating Pan-Africanism (all people of African descent should work together in the struggle for their freedom).

DuBois' activism clashed with the ideas of another influential Black leader of the period, Booker T. Washington. Washington's position was that Blacks should accept discrimination for the time being, but work to gain the respect of whites through hard work and economic gain. DuBois believed that strategy would only contribute to keeping African-Americans as "second-class citizens."

One of DuBois's key beliefs was that, in addition to political activism, education was a critical factor in bringing about social change. DuBois said:

"The Negro Race, like all races, is going to be saved by its exceptional men."

He argued for "the Talented Tenth": a small group of college-educated Blacks who would be the exceptional ones needed to provide the leadership to fight against prejudice and discrimination and ultimately change society.

Another of his key beliefs was that it was important for African Americans to develop their own literature and art; as the editor of *Crisis,* the newspaper of the NAACP, he urged his readers to see "beauty in Black."

During the 1950s, DuBois was drawn into leftist causes. He chaired the Peace Information Center, which refused to comply with the Foreign Agents Registration Act. Consequently, he was indicted with four others by a federal grand jury in 1951. Although all five were acquitted, the accusations of Communist associations caused him to be shunned by colleagues and harassed by federal agencies. In 1961, DuBois, disenchanted with America, settled in Ghana and began work on the *Encyclopedia Africana*, a compendium of information on Africans and peoples of African descent throughout the world. He died there in 1963.

W.E.B. DuBois was one of the most important African-American intellectuals, social thinkers, and protest leaders in the United States during the first half of the twentieth century. His career spanned seventy years of scholarship, teaching, and activism in liberation struggles. His influence culminated in the explosion of the civil rights movement of the 1960s.

YOUNG LIONS

Frederick Douglass

Born a slave in 1817 or 1818, Frederick Douglass, born Frederick Bailey, knew very little about his mother, who worked as a field hand on a plantation twelve miles away and died when he was eight or nine years old. He knew even less about his father, who may have been his white slaveholder. Young Frederick was ill-treated and, at times, ate from the food thrown to his master's dogs. At the age of eight, he was sent to be a houseboy in the home of Hugh and Sophia Auld in Baltimore, Maryland. Mrs Auld grew fond of him and taught him to read and write. However, her husband found out and stopped the lessons. Frederick continued his lessons by himself.

At the death of his slaveholder, Frederick, now 15, was passed along to the possession of Thomas Auld. There he experienced the harshness of slavery, and his hatred of the institution deepened. Infuriated by Frederick's refusal to call him "Master," Auld hired him out to a slave breaker who worked and whipped him mercilessly. One day he could stand it no longer and fought back.

When Frederick was sent back to Baltimore, he met Anna Murray, a free Black woman. Loving her made his desire to be free stronger. On September 3, 1838, dressed in a sailor's uniform and carrying false identification papers, he managed to reach New York City. An abolitionist sheltered Frederick. Then Frederick married Anna and moved to Massachusetts. He changed his last name to Douglass.

Douglass began reading *The Liberator* and attending anti-slavery meetings. On one occasion he had the opportunity to tell his story. After that, he was asked to be a lecturer for the movement against slavery. He was well-spoken, and he filled his story with evocative images of what it was like to be a slave. His ability to speak, his dignity, his strength of character, and his powerful voice gave Douglass a commanding presence.

So eloquent were his speeches that after a while the public began to wonder if this articulate man could ever have been a slave. To remove the doubt, Douglass published an account of his slave experiences, *Narrative of the Life of Frederick Douglass,* in 1845. As a result, he was at risk of being captured. He fled to England and stayed there for two years.

With the financial help of his European friends, Douglass returned to America, legally secured his freedom, and launched his newspaper, *The North Star.* He wrote scathing editorials on a variety of topics. Slavery was just one of his targets; job discrimination against free Blacks was another. He wrote, "We need mechanics as well as ministers; we must build as well as live in houses; we must construct bridges as well as pass over them." He also published his autobiography, *My Bondage and My Freedom*, in 1855.

Douglass was a man of action, as well. He gave his money to aid fugitive slaves and used his printing shop in New York as an Underground Railroad station. During the Civil War, he wrote for the Union cause and emancipation, recruited Black troops, and met twice with President Lincoln. After the war, he brought attention to Jim Crow laws in the North by entering forbidden public places, risking being physically thrown out. He worked against lynchings. He also championed women's rights. He continued to speak out and to write persuasively on racial issues and social justice. He died in 1895.

From AFRO-American Almanac, © 1996 by The Digital Development Group. All rights reserved. See www.toptags.com/aama for more information.

Mary Jane McLeod Bethune

Born in 1875 to former slaves, Mary Jane McLeod (later Bethune) was one of seventeen children. As a child, she had a strong desire for knowledge, but there were no schools for her in Mayesville, South Carolina. It was not until she reached age eleven that a school opened some five miles from her home, and she walked the distance daily.

After graduation, she was awarded a small scholarship by a white woman in Denver, Colorado, who wanted to help one Black child attain more education. With the scholarship, her own part-time jobs, and sacrifice on the part of her family, she graduated from Scotia Seminary in 1893. Because she longed to become a missionary to Africa, she went on to study at the Moody Bible Institute. As soon as she graduated, she asked the Presbyterian Board of Missions for a position in Africa. The Mission Board turned her down. She later accepted a teaching position and married Albertus Bethune. The couple had a son, Albert. Her husband died soon after.

In 1904, convinced that education was the most powerful weapon in the fight against Black powerlessness and racial subordination and with $1.50, she founded a school for girls in Daytona Beach, Florida. Her student body consisted of her four-year-old son and five little girls, who each paid 50 cents a week tuition. Her school began in an old house near the city dump. She used a packing crate for her desk, and her students' chairs were salvaged from the dump.

Bethune recalled, "The school expanded fast. In less than two years, I had 250 pupils. . . . I concentrated more and more on girls, as I felt that they especially were hampered by lack of educational opportunities." In 1923, however, she agreed to merge with Cookman Institute, a Methodist school for African-American boys, forming the Bethune-Cookman College. At the time of the merger, she had a student body of 632 faculty members, and an $800,000 campus free of debt.

Bethune's pioneering work in Black education earned national acclaim. She stressed teacher preparation, industrial training and domestic arts, good manners, and Christian virtue. She soon attracted the attention of white political leaders, serving as adviser to the White House on Black education and racial affairs. She served, in various capacities, the administrations of Coolidge, Hoover, Roosevelt, and Truman. She well understood the need for Blacks to marshal political power and acquire advanced education as strategies in the ongoing struggle for equal rights.

In 1935, she founded—and served as president until 1949—the National Council of Negro Women, a federation of Black women's organizations. The NCNW was dedicated to achieving "the outlawing of the poll tax, the development of a public health program, an anti-lynching bill, the end of discrimination in the armed forces, defense plants, government housing plants, and finally that Negro history be taught in the public schools of the country."

Bethune is a pivotal figure in twentieth-century Black women's history. Her life and work formed a major link connecting the social reform efforts of post-Reconstruction Black women to the political protest activities of the generation emerging after World War II. Champion of human rights, a woman beloved by all regardless of race, color, or creed, Mary Jane McLeod Bethune died in 1955.

From AFRO-American Almanac, © 1996 by The Digital Development Group. All rights reserved. See www.toptags.com/aama for more information.

YOUNG LIONS

Malcolm X

Malcolm X began life in 1925, in Omaha, Nebraska, as Malcolm Little, the son of a Baptist preacher. His father was an outspoken proponent of social and economic justice for Blacks and a follower of Marcus Garvey (see page 269). When Malcolm was only six, his father was murdered by white terrorists for his activism.

The family never recovered from the death. Mrs. Little suffered a nervous breakdown. The children were split up; Malcolm went into a foster home. After the eighth grade, he dropped out of school. He fell into a life of crime, including peddling drugs; and at age 20, he was imprisoned for burglary.

While in prison he developed an interest in Elijah Muhammad, leader of the Nation of Islam (Black Muslims). Muhammad taught that all whites were evil, that God was Black, that Blacks should have an independent Black state, and that a Black revolution was needed. Black Muslims also stressed personal self-restraint (no alcohol, no drugs) and economic self-help. Malcolm became a loyal disciple and gave up his "slave name" and adopted X—symbolic of a stolen identity—as his last name.

After his release from prison, he became a prominent spokesperson for the Nation of Islam. During the 1955–1964 decade, while Black leaders such as Dr. Martin Luther King, Jr., were focusing on civil rights and non-violence, Malcolm X preached the opposite. However, he began to see problems with Elijah Muhammad and his teachings. His 1964 pilgrimage to the Muslim Holy City of Mecca brought about a profound change in his thinking.

Malcolm had discovered that orthodox Muslims preach equality of the races. He renounced the teaching that all whites are evil. He broke with the Nation of Islam and became an orthodox Muslim. He advocated for Blacks to work with one another, sympathetic whites, and Hispanics to overcome racism.

His popularity, outspoken criticism of the Nation of Islam, and change of tactics angered the Black Muslims. In February 1965, while making a speech, Malcolm X was assassinated. At the time, he had been working with writer Alex Haley (*Roots*) on his story. Published after his death, *The Autobiography of Malcolm X* is an important work and a story of radical transformation:

- From hustler and criminal to spiritual leader;
- From preacher of racial hatred to advocate of interracial brotherhood;
- From advocate of violence to man of peace;
- From one who rejected political solutions, including voting, to a political activist and champion of the vote.

The messages of self-respect ("Black is beautiful") and self-help (African-Americans must take control of their own destiny) are coupled with his rejection of racism in any form. These are the legacy of Malcolm X.

Black Panthers

Originally called The Black Panther Party for Self-Defense, the organization was founded in October, 1966, in Oakland, California, by Huey P. Newton and Bobby Seale. A chief goal was to protect Blacks from police brutality. The name was soon shortened to the Black Panther Party (BPP), and the group broadened its goals to include a fairer distribution of jobs, economic justice, and neighborhood control of education.

The Black Panthers had two fundamental elements that brought them trouble:

1. They favored violent revolution to bring about change in society. They supported the use of guns, both for self-defense and for retaliation against those who oppressed others. This stance brought them into armed conflict with police and resulted in several shoot-outs. It also brought them under the scrutiny of the government and led to trials on various charges, including conspiracy.
2. They began to work with white radical groups that shared their economic goals and philosophy of revolutionary change. This action brought them into conflict with other African-American organizations that worked through the political systems and that regarded the struggles of Blacks as racial.

The organization effectively spread its ideas and message of Black Power (symbolized by the clenched fist) through the newspaper *The Black Panther,* edited by Eldridge Cleaver. Cleaver spent several years in prison as a young man, but was paroled in 1966 and joined the party. In 1968, Cleaver's first book, *Soul on Ice,* was published. He also ran as the United States presidential candidate of the Peace and Freedom Party. Later, he was involved in a shooting incident and fled to Africa. Cleaver returned in 1975, having become a Christian. He described his conversion and his change in thinking in his book *Soul on Fire,* published in 1978.

Bobby Seale, a cofounder of the party, also became politically active. He ran for mayor of Oakland in 1973. Although he lost, he won a third of the votes. Huey P. Newton, the other founder, was shot to death in 1989.

Although the Black Panther Party had ceased to exist by the mid-1970s, it had had a positive impact through its community organization efforts. Throughout various cities in the United States, the Panthers mobilized communities to work for free breakfasts for children; free health clinics; rent strikes (which resulted in tenant ownership of the buildings); free clothing drives; community control of schools; and campaigns against drugs, crime, and police brutality. The principle the Panthers taught was self-reliance.

Marcus Garvey

Born in 1887 in Jamaica, Marcus Garvey originally emigrated to the United States in 1916, hoping to garner support for building a school in Jamaica similar to Booker T. Washington's Tuskegee Institute. However, the mix of man and opportunities quickly moved him to the forefront of leadership in the Black community of Harlem, New York, and from there to the world.

World War I and the 1920s fomented social upheavals, anticolonial movements, and revolutions that were changing existing power structures. In Harlem, a new surge of discussion and energy around music, arts, literature, education, and race (the Harlem Renaissance) provided fertile ground for the growth of Marcus Garvey's ideas. He connected with the people's growing desires for justice, wealth, and community.

But Garvey's vision was not limited to Harlem or even the United States. He founded the Universal Negro Improvement Association (UNIA), which grew to nearly a million men and women from the United States, the Caribbean, and Africa. He knitted together Black communities on three continents with his newspaper *The Negro World*. His goals were to end both imperialism in Africa and discrimination in the United States and to overcome class and national divisions.

Garvey attempted to unite mass organization and economic strength to achieve his goals. In 1919, he formed the Black Star Line, an international shipping company to provide transportation and encourage trade among the Black businesses of Africa and the Americas. In the same year, he founded the Negro Factories Corporation. However, the projects floundered and failed.

Garvey's determination to lead inevitably set him on a collision path with other Black leaders. His speaking ability and his dramatic flair attracted thousands, but his faltering projects added fuel to the fires of ideological and personality conflicts. In the end, he could neither unite Blacks nor accumulate enough power to achieve his goals.

Finally, the Justice Department (J. Edgar Hoover's Federal Bureau of Investigation) indicted Garvey for mail fraud. He was convicted in 1923, imprisoned in 1925, and deported to Jamaica in 1927. He moved to London, where he died in 1940.

More than one hundred years after his birth, however, Marcus Garvey still has influence. He has risen to the level of folk hero, continuing to inspire people through today's reggae music: "Marcus Garvey" (Burning Spear), "Right Time" (Mighty Diamonds), "So Much Things to Say" (Bob Marley), and "Rally Round" (Steel Pulse).

Queen Makeda

Known to her people as Makeda, she has been known by various names: To the Moslems, she was Bilqis; to King Solomon of Israel, she was the Queen of Sheba, or Saba; to the ancient Greeks, she was the Black Minerva and the Ethiopian Diana.

Makeda was the queen of both Ethiopia and Saba, in southern Arabia. It is believed that Axum, the capital city of her empire, was founded one hundred years after the Great Flood. Makeda made many changes and rebuilt the territory of Saba during her reign.

Queen Makeda was very beautiful and exceedingly rich. She had heard from her royal merchants a great deal about the wealth of Israel and the wisdom of King Solomon. The more she heard, the more she desired to go to Jerusalem. One day she announced to her constituents that she intended to visit the wise King Solomon. Makeda departed for the Holy City with a caravan of almost eight hundred camels, donkeys, and mules, which were loaded with precious stones, metals, and other valuable items.

During her six-month stay, Makeda met frequently with King Solomon. She was so impressed with his wisdom that she gave up her religion and adopted his, Judaism. King Solomon wanted to have many sons who would rule in the name of the God of Israel; he and Makeda became intimate. Shortly thereafter, she requested to return to her own country. Although Solomon wanted her to stay, he allowed her to go but gave her a special ring. The ring was both for remembering their love and to be a sign if she had a son. She agreed that if she had a male child, she would crown him king of Ethiopia. Her promise was significant because at that time, the areas where she reigned were matriarchies (ruled only by women). The queen departed for home, and nine months and five days after Makeda left King Solomon, she gave birth to a male child. She named him Ibn al-Hakim, "son of the wise man." His royal name was Menelik.

At the age of twenty-two, Menelik traveled to Jerusalem to visit his father. He did not need the ring Solomon had given his mother for identification; because when he arrived in Gaza, the people knew by his appearance that he was Solomon's son. When Menelik finally reached his father, Solomon stated, "He is handsomer than I am; and his form and stature are those of David, my father, in his early manhood." Solomon kissed and embraced his son, and asked him to stay. He promised Menelik the kingdom of Israel upon his death, but Menelik stated that he was unwilling to abandon his own country and that he had promised his mother that he would return.

Solomon anointed Menelik King of Ethiopia, bestowed upon him the name of David, and provided him with counselors and officers for the founding of Israel's new kingdom in Ethiopia. Except for a brief period during the ninth and tenth centuries, and until the death of Haile Selassie in 1975, Queen Makeda's descendants have ruled the throne of Ethiopia.

From AFRO-American Almanac, © 1996 by The Digital Development Group. All rights reserved. See www.toptags.com/aama for more information.

YOUNG LIONS

King Shaka

Warrior-king of the Zulus, Shaka was born in 1787 to Senzangakona, a Zulu chieftain, and Nandi, an orphaned princess of the Langeni clan. At age six, Senzagakona and Nandi separated. Nandi took Shaka back to the Langeni. Around 1802, the Langeni drove Nandi and her son out and she found shelter with the Dletsheni, a subclan of the Mtetwa. When Shaka was twenty-three, Dingiswayo, the Mtetwa chieftain, called up Shaka's age group for military service.

As a young man serving in the army of Dingiswayo, Shaka's acts of bravery won him Dingiswayo's admiration. Upon Senzangakona's death, Dingiswayo gave Shaka the military assistance to ascend to power. In 1816, he became chief of the Zulu clan. It was Shaka's aim to rule all Africans.

Shaka implemented a new system of military organization that incorporated regiments from defeated tribes. When a chiefdom was conquered, it became a territorial segment of Shaka's kingdom-at-large. The warriors became a part of his royal army. They were drilled, and they fought beside combatants from other chiefdoms.

To maintain his royal army, Shaka established military towns and provided his army with the best training and provisions. He demanded the strictest of discipline and perfection from his regiments. His soldiers were required to remain celibate during their period of enlistment. Any violation of this rule was punished by death. He also killed any soldier who exhibited signs of fear.

Shaka turned the Zulus into a powerful military nation. He unified many tribes of the South African region, and his efforts are directly credited with saving that region from European domination during his lifetime. In 1829, Shaka met with a violent death at the age of forty-two at the hands of his half-brothers.

Nelson Mandela

Born in 1918 in South Africa, Nelson Mandela grew up in a tribal village. As a foster child of a Thembu chief, he was being prepared to rule. However, growing up Black in South Africa meant being severely limited by *apartheid,* the legal system that kept the races separated and oppressed the Black population. The injustice and the day-to-day grimness that Blacks lived with moved Mandela to pursue change through politics and law. As a college student, he participated in a protest boycott and was suspended from the university. However, he finished his degree through correspondence.

Mandela joined the African National Congress (ANC), the Black nationalist movement, and helped write the policy statements for changing the distribution of land, giving trade unions rights, and providing education. He also recruited people for a massive campaign for civil disobedience, a form of protest. For that, his freedom to travel was taken away. He continued his study and passed the bar exam to become a lawyer. With Oliver Tambo, another political activist, Mandela formed the first Black law partnership in South Africa.

His activism expanded to forming an underground military wing of the ANC and traveling abroad to arrange for guerrilla training. His activities alarmed the government and he was arrested for illegal travel and convicted of conspiracy to overthrow the government. He was sentenced to life imprisonment.

Mandela spent twenty-seven years in prison. But he didn't allow that injustice to make him bitter or give up. He continued to read and to write. Others smuggled out his writings, and he became an international symbol of the evils of apartheid. In the meantime, he thought of the prison situation as a reflection of the larger society with one race over the other. Consequently, he worked toward establishing a conciliatory atmosphere within the prison between the jailers and the jailed. His efforts paid off in better conditions within the prison but also taught him much that would guide him in the next phase of his leadership.

Released in 1990, he led the ANC in its negotiations with South African President F.W. de Klerk for an end to apartheid and the establishment of a multiracial government. Mandela and de Klerk were jointly awarded the 1993 Nobel Prize for Peace. After South Africa's first multiracial elections (1994), Mandela was elected president.

When Mandela left the prison, he stated that he regretted that he had forgotten to thank his guards. But as the new president of South Africa, he consulted regularly with his former captors about ways to construct a racially integrated and democratic society. With the aid of his statesman-like qualities and commitment to reconciliation, President Nelson Mandela led his country through a remarkable transition from tyranny to democracy without a violent upheaval or bloodbath. He retired in 1999. South Africa is still troubled by the legacy of racial injustice, but the legacy of Mandela has helped to set the course for change.

YOUNG LIONS

Crispus Attucks

Because Crispus Attucks was a slave, it is not known exactly when he was born; but the commonly held year is 1723. What is known is that he died on March 5, 1770, one of the first men to be killed in America's struggle for independence.

Attucks grew up in Framingham, Massachusetts, working in the fields with the other slaves but longing to be on the sea. At age 27, he slipped away and became a sailor, mostly working on whaling ships sailing from Boston Harbor. Being a sailor, he was aware of the British navy's practice of impressment (forcing men into service without their agreement). Nearly twenty years later, Crispus Attucks was back in Boston as a laborer, where he also experienced competition for jobs from British soldiers who were willing to work part time for lower wages. That practice threatened the livelihood of many of the colonial laborers like Attucks and added fuel to the growing fire of rebellion.

In 1770, tensions between British soldiers and the Americans were also rising over issues of taxation. The Americans resented paying taxes to a government 3,000 miles away, in which they had no say. It was not uncommon for people, even children, to taunt the redcoats and throw things at them. Some, possibly even Attucks (a former slave who knew firsthand about not being free), spoke out for freedom from Britain.

On March 5, 1770, a group of about thirty colonists were harassing a guard. Seven other soldiers came to the guard's rescue. Someone fired, and Crispus Attucks died. Four others also were killed that day. Patriots and propagandists dubbed the event the "Boston Massacre" and the men who died, "martyrs" and "symbols of liberty."

John Adams, later the second President of the United States, defended the soldiers in court on the charges of murder. The court acquitted them. But the colonists were only further angered by the verdict. Every year leading up to the Revolutionary War, the citizens of Boston observed the anniversary of the day Attucks was killed. Speeches in subsequent years praised the bravery of Crispus Attucks and the fact that even a person who was not treated equally had the courage to fight for his country.

In 1888, the Crispus Attucks monument was unveiled in the Boston Common.

Medgar Evers

Born in 1925, sixty years after slavery ended and Black people were "free," Medgar Evers grew up in Mississippi where humiliating Blacks was an everyday occurrence. As a child, he witnessed the lynching of a friend of the family for supposedly insulting a white woman.

During World War II, Evers left high school to join the Army with his brother Charles. Assigned to an all-Black unit, he experienced freedom and respect from the French. But when he returned home, not much had changed.

Evers went to college and proved his leadership ability: member of the debate team, choir, football team, track team; junior class president; editor of the yearbook and of the newspaper. After college, he and his wife, Myrlie, began working for Magnolia Mutual Insurance Company, one of the few Black-owned businesses. As he traveled around the state of Mississippi for the company, he saw the extreme poverty, the indignities, and the injustices that Blacks, especially the sharecroppers, were subject to. He determined to go to law school to make a difference.

In 1954, Medgar Evers became the first African American to apply for admission to the University of Mississippi ("Ole Miss"). However, he was denied admittance. He asked the National Association for the Advancement of Colored People (NAACP) to file a suit on his behalf; but the organization asked him, instead, to work with them.

As the first NAACP field secretary in Mississippi, Evers organized boycotts against gasoline stations that refused to allow African Americans to use their restrooms and against merchants in Jackson, Mississippi, that did not show respect to African-American customers. He publicized racist brutality, promoted voting rights, and pushed for desegregation of public accommodations. He was successful in getting James Meredith admitted to Ole Miss eight years after his own attempts had been rebuffed.

Successfully drawing national attention to the injustices practiced so pervasively in Mississippi, Medgar Evers became a target. On June 7, 1963, he was ambushed and shot in the back. He was taken to the closest hospital, which refused at first to admit him because he was Black. When the doctors found out who he was, they treated him; but it was too late.

He was buried in Arlington National Cemetery with full honors. Twenty thousand people came to honor him and to stand with him for change.

White supremacist Byron De La Beckwith was arrested and tried for Evers's murder. Despite the clear evidence against him, he was set free after two all-white juries could not reach a verdict. Finally, in 1994, thirty-one years after the murder, De La Beckwith was convicted and sentenced to life in prison.

Charles Evers, Medgar's brother, continued his work on voter registration; Charles later became the first African-American mayor in the state of Mississippi. When Medgar died, only 28,000 Blacks were registered to vote; twenty years later the number had risen to 500,000. Ten years after his death 145 African Americans were in elected positions. The numbers have continued to grow.

Shirley Chisholm

Shirley Anita St. Hill Chisholm was the first African-American woman to serve in the United States Congress. Born in 1924 in Brooklyn, New York, she attended public schools and went on to receive her master's degree from Columbia University. She worked as a nursery school teacher, then as director of a childcare center, and became an educational consultant for the state of New York on daycare needs.

In 1964, Chisholm was elected to the New York state assembly; four years later, the state elected her to the United States House of Representatives, where she served until 1983.

Originally, she was assigned to the House Committee on Agriculture. She protested the assignment as inappropriate for the representative of an inner-city district. She won a transfer to a committee on which she felt she could be of greater service to her Brooklyn constituency. Chisholm also served on the Rules Committee and the Education and Labor Committee during her seven terms in the House.

Her tenure in the House saw her actively working for causes she believed would help people; much of her work is reflected in today's life that we take for granted:

- ending the draft and creating an all-volunteer military force;
- establishing a national commission on consumer protection and product safety;
- ending discrimination in the hiring practices of food store chains and automobile manufacturers;
- increasing daycare programs, expanding those services to working mothers of both middle-class and low-income families;
- guaranteeing an annual income to families;
- expanding the coverage of minimum wage legislation to include domestic workers. (She gathered support from organized labor and the women's movement and on the House floor delivered an impassioned speech recalling the hardships of her own mother's work as a domestic worker.);
- working for federal health, safety, and personnel standards for daycare centers;
- standing against tax credits to defray tuition to private schools, arguing that such credits would undermine the public school system.

In 1972, Chisholm declared her candidacy for the Democratic presidential nomination. Although she did not win it, she did receive 152 first ballot votes at the convention, a very respectable showing.

She has written an autobiography, *Unbought and Unbossed* (1970, out of print).

Ida B. Wells Barnett

Ida Bell Wells (later Barnett) was born in 1862 in Mississippi, a daughter of slaves. For her, overcoming racism and halting the violent murder of Black men were a central mission, among her wide-ranging struggles for justice and human dignity. She was educated at Rust University, actually a high school and industrial school. From 1884 to 1891, Wells taught in a rural school near Memphis and attended summer classes at Fisk University, in Nashville.

A pattern of resistance to racial subordination was set early in her life. In 1887, she purchased a railroad ticket in Memphis and took a seat in the section reserved for whites. When she refused to move, she was physically thrown off the train. She successfully sued the Chesapeake and Ohio Railroad for damages. Upon appeal, however, the Supreme Court of Tennessee reversed the lower court's ruling.

Wells first became a teacher in rural Mississippi and Tennessee; but in the late 1880's, she turned to journalism. Using the pen name "Iola," she wrote articles for Black-owned newspapers on such issues as the education of Black children. In 1891, she co-founded the militant newspaper *Free Speech,* in Memphis.

Later that same year, however, after Wells denounced in her editorials the lynching of three of her friends, the newspaper's office was mobbed and destroyed by local whites. Undaunted, she began a crusade to investigate the lynching of Blacks in the American South. She argued that lynching stemmed not from the "defense of white womanhood" but from whites' fear of economic competition from Blacks. With a death threat hanging over her in Memphis, Wells decided to remain in the North. During her exile, she wrote the pamphlet *A Red Record* (1895), a statistical account and analysis of three years of lynchings. She subsequently traveled throughout the United States and England, lecturing and founding anti-lynching societies and Black women's clubs.

In 1893, Wells organized a Black women's club in Chicago; later she was a founder of the Chicago Negro Fellowship League, which aided newly arrived migrants from the South. She was also a women's rights advocate, starting what may have been the first Black women's suffrage group. She worked with Jane Addams to block the establishment of segregated public schools in Chicago and served as a probation officer from 1913 to 1917 for the Chicago municipal court.

In 1895, Wells married Ferdinand Lee Barnett, a lawyer and editor of *The Chicago Conservator.* She died in 1931. Her autobiography, *Crusade for Justice* (University of Chicago Press, 1991, ISBN: 0226893448), was published posthumously in 1970.

James Weldon Johnson

James Weldon Johnson was born in 1871 in Florida. He is best known for being a poet, composer, diplomat, and anthologist of Black culture. He also played a major role in articulating goals, devising strategies, and organizing people in the struggle for racial equality.

Johnson was trained in music and other subjects by his mother, a school teacher. A product of the Black middle class, he was widely traveled and multilingual. He graduated from Atlanta University in 1894 and later obtained a master's degree from Columbia. For several years, he was principal of the Black high school in Jacksonville, Florida, expanding educational opportunities there for Blacks. He read law at the same time, and was admitted to the Florida bar in 1897.

His training in law helped prepare him for appointments as U.S. consul to Venezuela and Nicaragua (1906–1912) and equipped him for distinguished leadership (1916–1930) in the National Association for the Advancement of Colored People. As NAACP field secretary (1916–1920), Johnson worked tirelessly to increase the group's membership and expand its geographic representation, transforming a fledgling interracial civil rights group into a visible, vocal, and credible national force. His investigations of lynchings, peonage, and race riots raised public awareness and won the attention of national leaders. During Johnson's tenure as NAACP executive secretary (1920–1930), the organization defined the Black agenda largely in legal and political terms, focusing on publicity; lobbying; and litigation in such areas as lynching, criminal justice, and residential segregation.

Johnson rejected both the vocational self-help philosophy of Booker T. Washington and the more radical economic measures advocated by W.E.B. DuBois. He believed that African Americans could advance their position in American society by demonstrating "intellectual parity . . . through the production of literature and art." Johnson himself helped shape the body of African-American literature during the Harlem Renaissance of the 1920s. He reached wide interracial audiences with his own poems, including "God's Trombones." Johnson promoted art competitions and secured major sources of funding for Black artists and writers. His novel *The Autobiography of an Ex-Coloured Man* remains a classic. Its main character, a light-skinned Black pianist, succumbs to racism, passing for white, choosing an artistically compromised but less restricted musical career.

Johnson was also a musician. His work ranged from a libretto for the Metropolitan Opera to some 200 songs for the Broadway musical stage, most of which he wrote in collaboration with his brother, J. Rosamond Johnson. The brothers published two best-selling collections of traditional spirituals, documenting and spotlighting an overlooked but important American musical tradition. Best known of all their works may be "Lift Every Voice and Sing." Considered to be the unofficial "Negro National Anthem," it was a bold piece of work that spoke of the struggle of the African Americans in America and of hope for a better future. (The song is found today in many contemporary hymnals.)

Johnson's introductions to his anthologies contain some of the most perceptive assessments ever made of Black contributions to American culture. *Along This Way* (Da Capo Press, 2000, ISBN: 030680929X), published in 1933, is his autobiography. He died in 1938.

Bill Cosby

The year 1937 marked Bill Cosby's entrance onto life's stage. Since then, his stages have included comedy clubs, recordings, TV drama, TV sitcoms, movies, commercials, and books. He has garnered five Emmy awards and eight Grammys as well as numerous other recognitions.

Beginning as a stand-up comic telling funny stories of Old Weird Harold, Fat Albert, and others, Bill Cosby broke a color barrier early in his career. He became the first African American to star in a weekly TV drama (*I Spy*). From there he moved to his own shows. In 1984, he pitched a series concept to one of the major networks, but ABC didn't think viewers would accept the idea of a wholesome, Black, middle-class family. Fortunately, NBC was willing to take a chance and contract for just six episodes. The rest speaks for itself. The *Cosby Show,* with the Huxtable family, hit number one in the ratings and remained there for years.

Listed officially as an entertainer, Cosby is truly an educator. In the beginning, however, education didn't seem to matter. He dropped out of high school and joined the Navy. Later, he went to college on a football scholarship. And later still, he went on to graduate from college. He has both a master's and a doctorate in education. His focus in his studies has been on how children learn.

Instead of forgoing his stage career in order to teach, Cosby has successfully brought together both. The Huxtable family successfully entertained and taught a different view of African Americans. Previously, TV portrayals of Blacks had been largely as poor people, custodians, maids, buffoons, or bad guys. However, people of all ethnic and social backgrounds could identify with the Huxtables' problems and triumphs. The *Cosby Show*'s story lines and family relationships taught positive values such as showing respect, accepting responsibility, sharing, celebrating accomplishments, facing problems, honoring parents and grandparents, and caring for one another. The hit show created a new awareness and positive image of Blacks, breaking old stereotypes.

> **"The brilliant thing Cosby did was to put race and economic issues on the back burner so we could see a Black family dealing with all the things Black people deal with the same as all other people."**
> —Henry Louis Gates, Jr., Chairman of African-American Studies at Harvard

Bill Cosby's own family suffered the murder of his only son. While Ennis Cosby was changing a flat tire, he was shot and killed in a robbery attempt. The Cosby family has established the Hello, Friend/Ennis William Cosby Foundation to fulfill the dreams of their son, who was a doctoral student in the field of special education. He had planned to teach and to found a school for people with learning differences, which he also had faced. The foundation is dedicated to being a friend to all people with dyslexia and language-based learning differences, recognizing and celebrating their gifts, opening the doors of learning to them, and helping them to reach their full potential.

YOUNG LIONS

African-American Authors

The following are descriptions of the three books to be used for the African-American Heroes presentations of Unit 6: Growing Up. You will need to obtain a copy of each of the books in order to make the presentations about the authors' growing up years.

BLACK BOY: (AMERICAN HUNGER)

First published in 1945, *Black Boy,* by Richard Wright, tells of his coming of age in the Jim Crow South. It is a story of what it meant to be a man, Black, and southern in America during that time. Reviewer Karim Walker, a student at Rutgers University, wrote this review for Amazon.com:

"Of my four years in high school, none was as difficult as my sophomore year. Filled with uncertainty and soul-searching, I am happy to have found solace in the books that I had read during those times of unrest. One such book was Richard Wright's autobiography, *Black Boy.* Wright exposes the haunting and outrageous 300-year-old lies that Americans had lived. He shows the brutality of growing up in the American South and the sorrow of growing up with neither true friends nor true family. This should be mandatory reading for all Americans, Black or white. Everyone will get something out of it." (Reprint paperback edition published in 1998 by Harperperennial Library; ISBN: 0060929782.)

MANCHILD IN THE PROMISED LAND

First published in 1965, *Manchild in the Promised Land: A Young Black Man in America* is a thinly fictionalized account of Claude Brown's childhood as a hardened, streetwise youth trying to survive life in the Harlem ghetto. Praised for its realistic portrayal of Harlem's poverty, hardworking folks, hustlers, drug dealers, prostitutes, pimps, police, sex, and violence, the book continues to appeal to new generations. Not only is it a story filled with the struggles of urban youth, which are as relevant today as in the author's time, but it is also a story about the one who "made it," the boy who kept landing on his feet and became a man. (Reprint paperback edition published in 1999 by Simon & Schuster; ISBN: 0684864185.)

MAKES ME WANNA HOLLER: A YOUNG BLACK MAN IN AMERICA

Makes Me Wanna Holler: A Young Black Man in America, by Nathan McCall, is a story of the author's transformation from teenage gang-banger (rapist) and stick-up artist to prison inmate, and, finally, after much struggle, to a job as a reporter at the prestigious *Washington Post.* The *San Francisco Chronicle* called the book an "honest and searching look at the perils of growing up as a Black male in urban America." (Paperback edition published in 1995 by Random House; ISBN: 0679740708.)

Thurgood Marshall

Born in 1908, Thurgood Marshall grew up in a Black community within Baltimore, Maryland, that had been actively working for civil rights since the Civil War. His family was often at the forefront of those efforts.

His early education was in racially segregated public schools. An outstanding student, Marshall graduated from law school (magna cum laude) and began work for the National Association for the Advancement of Colored People (NAACP). Issues of racial justice were his specialty. Learning from his mentor, Charles Hamilton, the first Black lawyer to win a case before the Supreme Court, Marshall ultimately argued thirty-two cases before the Supreme Court and won twenty-nine of them.

His most famous case was *Brown vs. the Board of Education.* Winning that case took away the legal basis for racial segregation in the public schools and sparked the 1960s civil rights movement. Other cases Marshall argued and won broke the color barrier for housing, transportation, and voting, ending the "separate but equal" legal apartheid in America. The changes these cases brought about included access for more African Americans to college educations and the growth of the Black middle class.

In 1961, President John F. Kennedy appointed Marshall to the U.S. Court of Appeals. During that time, he wrote 112 opinions, none of which were overturned upon appeal. In 1965, President Lyndon B. Johnson appointed him as the first African American to serve as Solicitor General. In 1967, Marshall became the first African American appointed to the Supreme Court, the very body he knew so well from the other side of the bench.

As a Justice, Thurgood Marshall promoted affirmative action; individual rights; and protection under the law for women, children, prisoners, the homeless, the press, and African Americans. He served the nation as a Supreme Court Justice for twenty-four years, from 1967–1991.

Thurgood Marshall did not have the high visibility of some of the other champions of civil rights, but his work in the courts forever changed American society and laid the foundation for racial justice. Marshall died in 1993.

Marian Wright Edelman

Marian Wright (later Edelman) was born in South Carolina in 1939, the youngest of five children of a Baptist minister. She graduated from Yale Law School in 1963 and opened and ran the Mississippi office of the National Association for the Advancement of Colored People (NAACP). She was the first Black woman admitted to the Mississippi Bar. She brought Robert F. Kennedy, at that time the Senator for New York, to Mississippi so that he could see firsthand the homes of the poor. Her strategy effectively drew attention to the problem of hunger and the need for federal help in the form of food stamps.

She moved to Washington and worked with Martin Luther King, Jr., to plan the Poor People's March on Washington, which took place after his death. Soon after, she founded the Children's Defense Fund (CDF). The mission of the Children's Defense Fund is to

Leave No Child Behind®

and to ensure every child a Healthy Start, a Head Start, a Fair Start, a Safe Start, and a Moral Start in life.

Through the Children's Defense Fund, she organized the Stand for Children march, which drew more than 200,000 people to Washington in June, 1996, and more important, drew attention to the needs of disadvantaged Americans of all colors. Under Edelman's leadership, the CDF has become a strong national voice for children and families.

Edelman served on the Board of Trustees of Spelman College, where she was an undergraduate, and was the first woman elected as a member of the Yale University Corporation. In addition to many other honorary degrees and awards, in 2000, she received the Presidential Medal of Freedom, the nation's highest civilian award, and the Robert F. Kennedy Lifetime Achievement Award for her writings, which include five books: *Families in Peril: An Agenda for Social Change*; the #1 *New York Times* bestseller *The Measure of Our Success: A Letter to My Children and Yours*; *Guide My Feet: Meditations and Prayers on Loving and Working for Children;* a children's book entitled *Stand for Children;* and most recently, *Lanterns: A Memoir of Mentors,* published in 1999. Her best-selling book *The Measure of Our Success* grew from a letter she wrote to her son, Joshua, on his 21st birthday.

A strong voice for the things she believes in, Marian Wright Edelman has had critics from time to time; but she says, "I know people talk about my not being willing to compromise. On the other hand, I don't know what middle ground there is between immunizing a child and not immunizing a child, between children dying from guns and not. If that's self-righteous or holier than thou, then I'm sorry."

Jesse Jackson

Born in 1941 in South Carolina, Jesse Jackson grew up keenly aware of racial inequities. He was a good student and an athlete and earned a scholarship to the University of Illinois; but when he was not allowed to play quarterback, he transferred to North Carolina Agricultural and Technical College. He later attended Chicago Theological Seminary. He left seminary to work with Dr. Martin Luther King, Jr., and was present when King was assassinated. In many ways, Jackson has stepped into the visible leadership vacuum that the loss of Dr. King created.

Ordained a Baptist minister, Jesse Jackson is noted for his ability to speak persuasively. His words have the power to motivate and move people. He combined that skill with his ability to organize and produced some significant changes in society in the areas of civil rights, empowerment, economic and social justice:

- In 1966–1971, he headed Operation Breadbasket, which as part of the Southern Christian Leadership Conference (SCLC), focused on economic issues.
- In 1971–1984, he founded Operation PUSH (People United to Serve Humanity). Through both of these organizations, he persuaded many white-owned companies to hire Blacks and other minority persons, to sell products made by Black-owned businesses, and to open up other economic opportunities.
- In 1984, he pulled together the Rainbow Coalition, appealing to all races. Working through this organization, he conducted two presidential campaigns. Although he did not win, the number of persons voting for him in the two elections went from three million to seven million. And because of his candidacy and the work of his organization, one million new voters registered in the 1984 election and two million in the 1988 season.

Although his efforts were controversial, Jesse Jackson stepped into some tense situations and successfully won freedom for prisoners caught in the middle of international power struggles:

- In 1984, he obtained the release of a captured U.S. pilot shot down in the Middle East.
- In 1984, he negotiated the release from Cuba of 46 Cuban and American prisoners
- In 1990, he brought American hostages out of Kuwait and Iraq.
- In 1999, he helped arrange the release of three U.S. soldiers taken prisoner in Yugoslavia.
- In 1999, Jackson took on the "zero tolerance" policy of a school that had expelled six African-American students for allegedly starting a fight at a football game. Later, the school reduced the expulsions to one year. Jackson has been a friend to youth, visiting thousands of schools, urging young persons to stay away from drugs and encouraging excellence in their education.

Jackson's son, Jesse L. Jackson, Jr., continues to work for justice for all people in his role as a U.S. Congressman.

YOUNG LIONS

Madame C.J.Walker

Born Sarah Breedlove in 1867, the daughter of Louisiana sharecroppers, Walker was orphaned at six, married at fourteen, and widowed at twenty with a two-year-old daughter to care for. She resettled in St. Louis and went to work as a laundress. Her early years reflected patterns all too common for Black women of her generation.

In 1905, Walker, who had been losing her hair, sought a treatment for the condition. The method of beauty culture she developed revolutionized Black hair care. The combination of scalp preparation, application of lotions, and use of iron combs became known as the "Walker system." She distinguished her products from the hair straighteners advocated by white cosmetic firms, arguing that her treatment was geared to the special health needs of Blacks. She sold her homemade products directly to Black women, using a personal approach that won her customers and eventually a fleet of loyal saleswomen.

Walker trained her "beauty culturalists" after establishing her business headquarters in Denver, with a branch in Pittsburgh managed by her daughter A'Lelia. Her second husband, Charles J. Walker, a journalist, helped promote his wife's flourishing enterprise. Her lectures and demonstrations won thousands of customers, and in 1910 she moved her headquarters to Indianapolis. Her business employed over three thousand workers, mainly door-to-door saleswomen. Her product line of nearly twenty hair and skin items was widely advertised in the Black press.

Walker, whose talent for self-promotion made her one of the best-known Black Americans during the first quarter of the century, was lauded as "the first Black woman millionaire in America." Her largesse was legendary, and she spent extravagant sums on her Manhattan townhouse. When her daughter inherited the mansion in the 1920s, it became a salon for members of the Harlem Renaissance. Walker also owned a luxurious country home, Villa Lewaro, in Irvington-on-Hudson, designed by Black architect Vertner Tandy.

Walker was as generous as she was successful, establishing a network of clubs for her employees and offering bonuses and prizes to those who contributed to their communities through charitable works. She promoted female talent: the charter of her company provided that only a woman could serve as president. She was a standard-bearer for Black self-help, funding scholarships for women at Tuskegee Institute and donating large sums to the NAACP, the Black YMCA, and dozens of Black charities.

Madame Walker's plans for her headquarters, the Walker Building, were carried out after her premature death at fifty-one, in 1919. The structure, completed in 1927, today is part of a historic renovation district in downtown Indianapolis.

By Catherine Clinton. Reprinted by permission from *The Reader's Companion to American History*, Eric Foner and John A. Garraty, editors. Copyright © 1991 by Houghton Mifflin Company. Published by Houghton Mifflin Company. All rights reserved.

Booker T. Washington

Born into slavery in Virginia in 1856, Booker T. Washington did not see the end of back-breaking work and poverty with emancipation. As a free Black at age ten, he began working long exhausting days packing salt and going to school in his spare time. But he longed for a greater education. At age 16, he showed up penniless and hungry at the door of the Hampton Institute, one of the first schools for free Blacks.

Later, as the principal of a new school, Tuskegee Institute, founded in 1881 in Alabama, Washington modeled the school after the Hampton Institute and continued the values he had learned there from its founder, General Samuel Chapman Armstrong: self-discipline, self-reliance, work, study, good hygiene, and morality. The financial support the school received from the state was not enough, so Booker T. Washington began speaking tours to raise money.

An effective speaker, he was successful in getting donations from white northerners, including millionaire industrialists Andrew Carnegie and John D. Rockefeller. White contributors were impressed with what Tuskegee Institute was doing, but they were also comfortable with Washington's racial views.

Washington advocated for Blacks to improve their economic skills and their character in order to win the respect of whites; he did not believe that they should push to attain equal political and civil rights. This stance opened doors for him in the white community. Not only was he able to raise the funds he needed for the school, but he also became an adviser to presidents Theodore Roosevelt and William Howard Taft. He became the first African American to dine at the White House. However, many white people believed that the races should not mix socially; and the action created a scandal. President Roosevelt continued to consult with Washington but never invited him back for dinner.

Washington's racial views pleased whites; but increasingly as African Americans realized their status was not improving no matter how hard they worked, they turned away from Washington's leadership. They believed that a more forceful approach was needed and began to follow W.E.B. DuBois and the National Association for the Advancement of Colored People (NAACP).

Not well-known during his lifetime were Washington's actions behind the scenes on behalf of social change. He worked secretly against lynchings and other racial violence and against the laws (Jim Crow) that made it legal to keep African Americans separate from the rest of society.

Booker T. Washington's autobiography, *Up From Slavery*, is a classic narrative of a self-made man. It was a bestseller in its time and is available in current editions. (Signet Classic, 2000; ISBN: 0451527542.)

YOUNG LIONS

Reading Resources

GENERAL

Black Children: Their Roots, Culture, and Learning Styles, by Janice E. Hale-Benson (The Johns Hopkins University Press, 1986; ISBN: 0801833833). Hale offers solutions for how to better reach and teach African-American youth.

The Black Christ (The Bishop Henry McNeal Turner Studies in North American Black Religion, Volume 9), by Kelly Brown Douglas (Orbis Books, 1994; ISBN: 0883449390) A challenging and accessible introduction to an image of a long historical and deep religious significance among African Americans: the Black Christ. The author demonstrates the importance to the community of viewing Christ as one who identifies with the community and in whom the community finds strength.

Black Fatherhood: The Guide to Male Parenting, by Earl Ofari Hutchinson (Middle Passage Press, 1995; ISBN: 1881032094). Hutchinson guides the Black male to fatherhood.

A Black Theology of Liberation, by James H. Cone (Orbis Books, 1990; ISBN: 0883446855). First written more than 20 years ago, this book indicts white society and theology. Cone has updated this version to show the evolution of his thinking over the years to include liberation theology and feminist theory.

Coming of Age: The African-American Male Rites of Passage, by Paul Hill, Jr. (African-American Images, 1997; ISBN: 0913543284). Hill documents research on the rites-of-passage movement and reviews various operating programs.

Coming Together: The Bible's Message in an Age of Diversity, by Curtiss Paul DeYoung (Judson Press, 1995; ISBN: 0817012265). DeYoung's purpose in writing this book is to work toward reconciliation by addressing racial and cultural diversity from a biblical perspective.

Countering the Conspiracy to Destroy Black Boys, Volumes 1–4, by Jawanza Kunjufu (African-American Images, 1995; ISBN: 0913543446). Kunjufu's series identifies and examines the issues facing Black boys in American society and offers suggestions for addressing those issues.

Developing Positive Self-Images and Discipline in Black Children, by Jawanza Kunjufu (African-American Images, 1997; ISBN: 0913543012). This book discusses the relationship between self-esteem and student achievement.

Help! I'm an Urban Youth Worker: A Survival Guide to Ministry in the Big City, by Ginger Sinsabaugh (Zondervan, 2001, ISBN: 0310236096). Sinsabaugh offers key insights into the urban youth culture. She also provides suggestions for how to instill values, ignite creativity, and develop a work ethic that will empower your ministry and youth.

How Black Is the Gospel? by Tom Skinner (1976; out of print). An incisive commentary on the gospel's relevance to the Black experience.

Men to Men: Perspectives of Sixteen African-American Christian Men, by Lee N. June, Ph.D., and Matthew Parker, eds. (Zondervan, 1996; ISBN: 0310201578). This book for Black men by Black men offers advice, challenges, encouragement, and inspiration for issues they face.

Rosa Parks: My Story, by Rosa Parks with Jim (Puffin Books, 1999; ISBN: 0141301201) "The only tired I was, was tired of giving in."

Salute to Black History series, Empak Enterprises: *A Salute to Historic Black Women* (Volume 1, 1996; ISBN: 0922162018); *A Salute to Black Scientists and Inventors* (Volume 2, 1996; ISBN: 0922162026); *A Salute to Black Pioneers* (Volume 3, 1996; ISBN: 0922162034); *A Salute to Black Civil Rights Leaders* (Volume 4, 1996; ISBN: 0922162042); *A Salute to Historic Black Abolitionists* (Volume 5, 1996; ISBN: 0922162050); *Salute to Historic African Kings and Queens* (Volume 6, out of print); *A Salute to Historic Black Firsts* (Volume 7, 1996; ISBN: 0922162077); *A Salute to Blacks in the Arts* (Volume 8, out of print); *A Salute to Blacks in the Federal Government* (Volume 9, 1996; ISBN: 0922162093); *A Salute to Historic Black Educators* (Volume 10, 1996; ISBN: 092216214X).

The Souls of Black Folk, by W.E.B. DuBois (Dover Publications, 1994; ISBN: 0486280411). The book's largely autobiographical essays take the reader through African-American life after the Emancipation Proclamation: from poverty, the neoslavery of the sharecropper, illiteracy, miseducation, lynching, and the spiritual "sorrow songs" that gave birth to gospel music and the blues.

Sugar in the Raw: Voices of Young Black Girls in America, by Rebecca Carroll, ed. (Crown Publishing, 1997; ISBN: 0517884976). Fifteen girls tell their own "stereotype-breaking" stories.

FOR UNIT 1

Autobiography of W.E.B. DuBois: A Soliloquy on Viewing My Life From the Last Decade of Its First Century, by W.E.B. DuBois (International Publishers Co., 1968; ISBN: 0717802345). The story of DuBois's battle against oppression, continuing where *The Souls of Black Folk* left off.

My Bondage and My Freedom, by Frederick Douglass (Dover Publications, 1988; ISBN: 0252014103). Douglass details his life from slave to noted author and speaker on slavery.

 YOUNG LIONS

FOR UNIT 2

Martin and Malcolm and America: A Dream or a Nightmare? by James H. Cone (Orbis Books, 1992; ISBN: 0883448246). King saw America as "essentially a dream . . . as yet unfulfilled"; Malcolm viewed America as a realized nightmare. James Cone cuts through superficial assessments of King and Malcolm as polar opposites to reveal two men whose visions were complementary and moving toward convergence.

FOR UNIT 3

Ashanti to Zulu: African Traditions, by Margaret Musgrove (1977 Caldecott Award Winner, Dial Books for Young Readers, 1992; ISBN: 0140546049). Musgrove describes the ceremonies, celebrations, and day-to-day customs of twenty-six African tribes.

Jambo Means Hello, by Muriel Feelings (Dial Books for Young Readers, 1992; ISBN: 0140546529). It may be found in the children's section at bookstores or in the public library. Use the book to introduce Swahili, the language most spoken in eastern Africa, to the Young Lions group. The book is an excellent tool for exploring African culture also.

FOR UNIT 4

Unbought and Unbossed: An Autobiography, by Shirley Chisholm (1970; out of print).

Before the Mayflower: A History of Black America, by Lerone Bennett, Jr. (Penguin Books, 1993; ISBN: 0140178228). A history of Blacks in America from African roots to the civil rights period.

FOR UNIT 5

Along This Way: The Autobiography of James Weldon Johnson, by James Weldon Johnson (Da Capo Press, 2000, ISBN: 030680929X). Johnson chronicles his life as an educator, lawyer, diplomat, newspaper editor, lyricist, poet, essayist, and political activist.

Crusade for Justice: The Autobiography of Ida B. Wells, by Ida B. Wells (University of Chicago Press, 1991; ISBN: 0226893448). Wells tells the story of herself as mother, teacher, lecturer, and journalist in her fight against attitudes and laws oppressing Blacks.

FOR UNIT 6

Black Boy, by Richard Wright (Harperperennial Library, 1998; ISBN: 0060929782). Wright tells of his coming of age in the Jim Crow South.

Makes Me Wanna Holler: A Young Black Man in America, by Nathan McCall (Random House, 1994; ISBN: 0679740708). An African-American man tells his story about growing up Black in America and the path he took through violence, prison, and relationships.

Manchild in the Promised Land, by Claude Brown (Simon & Schuster, 1999; ISBN: 0684864185). Brown wrote a thinly fictionalized account of his childhood as a hardened, streetwise youth trying to survive life in the Harlem ghetto.

FOR UNIT 7

Lanterns: A Memoir of Mentors, by Marian Wright Edelman (HarperCollins, 2000; ISBN: 0060958596) Edelman tells stories from her life at the center of this century's most dramatic civil rights struggles. She pays tribute to the extraordinary personal mentors who helped light her way, including Martin Luther King, Jr.; Robert F. Kennedy; Fannie Lou Hamer; William Sloane Coffin; and Miz Tee; Miz Lucy; and others.

The Measure of Our Success: A Letter to My Children and Yours, by Marian Wright Edelman (HarperCollins, 1993; ISBN: 0060975466). Edelman outlines principles for success and achievement, such as never stop learning and improving your mind, setting goals and working quietly and systematically to achieve them, and never giving up no matter what happens or what struggles you face.

Skillstreaming the Adolescent: New Strategies and Perspectives for Teaching Prosocial Skills, by Arnold P. Goldstein and Ellen McGinnis (Research Press, 1997; ISBN: 087822369X) to bring out issues of anger, aggression and violence. The series includes using self-control, problem-solving, and accepting consequences. Each session involves roleplaying and working through steps to resolution.

FOR UNIT 8

Up From Slavery, by Booker T. Washington (Signet Classic, 2000; ISBN: 0451527542). This autobiography is a classic narrative of a self-made man.

 YOUNG LIONS